DIRTY WORDS ON CLEAN SKIN

Sexism and Sabotage
a Hillary supporter's rude awakening

ANITA FINLAY

Golden Middleway Books

ISBN:0615615066
ISBN-13:9780615615066

Cover Photo: Associated Press/Charles Dharapak
Cover Design: Kelly Rice, TreeFrog Marketing

For Mom,
who always got up early.

CONTENTS

ACKNOWLEDGMENTS

For David Givens, my partner, my champion, my love.

For Elisa Goodman, who taught me the meaning of friendship.

For Benée Knauer, for her support, editorial assistance and sage counsel.

For Linda Anselmi, who generously gave of her time and talent.

For Kelly Rice and Iris Goldfeder for their design and marketing expertise.

For Susan, Larry, Amy, UppityWoman, Valerie, Kathy, Julie, Jim, Shelby, Tricia, LisaB, Camille, Will, Emily, Thom, TD, Sisterdo, Robin, Barbara, John, Bill, Ray, Lynn, Valorie, Jasmin, Marilee and all the dear, supportive souls who encouraged me to express myself.

For the 18 million…

1 AN UNLIKELY CHAMPION

Lightning struck me the night of January 31, 2008.

It was the first solo debate between Hillary and Barack at the Kodak Theatre in Hollywood. The tension filling the air of the cavernous, gilded auditorium could not have been greater than what was burning at the base of my neck.

I was riveted to these two Senators as if our fate hung on their every word. They were duking it out just six miles away from my home. Either a woman or a black man was going to be our Democratic Presidential nominee. We had come to the point in our nation where such a momentous thing was possible.

The town so clamored for tickets, the Oscars paled by comparison. Five hundred journalists were credentialed to cover the debate that evening.[1] This was for all the marbles. Super Duper Tuesday was only a few days away with twenty-two states to vote.

I hugged my thumbs in my fists, forcing myself to watch the coverage on CNN. Would Wolf Blitzer be a fair moderator? I couldn't stay planted on the sofa. I paced. I got a snack. No amount of chocolate would help. I called my "brother from another mother" and we compared notes.

Hillary had to do well. No. She had to be perfect. By the scrutiny she received daily, nothing less would do.

Their competition for the nomination was billed as mortal combat from the beginning. That sold a lot of copy. Judging by the commentary I'd already heard from many in the pundit class, I had a pretty good idea who they preferred be left bloody and battered by the side of the road.

Some were already telling her to go away. Somewhere, somebody was laughing that I was seething – probably Rush Limbaugh. He said Hillary had a "testicle lockbox."

At an earlier debate, she was asked how she felt about not being likeable. Respected journalist Carl Bernstein unearthed complaints about her "thick ankles." Would her ankles be an obstruction to her becoming President? The *New York Times* tore into her for her "cackle."[2] The most prepared candidate with comprehensive answers to every policy question could be undone by her laugh.

The American people were looking to elect a President. Commander in Chief of the Armed Forces and leader of the free world. Big media was concerned with ankles and cackles.

Hillary was engaged, plain-spoken and smart as hell. She talked to me, not at me. Not a stump speech, just the laundry list. She discussed the logistics of getting us out of Iraq. Methodical. Sensible. Sharp. She was on message. No one could take that away from her.

The audience applauded. Was her applause louder than his? Was it the other way around? Thank God for TiVo.

Senator Obama was undeterred. He pointed his face upward. A mischievous grin threatened the corners of his mouth. He was going places.

Then Hillary said, "If you don't start by saying you're going to achieve universal healthcare, you will be nibbled to death."[3]

The camera cut away to Chelsea. Proud of her mom, she watched with unwavering focus, so filled with emotion I thought she would burst from her chair. I could not forget her expression, her intensity, her faith in her mother.

I wondered if my mom could tolerate me looking at her the same way. Would she internalize my pride in her? I had for years challenged myself to find the proper words of appreciation. Then I saw Chelsea look at her mother, so proud of what she had accomplished. Such deep admiration was not a given. It was earned.

I knew that much in my cells. In her expression, I saw their entire relationship.

Chelsea did it for all of us at that moment. Proud of mother. Proud of woman.

* * *

I'd first considered supporting Senator Clinton because she received the early endorsement of someone I respected so I started to do some research. I was surprised to learn how much work she had done on behalf of children's development, abuse prevention and foster care over the years. She was also instrumental in turning the Arkansas education system into a top ten concern.

Her advocates kept saying one thing over and over: "She steps up."

As Senator, she'd fought for and won extended benefits for military families and health benefits for our troops in the National Guard and Reserves. She fought off large cuts to Medicaid and the State Children's Health Insurance Program (SCHIP). Her ability to reach across the aisle, collaborating on health insurance legislation with the man who had been her husband's nemesis years before, was impressive.

For eight years in the White House, she stood next to the world's most powerful decision maker and was privy to information and an understanding of the demands of governing most of us could only guess at. That knowledge was a formidable advantage for any candidate, and for the nation, I thought.

The divide in opinion about her was so vast as to defy all reason. There were those on both sides of the aisle who had long ago rejected her as too outspoken, too ambitious, with an "I don't bake cookies" attitude. While I'd never acknowledged this out loud, their brainwashing worked. Over the years, I'd been suckered into the "Hillary is divisive and polarizing" narrative, too. "Ooh, I don't like her." Why don't I like her? "I don't know. I just don't."

I had even found myself using their favorite word on occasion when I'd heard her speak over the years: "strident." I'd sure as hell never heard a man described that way.

Perhaps this negative characterization took hold because her lack of a lyrical vocal sound prevented many from looking past style to see substance. Perhaps some had a problem with a woman who didn't come across as dainty. The tenor of these condemnations rang too many old bells for me to ignore.

> "...[T]he reason she's a U.S. Senator, the reason she's a candidate for President, the reason she may be a front-runner is her husband messed around. That's how she got to be senator from New York. We keep forgetting it. She didn't win there on her merit."[4]
>
> -- Chris Matthews, MSNBC

Well before the Primaries, political pundits, even some news anchors, were a little too eager to discredit Hillary Clinton. I asked myself, "Who benefits?" The harder they pounded, the more curious I became. I began to question big media's addiction to painting Hillary as a shrew.

"Dedicated" and "worker bee" were not attributes that matched with "harpy." As I listened to her that night, I finally saw Senator Clinton as a person. To me, she more closely resembled the woman reflected in her daughter's eyes than the creature painted by fifteen years of spin.

Seeing two such attractive candidates on stage at the debate, I had first hoped for a unity ticket with Hillary on top. Yet the battle lines had been drawn months before:

Hillary said she was "Ready on Day One."

Obama countered that he was "Right on Day One."

Senator Obama only allowed that the Clintons achieved "some good things." Of necessity, his strategy had to be to make us forget the peace and prosperity of the Clinton years and dwell on Clinton Derangement Syndrome instead.

After seven years of President Bush, Democrats, starved to retake the Presidency, were tired of partisan infighting. As soon as the Clintons arrived in the White House in 1993, the hunt by the right wing opposition began and continued with little let up for eight years. I'm sure some were afraid the Clinton name meant the "hunt" by conservatives would start all over again.

Then Hillary let fly with what would become one of her most popular campaign slogans:

"It took a Clinton to clean up after the first Bush and I think it might take another one to clean up after the second Bush."[5]

But Mrs. Obama had already told Vanity Fair, "It's now or never."[6] Mentioning the "inconvenience factor" and the stress such a run would place on their family, she said her husband would only run for the Presidency if he could win now and "change the world."[7]

It seemed Senator Obama was not going to accept second position to anyone, even someone more experienced than he.

In fairness, I didn't get the sense Senator Clinton would take VP to him either. She had specific ideas about getting our country back on the right track. Her policy prescriptions were not in lock step with Senator Obama's.

Together Hillary Clinton and Barack Obama would have been unstoppable. But there would be no "Dream Ticket." That much was clear to me.

Most Democrats I knew were jubilant. With two such exciting choices, what could be better? Yet I got a prickly feeling ruminating over our seeming embarrassment of riches: the first viable bi-racial male versus the first viable woman. The divide was going to be huge. I smelled disaster.

The Presidency is bigger than sex, race or age. It could not be reduced to identity politics. Some were married to an idea, to the inspiration they felt Barack Obama would provide. While I understood their yearning in that regard, there was a difference between romance and reality. I decided to forego the romance of inspiration for the reality of knowledge, competence, wonkishness and hard work.

I ignored my scattershot but steady career as an actor to work on Hillary's campaign. I ignored everything else, too. The mail, the cooking, watering the plants, getting a mammogram. Auditions became an inconvenient distraction. Acting is the only calling I have ever had or loved. Setting it aside was out of character.

Prior to my political metamorphosis, I had spent far too much time with my head buried in the Arts & Leisure section. My career was nothing fancy but I'd made a living as an actor for many years. Most of my jobs were on television yet my greatest satisfaction came

5

from working in the theatre as a solo performer. It felt like inhaling pure oxygen to share a journey by connecting with the audience one on one, perhaps even making a dent.

One month before the debate, I had a mind to write a performance piece as a tribute to my mom. This was never meant to be about politics. As John Lennon once said, "Life is what happens to you while you're busy making other plans."[8]

If you told me I would immerse myself in this effort, become a blog writer for the first time in my life, build a following on various political websites and most shocking of all that I, a lifelong Democrat, would walk away from my party in protest of their questionable shenanigans, I would have said you were potzo.

Did I want Hillary to win because she was a woman? No. Did I want her to win because I thought she had the best chops for the job? Yes. She was my candidate. But the long knives were out for Hillary, the media bias appalling. Her party turned a deaf ear.

In 2008, my reluctant odyssey into the world of politics forced me to examine the way women are treated in a "post-feminist" world, especially women with high aims and hard heads. I questioned the bias against women in authority, the limitations women placed on themselves, my own preconceptions about party, my choice of career, and even some of my friendships as I discovered a society not as evolved as advertised.

If the words "post-feminist" mean that misogyny is still acceptable, then post-feminism isn't what it's cracked up to be.

The definition of misogyny is simply a hatred of women. I came across quotations, some of which were hundreds of years old:

> "There are some meannesses which are too mean even for man - woman, lovely woman alone, can venture to commit them."
>
> -- William Makepeace Thackeray

> "Cunning women and witches we read of without number, but wisdom never entered into the character of a woman. It is not a requisite of the sex."
>
> -- Samuel Richardson

"Women exist in the main solely for the propagation of the species."

-- Arthur Schopenhauer

Kneecapping a woman with poisonous derision was an ancient practice simply refreshed with new verbiage in 2008. Throughout the campaign, political pundits acted the part of the abusive husband with the DNC as their enablers. The cost reached far beyond Hillary. All women were harmed when they saw one woman could be debased by these tactics. Woman-hate. I saw it and I could name it.

The predisposition of sexism is to elevate the male and diminish the female. But was misogyny the motive or merely the method of discrediting a qualified female candidate? And why did it work? Was the behavior of pundits and journalists unconscious, or were they capitalizing on innate biases that existed in our psyches to push their favored candidate? Either the good ole' media boys were (and are) sexist, egged on by women who side with them to maintain a seat at the table, or they used sexist tropes in their coverage believing the average voter would willingly ingest such poison. The latter possibility is even more Machiavellian because it is intentional.

Hearing pundits refer to Hillary Clinton as a hellish housewife, Nurse Ratched, she-devil and bitch, I felt I was back in my childhood nuthouse where the only thing as predictable as the abuse was the denial that followed.

Growing up, I witnessed my tireless mother being daily devalued and shamed to devastating effect at my father's hands so that he could maintain superiority in our home. His practice of denigrating my mother worked its evil magic. To this day, she is terrified of talking to new people, afraid her inadequacy will bleed past her beautiful smile. I knew from experience a woman could daily do a good turn for others yet still be tagged vile or self-serving.

I could never have imagined that the painful culture of my upbringing would be echoed in the media, on the street, and by the very party Hillary Clinton had long fought for.

Why were so many averse to trusting the position of ultimate power to a woman? How was it possible that large sections of the media went unchecked as a double standard for male and female contenders thrived? Why would the DNC stand silent as Senator Clinton's record was diminished, her character besmirched and her policies misrepresented, allowing one of their most valuable assets to be damaged? And why would a corporate-owned media perpetuate sexist attitudes toward women in the public sphere?

Since those questions seemed to run contrary to the narrative the bulk of mainstream news outlets fed to the citizenry daily, I had to dig for the answers myself.

Far from being thrilled with my new mission, my mother grew mortified by my growing outspokenness about the campaign. She regarded me with a mix of curiosity and dread as if to say, "Who ingested my daughter and spit out this strange woman I see before me?" For me to dare to stand up or stand out was unthinkable to her.

Suddenly my fist was in the air and I was on a crusade. Watching Chelsea's two-second close-up on CNN had changed me irrevocably. My old pattern of watching safely from the sidelines would no longer do.

On that electric night in January, I realized I would regret not doing everything I could to get Hillary Clinton elected. Judging by everything I had been reared to believe, I was an unlikely choice to champion Hillary in her historic run.

2 WHERE DIRTY WORDS BEGAN

My upbringing offered me an advanced degree in the mistreatment of women. There was a grave cost to insisting that the female is a lower life form. It wasn't the first insult that took you down. It was the repetition.

I was trained to be "a good little soldier." Revere authority. Don't complain. Never make a mistake. Under my father's tyrannical reign, women existed only to be of service and obey. He had also declared "there is no worse bird than one who shits in his own nest." To have dreams or goals that did not put family first was verboten. Earning his approval was a near impossible task; the rules forever shifting with his erratic moods. The effects of his behavior still reverberate with my mother, sister, and me. Much of who we are was defined by either our success or failure at breaking free of his overbearing influence.

My father came from a well-to-do Hungarian family. His parents had passed away while he was relatively young and I never learned if his four sisters escaped incarceration in concentration camps. My dad did not. Captured late in 1943, he often repeated the story of his liberation from Mauthausen. He told me he was a skeleton, too weak to stand, and that he had to crawl out on all fours. It took fifteen months for him to regain his strength as he recuperated in an Austrian hospital. He married soon after, but his wife died in childbirth leaving him with a newborn baby girl to care for. Five months later, my father swept into my mother's life.

Born in northern Italy, my mom was and is not unlike a Tennessee Williams' heroine, her hands "fluttering about her like restless birds,"[9] her hair a flowing black mane. Her lilting, expressive mezzo voice attracted patrons who had wanted to sponsor her in a professional singing career. Her parents would not allow it. It was no life for a proper girl, they said. Instead, she sang in the church choir and was trained to be an expert seamstress. The second eldest in a family of ten, she was accustomed to putting everyone before herself.

Always a looker, Mom never lacked for suitors. But she hadn't known anyone like my father. Almost twenty years her senior, he was elegant and cultured. She fell for him but fell even harder for his baby and was determined to give his child a mother. In 1949, they wed after a three-week courtship. On their voyage across the Atlantic with my then six month old sister in tow, Mom sang on that enormous ship for all the passengers.

My mother in particular loved all things American and was thrilled they were to become citizens. She had no idea what was in store for her.

No matter what promises he had made to my mother for a better life, once they settled in New York, my father's bon vivant manner evaporated. By trade, my father designed and cut furs but he was unable to regain the success he'd had in his family's fur business. Trapped in an environment too poor for the way he remembered himself, he was furious at having to start over again with nothing. He would come home and explode. He raged that his coworkers were spying on him. They didn't give him his due. Then he would turn his rage on my mother. The cooking wasn't right. The cleaning wasn't good enough. It didn't matter really. The compulsion to punish was far more important than the offense.

A brilliant but emotionally disturbed man, he thought people were watching him through the walls, and kept the lights off in our tiny apartment in more ways than one. My dad literally believed, "Live small or you'll be killed." By the time I came along ten years after their arrival in the U.S., my father's paranoia and misanthropic behavior reached a level where he could no longer hold down a job and rarely left our apartment.

Mom was already our sole support and worked until two days before I was born. Two weeks later, when my father wouldn't return to work, my mother went back to being a finisher in the fur business, hand-sewing fine linings into the coats.

Dad took good care of me all things considered, feeding me, washing my diapers, making me paper airplanes.

Usually, the person who controls the purse controls the relationship. My father made sure that was not the case. He told my mother that though she often worked sixty hours a week to support us, she needed him to handle paying the bills because she was too stupid to write a check. By making her out to be incompetent, he made himself necessary. He would scream degrading curses at her in languages we were lucky enough not to understand. His favorite nickname for her was Nightmare.

According to my father, my mother was dirty. She was crazy. She drove others crazy. She was a whore. She was out to ruin him.

Devaluing my mother was also the antidote to his great need for her. The long buried pain of watching my mom on her knees before my father, holding her arms above her head to protect herself from his raised hand, is a memory my four-year-old brain retains to this day. Physical violence was by no means a constant, but the threat was ever present.

I needed to believe my dad loved my mom. But by the way he spoke to her face to face and behind her back, how he relentlessly complained to me about her, I couldn't fathom that he did. It was as if he was programming me to believe what he believed. The injustice of his remarks burned in me but there was nowhere I could go to appeal.

I once asked my mom why she chose to stay. She said, "How could I leave him? He couldn't take care of himself." The word workaholic wasn't part of the American vernacular back then, but she qualified. Duty and family meant everything.

Her impish sense of humor stood in sharp contrast to her contempt for life's inequities. She voiced her opinions with a raised brow capped by a brisk hand gesture for added emphasis. Such judgments were in the main directed toward those who didn't pull their weight. She had no time for excuses.

No matter what you needed of my mother, she would always chirp, "No problem!" The job was done before you asked a second time. You could tell her to meet you anywhere. After three buses, four trains and a pack mule, you'd reach the mountaintop only to find her there ahead of you, smiling her party smile, smoking a cigarette and looking stylish. She looked like Saks' Fifth Avenue on a Woolworth budget. If you dressed her in a burlap sack, she'd find a belt and make it work. Anyone who met my mom referred to her as "the Countess." She was stunning and quietly charmed the crap out of everybody.

She knew how to pick a fight with my father and did that on a number of occasions to seek revenge for their unhappy home life. She had admitted as much. But no matter her provocations, she could never get more than ten percent of him. The rest was locked away somewhere out of her reach.

My father's explosions of temper were like bombing raids. We never knew when they would erupt or how long they would last. Sometimes the waiting was the worst. What new offense would set him off? In order to have the last word, my father would threaten to throw a bucket of ice water at my mom. My sister and I dreaded he would someday do it. He must have thought that was the worst way you could shame someone.

The unspoken truth was that if you stepped out of line you would get a taste of the treatment my mother received. My sister found that out. My father would often command her, "Think before you speak." Wanting to avoid being cursed as my mother had been, she barely said anything. Lacking in confidence, she remained a shadowy presence, avoiding contact with him wherever possible. I too learned the lesson well and made every effort to appear perfect in his eyes.

As my father's bridge to the outside world, our daily ritual never changed. After school was our best time together. He seemed to know everything and had a biting wit that could make me laugh until the tears rolled. I listened to his proverbs on every topic: "A rich girl can do what she likes. A poor girl has only her honor." He liked running my schooling and always greeted me at the door, eager to hear about my day.

When I was nine, I started fifth grade at a new school. At the end of the day, the announcement blared over the P.A. system, "All students are required to wear a white shirt for tomorrow's assembly in the auditorium."

I raced home to tell my father all about my new class. No sooner had I walked in the door than he cornered me in our narrow kitchen and slapped me hard across the face. I couldn't figure out what I'd done wrong. I was Daddy's little sunshine.

My nose started bleeding. I made no sound. Looking down, I saw blood all over my only white shirt. I thought blood was permanent. And assembly was the next day.

I'd gotten a couple of beatings from my father but he had trained me to be the perfect student, making me write the alphabet when I was almost too young to hold a pencil. Education was all that mattered so by now, I was more afraid of school than of him.

I stuck my chin out and barked, "Go ahead and hit me again, you big elephant. That's all you know how to do anyway!"

He reared back against the refrigerator, stunned. We stared at each other as another drop of blood dribbled past my lip onto my shirt. We stood frozen for what seemed like an eternity. He could have broken me in half. No one stood up to my father and won.

Then he looked away, breaking the spell. He lumbered out of the kitchen. It was the last time he hit me.

Our relationship was different after that. Maybe he respected that I stood up for myself. He must have loved me a great deal to grant me a special dispensation no one else in the family ever received.

Observing my parents' behavior, I saw all the different ways one could undercut a woman. Apart from withholding affection, making a woman feel unattractive, even ugly, was another method of destroying her confidence. As if to say, who else would want her? But for my father to allow all my mother's efforts to go without acknowledgement was the most devastating cut of all. No matter how hard she worked, it would never be good enough.

It wasn't until she collapsed from overwork at age fifty that he started to appreciate her. In January of 1977, I entered our near dark apartment one night just in time to see her crumple to the floor. After five months of surgeries, medications and a parade of clueless doctors, my mother wasn't getting any better. The workhorse we had relied upon so heavily was unable to pull the team. After my sophomore year in college, I took a leave of absence and became the breadwinner at eighteen. I went from being the perfect student to the perfect secretary.

Nine months after she fell ill, my father regarded my mother as she sat at the dining table staring at her array of pill bottles.

"She is a good woman," he said. Finally.

But I didn't know if my mother heard him.

In January, 1978, we celebrated my dad's seventieth birthday. He blew out his candles and stroked his moustache. He had his family around him and we were all in a rare good humor. I'd never seen him so happy. For once, he felt loved and honored. Content, he exhaled as he surveyed us all sitting around the table.

He died the following week of a massive heart attack.

At his service, Mom could barely walk across the room and we were worried she would follow him soon after. I didn't cry at my father's death. It had seemed logical to me that Dad decided to die so Mom could live. I figured he was so tough nothing could kill him unless he said so. That was the story I told myself to make it okay. Without the fights, without her having to worry over his health, she could focus on getting better herself.

We found doctors who restored our faith in the medical profession and when Mom returned to work in the fall of 1978, I returned to college to complete my B.A. It wasn't until after the loss of my father that I felt at liberty to pursue my childhood wish to become an actor. There would always be an empty place knowing Dad never got to see me doing the thing I loved the most, but my junior and senior years were the first time in my life I didn't feel like a soldier.

I was encouraged to apply to the Yale School of Drama, but going into debt on behalf of my career as an actor was a bridge too far. Though my father was gone, his influence remained. I could only pursue what I wanted as long as it wasn't real enough to cost anything.

The biggest dream he had for me was that I become a translating secretary at the U.N. Not *the* Secretary. *A* secretary. I imagined him reaching up from the grave, holding me at the ankles and I couldn't break free. But I was the one holding on. I never applied to Yale. I couldn't treat myself like I was worth it. For the next ten years, I struggled as an actor in New York, spending as much time working as a secretary trying to support myself.

On my mom's sixty-fourth birthday, she and her new beau visited a neighborhood pub that was also a piano bar of sorts. I accompanied them and was surprised the pianist had invited her up to sing. This must have been their ritual though as far as I knew my mother hadn't performed in public in forty years.

We were in an Irish pub. Lots of conversation, laughter and clinking glasses and it was a pretty large place. She sang "Mama" in Italian. As soon as she began, the place fell silent.

Her voice couldn't have been what it once was but she still had that warm, buttery sound. She sang with such expression, such feeling, the fact that no one in the joint understood a single word besides "Mama" didn't matter a damn. That was the only time I heard her sing in front of anyone besides me.

I knew my mom had given up on her dream just because someone told her to. I didn't want to be guilty of the same.

It was too much to hope, however, that I would have escaped the mistakes of my parents' relationship with my own. While my first marriage had its moments, in the main it offered a far milder version of the stifling criticism and emotional cruelty that plagued my mother's treatment at my father's hands. I grew to true adulthood in that union, but my evolution came at a price. Perhaps some part of me needed to live through my family's painful legacy in order to finally reject it.

I left New York for LA. That was the moment Dad, or my husband, stopped having the last word. It was the first choice I'd made that was not for anyone's benefit but my own. Moving those three thousand miles did more than provide physical distance from all my old ghosts in New York. One selfish act allowed me to open different doors. I found mentors, teachers and friends who would support rather than crush. They sounded out a different message than the dark world my father had presented on a daily basis.

In 1995, I met my second husband. He was the opposite of everything I had been used to in a relationship. It didn't matter how many facets of me there were. He was okay with all of them. David had and has a very healing effect on me.

When my mother was seventy-four, I asked her to retire. She refused. All but ignoring her, I packed her up, trunks and all, to move her to Los Angeles from New York.

We went to my father's gravesite at Flushing Cemetery to say goodbye. It was a sunny, muggy day in August. Dad was buried in one of the more affordable parts of the cemetery, but his patch of grass was well manicured. The surrounding trees were lush and still. His dark grey headstone protruded a couple of inches from the ground. It was nondescript for a man of his outsized personality.

I stepped back to let her have the space to herself. I heard her ask him why he didn't treat her better.

"I loved you, you know," she said.

The lettering on his headstone said Beloved Husband and Father. And he was, in spite of himself.

After Mom was settled near my husband and me, she hung her family photos on the wall of her new bedroom and put my father's portrait up, too. He was wearing a very stern expression. For five years, I saw the picture every time I went to visit. I asked, "Why do you want him staring at you when you sleep?"

She put the picture away. She never put away his brainwashing. Even now, when I get together with my mother for a girlie lunch, she still asks me if it's "okay" with my husband. I tell her, "He's not in the habit of making me ask permission."

While my father's dirty words for my mother did not stop her, she stood a little smaller. To be told she was worthless, to be isolated, removed from an environment where she might hear another message was a powerful control mechanism that took its toll on my mother, and on all of us.

You are less than me. You are not necessary. You are stupid. Everything that is wrong with my life is your fault. To berate another in this way is an indication of fear, not strength. But a bully has a way of neutralizing such observations. I can't help but wonder what a different person my mother might have become had she been treated with respect. And respected herself.

In 2008, domestic abuse played out on a national level. I felt compelled not to let the dirty words pass without comment when I heard them a second time.

3 THE WOMAN AS CITADEL

"...[T]hough Hillary Rodham Clinton has been on the periphery or in the middle of national life for decades ... she is one of the most recognizable but least understood figures in American politics."[10]

-- Jon Meacham, *Newsweek*

While women had attained positions of leadership, I observed our society still felt conflicted in its determination of what was acceptable or desirable conduct for a woman. We scrutinized a powerful or ambitious woman's every move, comfortable passing judgment on every part of her personal, physical and professional presentation.

I had experienced a microcosm of that ever-morphing criteria growing up. Having invented a persona that would please both my parents, I practiced image management to offer the appearance of perfection. Be coquettish like her, smart like him and don't piss anybody off in between. To my mind, only certain parts of me were acceptable and the rest were better left unseen.

Given a great deal of responsibility early, my take-charge nature came to me by default, and let me in for no end of teasing by my friends. I was frustrated with peers calling me the Rock of Gibraltar but dreading rejection, or looking incapable, I acted like I didn't need help. I talked about myself in the third person, as though referring to a character I was playing. That character was always prepared.

Long possessed of the ability to make anything sound scientific, I could tell you the Empire State Building is located in the middle of the East River and you'd probably go. Yet the voice which made me so believable caused me concern. It was different and I noticed. And others did, too. A mentor once declared, "You could address the U.N. on ten minutes' notice!" It took me years not to feel awkward about the sounds I made, and the authority my voice carried. While I liked the respect, I didn't like the resentment that sometimes went with it.

With my confident walk and outgoing personality, I carried myself like the CEO of a Fortune 500 company. Bystanders saw a very feminine person who could probably lead an army.

I saw myself as a fragile soul.

That got a huge laugh every time.

The truth was somewhere in the middle and helped me to understand how easy it was to misjudge others, particularly women, based on the protective patina or persona they wore when walking into the room.

Since my mom brought home the dough, she presented an atypical portrait of womanhood for the times. When "women's lib" was big in the early seventies, I found it odd. I didn't need a movement to tell me what I already knew. In my world, if you wanted something done, you counted on a woman to do it.

My mother was my hero, yet she never expected the deference that ought to have come with her position in the family.

To her, being pretty and pleasing was all that mattered. Rather than paying attention to my words, she was often busier examining my appearance. While she appreciated my "big brains," if I didn't look right the rest didn't mean much. Since I resemble her, I was indirectly her representative. If I didn't advertise properly, there was hell to pay.

I pretended her preoccupation with looks trumping accomplishment was a by-product of her generation, yet every magazine I opened I'd still see woman as Barbie doll. I loved Barbie but still wanted to be sheriff, so being pigeonholed never appealed to me.

Mom once referred to me as a cold cookie because I put my feelings aside in the moment to get the job done. She said this while she was ill and needed me most. I winced thinking my own mother didn't get me. Earnestness and warmth are not mutually exclusive traits. I had also made note that powerful did not translate to popular. Not for a female. My mother's discomfort with women asserting themselves made her resent a quality she had often thanked me for. Learning that the current world was often more in line with my mother's old-fashioned ideas of who a woman should be came as quite a shock.

I'd gotten a job in the mid-eighties as co-host of a show on The Travel Channel. There was lots of competition for the gig and about twenty people in on the decision. I pulled the producer aside one day and asked him why they chose me. He said, "You were the only one nobody *didn't* like." So that was the secret – offend no one.

In the nineties, I had several long-term spokesperson contracts for Fortune 500 companies. It was quite an effort to get producers to choose me over a male since men were considered "more trustworthy" in a suit. This credibility gap was puzzling, as if to say I did not have the same character, honor and principles of any man.

Since moving to Los Angeles, anytime I was on a film shoot and saw a woman director, or a far greater anomaly, a woman with her hands on the camera, I would nod and whisper, "Congratulations." The lady would offer a knowing smile. Nothing else needed to be said.

Soon after my husband and I bought our home in 2002, I was drafted to be president of our homeowners' association. I worried less about performing well than people having a "who the hell does she think she is" attitude toward my making decisions. An older male neighbor in our town-home complex got up in my face after I had been elected. Nose-to-nose, he said I needed to get some men on the board because "women don't know how to do anything." Answering him was pointless. I changed the subject.

Cleta Mitchell, Washington lawyer and former Oklahoma legislator, pointed out that from childhood, "it is an inherent male trait to assume he knows". She stated that women suffered not from being under qualified, but from lacking confidence in their own qualifications – women doubt women. Insecure men, to protect their own turf, teach women to doubt themselves:

> "Women always think that if they have one more piece of paper, or one more degree, or a few more years of this or that experience, then they will finally be 'qualified' for whatever next thing they are seeking. ...Instead, I've said to look at their male competition and ask this question: Can I do a better job than he can? And if the answer is yes, then forget the paper and the extra titles and go for it."[11]

Ms. Mitchell observed that in her second term as a state legislator,

> "[F]reshmen male legislators were not deferential to me, but were deferential to my male colleagues elected the same day I was. And I realized that men grant to themselves and each other certain 'credibility' that women have to earn."[12]

How good did a woman have to be to be considered good enough? And what would happen if you dared to acknowledge how much you brought to the table? Would the etiquette police blast their sirens if you stepped over the line and got too big for your bloomers?

All too late, I discovered Hillary, who never apologized for being the smartest girl in class. Wandering back through her life was a fascinating exercise. She had the fortitude to speak up from a young age and was named the first student valedictorian at Wellesley College.

Her commencement remarks were featured in *Life Magazine* in 1969:

> "We are, all of us, exploring a world none of us understands. . . . searching for a more immediate, ecstatic, and penetrating mode of living. . . . [for the] integrity, the courage to be whole, living in relation to one another in the full poetry of existence. The struggle for an integrated life existing in an atmosphere of communal trust and respect is one with desperately important political and social

consequences. . . . Fear is always with us, but we just don't have time for it.

...And you and I must be free, not to save the world in a glorious crusade, not to kill ourselves with a nameless gnawing pain, but to practice with all the skill of our being the art of making possible."

Couched in a middle-class upbringing, there was and is poetry in this woman, something for which she has rarely gotten credit. Hillary's otherwise plainspoken nature had gotten her into trouble more than once. It was something I understood well having on occasion failed to curb that trait in myself.

Striking many as abrasive when she first hit the national stage in 1992, Hillary gave the impression she had every expectation of being taken seriously. I don't think most people knew what to do with a woman who had that much belief in herself. I marveled that she was relatively unconcerned with how she was perceived and didn't wait for anyone's permission to make a contribution. Though she had taken her share of grief for being forthright, her mission statement, more than her polling, seemed to dictate her actions.

Hillary Clinton's longtime friends had said "she's utterly there for you" and "she is the first person they would call"[13] when in trouble, yet when Bill Clinton was first elected President, Hillary was accused by critics of having had a "personality transplant." Perhaps she was adjusting to living in the world's biggest goldfish bowl, trying to figure out how much of herself to share with the viewing public.

Hillary Clinton had been a target for people who thought she was overstepping herself long before she had the audacity to run for President. Margaret Carlson noted in her *Time Magazine* portrait of Hillary after her husband's election to the presidency in 1992,

"When Governor [Clinton] talked about "buy one, get one free" and possibly appointing Hillary to the Cabinet, her popularity took a dive."[14]

"...Without diminishing other First Ladies' intelligence, Hillary Clinton's is that of a trained killer lawyer, and the Governor says proudly that he wants her mind brought to bear on whatever he is doing, including being President. In any event, her influence is so pervasive that he has it with him whether or not she is in the room." [15]

Acknowledging Mrs. Clinton's many achievements as First Lady of Arkansas, Ms. Carlson quoted Conservative columnist John Robert Starr of the Arkansas Democrat-Gazette, "a rabid opponent of Bill Clinton's" who said ...

"...[T]he best thing that could happen would be to let Hillary run the country. I know that sounds ridiculous, but she has just never failed." [16]

During Bill Clinton's presidency, Hillary had a more overtly political and empowered role than any First Lady before her, save Eleanor Roosevelt, [17] and was more accomplished than any of her predecessors when she stepped into what was known as "the most ill-defined job in America." [18]

"There cannot be true democracy unless women's voices are heard. There cannot be true democracy unless women are given the opportunity to take responsibility for their own lives. There cannot be true democracy unless all citizens are able to participate fully in the lives of their country."

-- Hillary Rodham Clinton, July 11, 1997

She took the unprecedented step of having an office in the West Wing. First Ladies did not do that:

"Washington remains the heart of tea-pouring country, where Senate wives still hold Red Cross blood-bank drives and frustrated political wives have a long tradition of giving up their high-powered careers to advance their husbands." [19]

When Hillary and President Clinton worked to pass their health care overhaul in 1994, derisively dubbed "Hillarycare," insurance companies spent $100 million dollars to negatively characterize the bill and defeat it. The grief she got from the media for her attempts in this arena still haunt her today. Dusting herself off, Mrs. Clinton set about achieving smaller goals in healthcare reform and did.

Ms. Carlson saved her most prescient statement for last:

"...[Hillary] will make her own mistakes. And if history is any guide, for reasons as old as Adam and

23

Eve, some Americans will punish her for them out of proportion to their significance." [20]

Even with her acknowledged influence on policy in her husband's administration, many accused Hillary of putting her husband's career before her own. Given the times in which they were living, that was probably true. When Hillary Clinton at last claimed a political career for herself and ran for the U.S. Senate in 2000, the putdowns continued, as if her decision was somehow unseemly.

On a mission to prove she was not a dilettante, she went from district to district, especially in Upstate New York where there was a large Republican population, conducting a "listening tour." She set about with a dogged determination to win voters over and was elected by a twelve-point margin. In 2006, she was re-elected with 67% of the vote.

Looking at the sum total of Hillary Clinton's achievements, I was surprised at those who wished to denigrate her as nothing more than the wife of...

People overlooked a whole truckload:

Seven years with the Children's Defense Fund, research on early childhood brain development, taking on cases of child abuse, offering free legal services to the poor[21], working on President Nixon's impeachment, rebuilding the Arkansas education system, being named first woman partner at Rose Law firm and twice named one of the 100 most influential lawyers in the country.

As First Lady, working to successfully lower the rates of teen pregnancy, initiating and shepherding the Adoption and Safe Families act, helping to create SCHIP with Senators Kennedy and Hatch, helping to create the Office on Violence Against Women at the Department of Justice, playing a key role in bringing the issue of human trafficking to the forefront of United States policy...

As a senator, securing $21.4 billion in funding for cleanup and recovery after 9/11, providing health tracking for first responders and volunteers at Ground Zero and creating grants for redevelopment,[22] pushing President Bush to pass RU486, passing SCHIP with Newt Gingrich, getting increased benefits for the National Guard serving in Iraq, marching for Gay Rights, championing and fighting causes on behalf of NOW and NARAL, speaking around the world for the rights of women and children, becoming the first First Lady to become a US Senator and then win re-election. New York's first female senator. The list went on.

All due respect to President Clinton, those claiming Hillary moved forward through nepotism discounted that Bill Clinton may have been able to ascend to the heights he did because of her help. Despite the trash talk, it never looked to me as though she'd gotten a free ride.

Hillary had long been viewed as distant, foreboding and robotic, like a citadel. People usually have one of two reactions to a citadel. One, do not approach. Two, knock it down. Judgment of her hit close to home. When necessary, my own demeanor could intimidate, even ice over the room when necessary. It was a protection mechanism, nothing more.

For years, Hillary had been defensive when discussing her marriage and her husband's reported philandering. It seemed to me a mix of defiance, self-protection and "none of your hooting business." Her behavior worked against her but was another instance where her actions would have been judged harshly regardless. During her husband's impeachment hearings, she chose to stand by him and hold her head high. Her popularity shot up to its highest levels. Later, she was insulted and rejected for that same choice.

Her marriage was referred to as a "merger." The Clintons were often not credited with raising a lovely daughter, or for having other reasons to remain together that strangers could not possibly fathom. As Susan Estrich noted,

> "They made their share of mistakes. But Chelsea wasn't one of them...
>
> When she so famously crossed the White House lawn with one hand holding that of each parent, we saw not the most powerful people in the world, but a family fighting to stay together, and the girl in the middle fighting just as hard as either of them."[23]

I don't know what kind of choice I would have made in Hillary's place but for obvious reasons, I was prone to defending a woman who was blamed for the transgressions of her spouse.

"You know, people make a lot of money talking about me, don't they? They just get on those shows, and they talk away. There's nothing I can do. And that's one of the great lessons I try to convey in my book, which my mother implanted in me as a young girl... Is you can either be an actor in your own life, or a reactor in somebody else's."

-- Hillary Rodham Clinton

Finally, Senator Clinton had arrived at a sort of resigned humor, even a more humble, open tone, allowing us to share in the joke of all her turmoil that had been dragged out into the open and dissected.

"...I've been in this arena for a long time. I have a lot of baggage, and everybody has rummaged through it for years."[24]

-- Hillary Rodham Clinton

She was not easily pegged and though she was often accused of being more or less than human, she found a way to get her job done even when it got messy. Having a life that played out on such an immense stage was not for the squeamish. She was not unlike a "Joe Palooka" doll. If she was punched down, she'd spring right back up.

I learned a vital lesson from her resilience, one I wished I'd been able to act on much earlier. I had watched many women friends struggle with how to be in the world, fearing to be judged and thus rejected. To hear others say "not good enough" or "not right" when assessing a woman in public life was troubling, if not unpredictable.

Few could have stood up to the pummeling Hillary had been taking for nearly two decades. She grew even more successful. A lesser mortal would have caved long ago.

4 AN INTRODUCTION TO POLITICS

On September 12, 2001, I attended a vigil at the Pacific Design Center in Los Angeles. Several hundred people sat in the large esplanade, some held candles. All were numb. Everyone wanted to give blood, donate money, to do something. We were leaden, stealing glances at one another, frustrated at feelings of helplessness, grateful to hold hands with a stranger.

Seeing how terrorists had defiled New York City, I wanted revenge but didn't know where to direct my anger. Those gruesome moments played over and over on the news. The planes flying into the Twin Towers, the horror of people jumping from the windows, so many others covered with ash below, wandering in shock through the streets. I kept catching the numbers 9 11 every time I happened to look at a digital clock.

In the days that followed, I was never more proud to be an American. To watch first responders from around the country and volunteers of all stripes make their way to Ground Zero to help in the rescue and cleanup reminded me of the generosity, courage and tireless work ethic of my fellow citizens. The pictures posted on the walls near Ground Zero by those who had lost loved ones were a heartbreaking reminder that there was no one else left alive to save.

Even President Bush's megaphone moment at Ground Zero was a comfort. Mayor Giuliani's daily presence reinforced that someone was in charge and that we would continue.

I couldn't fathom the grit and guts of those in my old hometown. The thought of getting on a subway, going to work, getting into an elevator, buying groceries, any mundane activity must have been paralyzing.

When President Bush spoke to us from the Oval Office, visibly emotional, I allowed myself to forget everything else I felt about him, his candidacy, how I was not sold on the rhetoric of "compassionate conservatism." I even let go the way the election debacle of 2000 had transpired. He could have asked me for anything. Ninety percent of the country was with him. Our American flag was everywhere, suspended from apartment windows, attached to our cars.

The unprecedented global outpouring of good will was something of a comforting balm. Pictures that showed mountains of flowers laid at the gates of our embassies around the world presented an opportunity that in the end was squandered by our country's unilateral action in Iraq eighteen months later.

By countermanding Congress and not finishing the inspections requested by his Iraq War Resolution, I felt President Bush and his administration had betrayed our trust and those who voted in favor of the measures he had asked for. Only history would determine how those actions should be judged.

Even if one thought we were right to declare war on Iraq, I thought it better that we go in with an overwhelming force, not just to win the war but to maintain the peace, as some of his Generals had advised. They were fired for their trouble.

If in their hearts, the Bush Administration believed an invasion was morally correct, then the scope of it should not have been minimized and the true cost not hidden from the American people. We should all have been asked to sacrifice so as not to put an unfair burden on one small part of our citizenry. It could not be both morally right and swept under the rug.

Since the eight years prior had been peaceful and prosperous, the most important issue I recalled from the 2000 presidential campaign was Vice President Al Gore saying he would put Social Security in an "air tight lockbox." The direction our country took in the aftermath of 9/11 made me realize I had better pay closer attention to those minding the mint. I was embarrassed at how spoiled I had been in past years, thinking we were invincible.

I became a news junkie and via the Internet, jumped between a dozen news sites seeking both sides of a story. Finding objective reporting became an increasingly difficult task. During the 2004 presidential campaign, desperate to move on from President Bush, I pored over the news to see how people were reacting to news of the continuing Iraq war.

It had never occurred to me that President Bush would be re-elected. My friends and I, dyed-in-the-wool Democrats all, thought after four years of Mr. Nuk-u-lar, no one would ink the dot for him again. We couldn't see how someone who had sent us into Iraq, who refused to let us see the body bags with our precious soldiers in them while telling Americans to "go shopping" could win a second term.

I realized how effective the press could be in running interference for the President, moreover how effective fear is as a motivator to cull votes.

To be fair, the American people and the press were still in shock, reeling from the attacks. National security was the prime concern and many were terrified to go against prevailing authority.

I counted on the Fourth Estate to be effective regardless. George Bush was considered a wartime president and many were not anxious to stop him before they had "given him a chance to finish the job" in Iraq. He was a wartime president because he created the war; an inconsequential detail. Afghanistan, yes, I knew why we went there. Iraq, not so much.

I started to speak up in little ways, a letter here, an e-mail there, signing a petition to my Congressman.

By the time the California primary rolled around, Senator Kerry had it in the bag as the nominee. He seemed smart enough and decent enough. And anyone would be better than President Bush, right?

It was a sad day indeed when Senator McCain stood up at a Republican campaign event soon after to endorse President Bush. Lifting his stiff arms, broken many times by his captors in Hanoi years before, he held the President in an awkward embrace.

I couldn't fathom his actions. John McCain was a hero, a man I had always liked and respected even when we did not agree. He was in effect, embracing the same faction of the Republican Party that had eviscerated him years before, destroying his presidential hopes in 2000 with a whisper campaign in South Carolina, accusing him of fathering an illegitimate child. The truth was he and his wife Cindy had added to their large family by adopting a daughter from Bangladesh.

I looked back over Senator McCain's old campaign ads and platform. He was running as a moderate. That was not the prescription the neo-cons had in mind for our nation.

At the time, it occurred to me he must have been assured support for a 2008 election bid. But why he would trust his party after that, I could not imagine. Did his choice to embrace President Bush plague him when he looked at his clenched jaw in the mirror? Had he convinced himself that for the greater good he'd be willing to chow down on a dirt sandwich? He was not the only politician to have done so.

That was the first time I noticed the high cost of the herd mentality in our political culture. Republicans knew how to win elections because they stood in lock step. Senator McCain had been critical of the Administration's actions and those of Secretary of Defense Rumsfeld. Yet McCain and others in his party were still willing to offer up a full throated endorsement, standing for their party rather than standing for us, or so I thought.

That summer, I partnered with a friend to canvass for Kerry. Most voters I encountered were less excited about voting Senator Kerry in than they were about voting President Bush out.

Senator Clinton was interviewed in advance of the 2004 Democratic Convention. She was being goaded by a reporter, and asked if she was disappointed she was not running. Why were they trying to get a rise out of her? At that point, she was still only a first term Senator in her fourth year, doing a good job for New York. She said she was happy to stand with her party and that was that.

I also couldn't figure out why the keynote speaker at the Convention would be someone not even in the Senate or House, nor a Governor, but a little known state Senator from Illinois. Mr. Obama received quite a reception.

The Clintons had gotten a rock-star welcome when entering the Convention hall as well, and gave Senator Kerry a wonderful introduction. They had actually gotten me excited about him.

Senator Kerry, covered in flop sweat under the hot lights, was being introduced to the American people for the first time. He gave the speech of his life. But in his campaign, I could never figure out why he sounded so sleepy from the neck up. Put a little juice under it! The stakes couldn't be higher. I didn't want to admit it, but Kerry came across as patrician, elitist and stiff.

The most passionate or qualified candidate doesn't always make it to the nomination. The narrative is pushed by the media, the party pushes who it wants to push, and it is an illusion to think we are really picking the guy – or gal. But I'm getting ahead of myself.

As we got closer to Election Day, I complained that Kerry did not come out early to defend himself against the Swift Boat Veterans for Truth who had attacked his record in Viet Nam. Then I saw the photos of Kerry windsurfing and goose hunting. The picture of him windsurfing was unfortunate. The caption might as well have read, "Hi, I'm rich as Rockefeller."

His hunting picture struck me as absurd. Senator Kerry was walking through the woods with several other men, looking appropriately macho. He was holding the rifle under his arm but not the "kill," as if holding a weapon made him okay with gun owners, but having his aide hold the dead geese would make him okay with the lefties because he didn't have his hands on anything he had put a bullet in. What was he doing?

But how could I think anything negative about anyone in my own party? We were perfect…

When we found out President Clinton was going to need open-heart surgery that summer, I prayed for the surgeons but that gave birth to the frightening thought we were destined to lose. If a magnetic speaker and campaigner such as he was out of commission and couldn't drag the monotonous Kerry across the finish line, we were cooked. Superstitious, I was terrified to paint the devil on the wall lest he appear. I brushed this notion away like an annoying gnat too near to my eyes.

A gaunt President Clinton, recovering from quadruple bypass, faithfully campaigned for Senator Kerry in October but it was too late.

One week prior to the election, retired four-star General Wesley Clark was a panelist on HBO's "Real Time with Bill Maher". A war hero and ex-Supreme Allied Commander of NATO, with more medals, foreign honors and awards than he could stuff in a garage, Clark had a somewhat short lived presidential campaign in 2004. I didn't know much about him beyond that.

I about fell out of my chair when he went after President Bush in a way I had never heard before. He talked about President Bush's famous and premature "Mission Accomplished" moment, declaring victory in Iraq back in 2003.

Ruh roh.

Clark nailed President Bush for "prancing around in a flight suit on the deck of that aircraft carrier." Prancing, I say.

President Bush's cocky strut was off-putting. He seemed disconnected from the gravity of the situation. Confidence is one thing. Hubris is another. Did his administration think it was only going to take two weeks to defeat Iraq's army and peace would be restored in the land? My mother chimed in, "Look, he's playing president!"

General Clark said that if Bush was going to "take the glory of the men and women wearing the uniform, he ought to understand that in the Navy, it's a one strike and you're out system. If you're the captain of a ship and it runs aground, they don't care if you're on the bridge, eating lunch, asleep, chopping cedars in Texas, you're out."[25]

Who the hell was this guy? I got off my arse in an effort to find out.

His observation was a valid one. If 9/11 happened on a Democrat's watch, it is doubtful he would have been granted a second term, whether it was fair to assess blame on the President or not. I would have preferred someone with Clark's guts and intellect to be our nominee over John Kerry.

Actor Kevin Costner was also on the panel that night. I thought he was a bit full of himself at the time. He was advocating voting for

Ralph Nader and said that he might do so "if he had the balls." I rejected this notion, thinking it would be a wasted vote.

While I would not have voted for Mr. Nader, I owed Mr. Costner an apology. Defending his choice to vote third party, he said "sometimes you have to lose to win." Like Nader, he felt the parties had become too similar, both corrupt and too beholden to corporate interests. He had a point. He also stated a President should run for only one term, without having the obligation of getting re-elected. That person could get into office, clean up and be beholden to no one. I had sincere doubts we'd see a candidate offer to do that anytime soon.

On November 2nd, our next-door neighbors were throwing me a birthday/election night celebration. These were two dear and whip smart people who dubbed themselves the "Green Party." Soon after President Bush was elected in 2000 and sent his first rebate check to taxpayers in the amount of $300, our neighbor said he endorsed his stimulus payment over to the Democratic Party.

I wondered what the Treasury Department thought when they got the cancelled check.

We were joyous when the party started, thinking the tide had to turn. By the time we got to the cake, things had gotten pretty grim. The next morning, my actual birthday, I awoke to see Senator Kerry conceding. The perfectly coifed John Edwards stood by his side, looking rather pissed and tight.

Dumbfounded and miserable, I never got out of my robe that day – alien behavior to be sure. I'd have to bite my lip for another four years. And bite everything else.

Happy Birthday.

I remember the headlines in the British newspapers: "How Can 59 Million People Be So Stupid?" I didn't think the British were in any position to comment. I thought however unexciting Kerry appeared at the time, he was still the better choice. The elitist moniker and the swift boating stuck. Not to mention the old well-worn Republican tactic of using the threat of gay marriage and rampant abortion to rally the party faithful.

In February of 2005, I saw a woman standing in the parking lot of my neighborhood grocery behind a sign that said "Impeach Cheney."

I was sure he would sit at the left hand of Lucifer someday. During his tenure as VP, I kept waiting for the Devil to appear on the Senate floor and claim his soul on C-Span in payment for letting him live through those four heart attacks while making all that money from Halliburton. The Teflon Administration, nothing touches them. I saw the banner in huge red letters and if there was ever a place I wanted to add my name... I looked at the eager woman holding her pen over the petition but I couldn't sign.

I hadn't forgotten how President Bush's campaign architect Karl Rove made anyone who spoke out against the Bush administration seem like a traitor. You are unpatriotic! You don't support the troops! I support them plenty. I recoiled at reading that Secretary of Defense Rumsfeld did not hand-sign letters to the families of our soldiers who had made the ultimate sacrifice for their country. He had an electric signature generator. He had complained there were too many letters to sign.[26] After much criticism, he corrected that behavior.

Nonetheless – impeach Cheney? He's a big, scary guy. He had people everywhere. You don't know where those petitions go. I thought it would get back to him, he'd put me in Gitmo and you'd never hear from me again. "Whatever happened to that Anita?" "I don't know. Is she traveling?" "No, she never goes anywhere." "Well...maybe we should call her?"

Freedom of speech notwithstanding, in our post 9/11 world, protest did not seem welcome even though dissent and debate are two of our bedrock principles.

Of all the roles I'd ever invented for myself over the years, I realized I wanted to add a new one – political activist. But it was much easier to write brilliant articles and tell people off on imaginary talk shows if they didn't know where I lived, or that I even existed.

Since my father's cautioning voice was still with me, I was horrified contemplating writing an article, joining a protest where I might be photographed, having someone know my name, my opinion. A letter of complaint to my Senators made me downright queasy. They'll have my address. They'll know what I think. My childlike sense of justice stood in conflict with my need to remain anonymous and safe.

In years past, even appealing a denied unemployment claim felt life threatening. You'd have thought I was arguing a case before the Supreme Court. I imagined they would shine a light in my eyes like I was being interrogated by the Gestapo. How many more times before I could say I'm tired of being afraid, I will no longer live in a house of cards and it will take more than a brisk wind to blow away the house that Anita built.

When I scraped myself off the carpet a few months after the election, I found out that Wes Clark had formed his own political action committee, WesPAC. He was speaking out and encouraging those of us who were demoralized not to give up. The discussions on his website were intelligent and balanced so I started lurking there, though I never had the nerve to post anything. I had also made occasional small financial contributions to help keep the place going. A regular visitor, I found the site a safe haven from Republican spin.

I had no idea at the time what spin really was. I received a real education when 2008 rolled around. Especially when I saw who was doing a lot of the spinning. Finding out the Democrats are just as guilty as Republicans of these kinds of games dealt me a shock I am still reeling from. Was I hopelessly naïve? Yes, but I am being truthful.

Bestowing sainthood on one party and demonizing the other is indicative of what I have found from both sides in most political discussions – no gray area, no room for error and defense of one's own Kool-Aid at all costs.

I wouldn't have believed the Democratic Party capable of shenanigans back in 2006 when I worked with none other than MoveOn.Org to help Democrats take back Congress. I thought, finally! Give us back Congress and we'll have oversight.

It was a miracle that we had won back the House and had narrowly taken the Senate in the midterms. Democrats were back in control. Imagine my surprise when newly elected House Speaker Nancy Pelosi announced that "impeachment was off the table." More important, oversight was near nonexistent. And the out of control spending and lack of regulation continued.

When all Ms. Pelosi could do was bluster because the Democratic minority was powerless to affect change, she landed her punches. In fact, she was a bulldog and I cheered her on. Upon retaking Congress, she became much more polite. The expression 'I've been had' said it all.

* * *

On January 20, 2007, Senator Hillary Clinton declared her candidacy for President of the United States. In an interview with Katie Couric, Hillary was asked about her "electability":

> "I would say, give me a chance. As a friend of mine said the other day, I am the most famous woman that nobody really knows. Because I've been caricaturized to some extent, and I want to let people make their own decisions. And I think that I can do that as I have in here in our state."[27]

'Caricatured' is putting it mildly. As editor Amy Sullivan noted in the *Washington Monthly*:

> Edward Klein's *The Truth About Hillary: What She Knew, and How Far She'll Go to Become President* is, even by the low standards of the genre, vile. In seeking to portray Hillary Clinton as a cold, manipulative woman who will do anything for power, Klein relies on wholly unsubstantiated accusations of corruption, lesbianism, and marital rape.[28]...

> [On] "The Chris Matthews Show," a panel discussed Hillary's candidacy while calling her "Nurse Ratched" and a "castrating female persona"; things really got going when journalist Gloria Borger mimicked Clinton's laugh and mannerisms while her colleagues sniggered.

> And that's coming from members of the mainstream media."[29]

Throughout 2007, well before the first primaries, the media was carping about the "inevitability" of Hillary as the nominee. Their attitude seemed to be, "We're stuck with her. Gird your loins, fellas."

"…[W]hen I see her again, all my -- all the cootie vibes sort of resurrect themselves…I'm sorry. I must represent a lot of people… I actually find her positions appealing in many ways. I just can't stand her."[30]

--Andrew Sullivan,
Chris Matthews Show 1/28/07

Hillary Clinton's laugh is "loud, inappropriate, and mirthless. . . . A scary sound that was somewhere between a cackle and a screech."[31]

-- Dick Morris

"Any woman who has ever been the only female in the room knows the guys are always waiting for that perfect moment - the one that makes the woman look silly, stupid, weepy or best of all, witchy. The men running against Clinton are still waiting for such an opportunity."[32]

-- Joan Vennochi, Boston Globe

"In so many ways, this all women's college prepared me to compete in the all boy's club of presidential politics."

-- Hillary Rodham Clinton

Senator Clinton was characterized by her opponents as the establishment candidate, a tool of corporations, "Bush-lite" and worst of all, an iron maiden.

CBS' Katie Couric got into the act at one point and asked Hillary if she was referred to as "Miss Frigidaire" in high school.[33] It saddened me that Ms. Couric would feign cluelessness as to the possible reasons for some boys insulting a smart and proud girl. How many girls have had a guy say some version of, "don't be so uptight, baby," a line which was as amusing as it was self-serving.

When *Advocate* magazine spoke with Hillary, they wanted to know if she was gay. No matter their motives for asking the question, what did that have to do with her qualifications?

"One distressing thing is the way men react to women who assert their equality: their ultimate weapon is to call them unfeminine. They think she is anti-male; they even whisper that she's probably a lesbian."

-- Shirley Chisholm

Ms. Chisholm ran for President in 1972, yet this question was still being asked. How much in our attitudes had changed?

In advance of the primaries, PBS' Bill Moyers interviewed Kathleen Hall Jamieson, Professor of Communication and director of the Annenberg Public Policy Center at the University of Pennsylvania. Mr. Moyers asked her if the old argument that "you can't use your uterus and your brain" was still in effect. Considered one of the country's leading experts on political advertising and campaigns, Ms. Jamieson responded:

"[A]t one time there was actually an argument that if women became educated, they would become infertile....these kinds of attacks have actually been deployed against women as they began to run for public office in the United States before. So the assertion that a woman would have to be childless or she couldn't be voted into office because if she were in office, she would neglect her children.

But a man elected to office would not neglect his children. Men were supposedly going to be taking care of children. Long-lived attack.

[T]he assumption [is] that any woman in power will, by necessity, entail emasculating men and, as a result, be a statement of fundamental threat.

So, why shouldn't you vote for Hillary Clinton? Well, first, she can't be appropriately a woman and be in power. She must be a man. ...But also explicit statements that suggest castrating, testicles in lockbox. She's going to emasculate men. It's a zero-sum game in which a woman in power necessarily means that men can't be men."[34]

"Not much has changed. Dick Cheney is still a war criminal, Hillary Clinton is still Satan and I'm back on the radio!"

-- Imus

On September 23, 2007, Senator Hillary Clinton barnstormed all five Sunday morning talk shows.[35] She looked and sounded mighty presidential, and of course, unflappable. As reported, "There was no major news committed, but she did offer some illuminating details on a range of issues."

Hillary being über-capable almost worked to her detriment. She is not a cold person, quite the opposite, but perhaps gave this impression because at times her demeanor in interviews had a defended quality. I had thought Hillary was being over-handled. But given the dire straits our country was in at the time, substantive policies were more important to me than branding or slick delivery.

Hillary was almost a lone voice in the Senate sounding the alarm bell on the impending mortgage crisis back in 2005. No one listened. Her prescience on this issue far outweighed Andrew Sullivan's "cootie" vibes.

In early debates when seven other candidates were on stage, no matter how the pack of boys went gunning for Hillary as the frontrunner, they could not make a dent. Overall, Hillary's reviews were stellar.

Yet on October 16, 2007, Clifford May, a former Republican Party spokesperson, appeared on MSNBC with columnist Eugene Robinson when host Tucker Carlson declared,

"'You should vote for her because she's a woman. They say that all the time. That's like their rationale."

Clifford May responded:

"At least call her a Vaginal-American."[36]

So she had either become a man by virtue of her "testicle lockbox," or a "Vaginal American" or she had "cooties." Make up your mind, guys.

I sighed at the screen, rolled my eyes and shut off the TV. The election could not get here fast enough to suit me.

I had also decided MoveOn.Org was misguided after General Petraeus, Iraq's ground commander, testified before Congress in the fall of 2007, offering his progress report. MoveOn.Org took out a full page ad with the banner "General Petraeus or General Betray Us." Any factual content in the body of the ad was overshadowed by this insult to the man's character and name.

Even General Clark, a darling of the net roots crowd, pointed out what a poor decision this was. In larger numbers, Americans were feeling disaffected by the war in Iraq and President Bush's leadership. Insulting the integrity of a man who had spent his life in service to his country was not the way to get independents and moderates to stick a toe in their tent. Bad move. Frat boy move. The backlash was loud and hard.

When there was an outcry in the Senate to censure their organization, it was Senator Hillary Clinton who voted against a Republican measure. It passed 72-25. Senator Obama skipped the vote, though he was in the building at the time.[37] A more mildly worded reprimand proposed by Senator Barbara Boxer was voted for by most Democrats but failed to pass.

MoveOn.Org later polled their membership to see which Democratic candidate to "endorse," though they had never before done such a thing. They held a vote on a Thursday afternoon and 10 percent of their entire membership voted. As 7 out of 10 chose Obama, MoveOn.Org endorsed him the next day. Doing the math would indicate that about 7% of their total membership participated in this vote and they proclaimed that consisted of a majority on which to base their endorsement.

I dropped my membership to MoveOn.Org that day.

5 THE LONG KNIVES COME OUT

At the start of 2008, I felt buoyed by a sense of possibility. I started leafing through the President Bush countdown calendar one of my husband's students had given him. Unlike stand-ups who found President Bush provided endless fodder for their comic diatribes, I could not laugh. Nonetheless, January brought a smile to my face. Change was on the way. But hope for change did not come in the person of Senator Obama. I saw the chasm between his words and his actions.

I would turn fifty the day before the election and envisioned the gift of having Joan of Arc in a pantsuit as our next President. I came to admire the woman who showed up at the crack of dawn to share her message with plant workers at shift change. Hillary's policies were thoughtful and detailed. No matter how hard she was campaigning, she found time to propose new legislation or make a pertinent statement about a particular national or world event on her website. She had even made fun of her own know-it-all image on "The Colbert Report."

The media did not share my elation, at least not with her. The nightmare began in earnest the first week of the primaries and set the tone for everything that followed. The elbow jabbing, locker room antics of newscasters and pundits telegraphed to me that one should be ashamed to support Hillary.

I wanted to enjoy following her campaign, but almost from the beginning, Democratic bigwigs and columnists were screaming she should give it up. The long knives were not just for Hillary. I felt like they were for me, or any woman who had the nerve to make noise. Making an example of one person is an effective way to silence others.

Ridicule is a powerful weapon. I know what it is to be shamed for anything about me that is not the status quo, everything from my big personality to my get 'er done demeanor. That is, until my detractor is in need of my skill set.

Margerie Eagan of the *Boston Herald* noted that while she was "no fan of Hillary's," she could not turn a blind eye to the negative characterizations aimed not only at the Senator but at her supporters:

> "Look at the constant references to the struggling, older white women and the struggling, younger single women (as if they're somehow sawed-off, unfulfilled and slightly pathetic) who are going to vote for her.[38]

On January 3, 2008, the Iowa Caucuses sent out shock waves: Obama 37.6%, Edwards 29.7% and Clinton 29.4%. After Hillary's third place finish, news anchors and pundits raced to proclaim her early demise.

> "[T]he 48 hours before the New Hampshire primary were the most humiliating any national figure of Hillary Clinton's stature had to endure in recent political history. It was a political execution that was broadcast across the world in slow motion. And it was ugly."[39]
>
> -- Joe Scarborough, MSNBC

Hillary was laughed out of the building. Who would want to follow in her footsteps or stand up for her? To lose is one thing. To be treated as a pariah and mocked for even daring to step onto the stage is quite another.

A neighbor called me the weekend before the New Hampshire primary to ask if "our girl" was in trouble. My husband and I sent our first $100 donation and kept our credit card handy. We had all but maxed out by June 3rd. The most I had sent to any other candidate was $25. I wrote to the heads of NBC/MSNBC:

"Keep it up. The more hateful you are to her, the more money I send, the more phone calls I make, the more letters I write."

Big media's smug gloating after Iowa bordered on vindictive, but nothing was so much derided and analyzed as Hillary's "misty moment" on the eve of the New Hampshire primary.

Every major news outlet posted some variant of the headline "Clinton Chokes Up." Here is the exchange as reported by CNN:

At the close of a Portsmouth campaign stop, Marianne Pernold-Young, 64, asked Clinton: "How do you do it? How do you keep up... and who does your hair?" Clinton began noting that she had help with her hair on "special days," and that she drew criticism on the days she did not. Then she added:

> "It's not easy, and I couldn't do it if I just didn't, you know, passionately believe it was the right thing to do. "You know, I have so many opportunities from this country, I just don't want to see us fall backwards," she said, her voice breaking a bit. The audience applauded. "This is very personal for me, it's not just political, it's [that] I see what's happening, we have to reverse it," she said emotionally, adding that some "just put ourselves out there and do this against some pretty difficult odds. But some of us are right and some of us are wrong. Some of us ready and some of us are not. Some of us know what we will do on day one, and some of us really haven't thought that through enough...So as tired as I am — and I am. And as difficult as it is to try and keep up what I try to do on the road, like occasionally exercise and try to eat right — it's tough when the easiest food is pizza — I just believe so strongly in who we are as a nation. So I'm gonna do everything I can and make my case and you know the voters get to decide."

On CNN, Rep. Jesse Jackson, Jr., Senator Obama's campaign co-chair, intimated "she was crying about her appearance." He then raised his chin and declared "she never cried for Katrina victims." How would he know?

Time Magazine and others pondered whether Hillary's moment was genuine, yet male politicians who got emotional on the trail were neither derided as weak nor queried about being dishonest. FOX News' Glenn Beck had a contribution, too. "It cries," he said.

John Edwards, the Presidential candidate who cavorted with his mistress and fathered her child while his wife was struggling with cancer, wanted to discuss a President's need for "resolve":

> "I think what we need in a commander in chief is strength and resolve, and presidential campaigns are a tough business, but being president of the United States is also a very tough business."

He chose to perpetuate a myth that women are emotional and therefore not capable of logic, reasoning or, I presumed, governing capabilities.

When Senator Clinton was interviewed by PBS' Tavis Smiley, he asked her about the media's obsession with that misty moment. She said, "None of us have ever been here before. I'm sure the press doesn't know what to make of me either. We'll figure it out as we go. All I can ask is to be judged on the merits."[40]

Some viewed tears as a manipulation, yet having an emotional stumble while running to be Commander in Chief was the last thing I assumed would buy any woman votes. Labeling her a crybaby came hard on the heels of calling her plodding and robotic. I started a list: how many non-conflating behaviors could they accuse her of? It would have been an amusing distraction if it weren't so painful.

Hillary's businesslike demeanor worked to her detriment, yet all evidence showed that had Senator Clinton not been tougher or more knowledgeable than her male rivals, she would have been derided as weak, lacking gravitas and a moron.

Hillary as painted by the media was cold and impenetrable. Those sentiments were echoed by a You Tube ad called "Vote Different" which has to date been viewed nearly 6 million times. In it, she was on a movie screen speaking to an audience of drugged and imprisoned men, their faces ashen. A young, athletic blonde in racing shorts and a tank top with an Obama logo emblazoned on her chest runs in, swinging a large hammer. Hurling it at the screen, she shatters Hillary's face. The men are "freed" from their prison, their stupor, and presumably, bad mommy. The older woman was also being cast aside in favor of the new model.

Smashing an image of Hillary Clinton with a hammer likewise conveyed a disturbing message. Why was it necessary to destroy her to move forward?

Yet this felt no more or less charitable than Joel Achenbach of the *Washington Post* saying that Hillary Clinton "needs a radio-controlled shock collar so that aides can zap her when she starts to get screechy"[41] or columnist Andrew Sullivan and NPR's Ken Rudin who had both compared her to Glenn Close's character in *Fatal Attraction*,[42] a stalker and kidnapper who threatened to kill an entire family with a carving knife.

Hillary bashing reached a fever pitch. Joe Conason of *Salon.com* noted:

> "Bias is far too mild a term to describe the bullying she has endured on cable television as well as in print. Indeed, prejudice against her is evidently so ingrained in the culture of the political media by now that the most inflamed commentators and journalists no longer feel constrained to conceal their emotions in the name of objectivity. [T]he disparity in her treatment compared with that of her rivals -- especially the indulgent and even adoring coverage of Obama -- became simply too obvious to ignore."[43]

Dana Milbank of the *Washington Post* agreed, "The press will savage her no matter what, pretty much. There's no question they have their knives out for her."[44]

At the debate prior to the New Hampshire primary, Scott Spradling asked Hillary the now infamous question – how did she feel about the fact that she wasn't "likeable."

"Well, that hurts my feelings," she said, volunteering that Senator Obama was "very likeable."

Senator Obama looked down with a smirk. "You're likeable enough, Hillary."[45]

Undecided voters in New Hampshire broke for Hillary. Women having a snoot full of the treatment she was getting voted for her, too. Senator Clinton was supposed to lose by double digits. She didn't.

She made history.

Instead of jumping up and down to celebrate the fact that Hillary Clinton just became the first woman to ever win a binding presidential primary,[46] powerful media outlets implied an entire state was racist. Chris Matthews of MSNBC's "Hardball" piped up: "You remember the Lone Ranger and Tonto? Me think paleface speak with forked tongue. You hear me? Forked tongue."[47]

His implication was that voters lied to pollsters about who they were going to vote for. Big media carped about "The Bradley Effect," whereby one will overstate their support for a black candidate. Fourteen months later, an article in *Pollster.com* summarized the findings of the American Association for Public Opinion Research.[48,49]

It was revealed that flawed polling models were used during the primary. Due to their chosen calling times, pollsters were less successful reaching demographics that comprised Hillary voters. The Bradley Effect had little if anything to do with it. There were no apologies from the *New York Times*, CNN or other trusted sources for their error. Those who declared her loss before the fact were caught with their pants down.

The racist narrative began to take hold.

In his January 13th interview with Senator Clinton, respected journalist Tim Russert of NBC's *Meet the Press* played gotcha, offering up truncated quotes of the Clintons out of context. On the campaign trail, Senator Clinton said:

> "I would point to the fact that that Dr. King's dream began to be realized when President Lyndon Johnson passed the Civil Rights Act of 1964, when he was able to get through Congress something that President Kennedy was hopeful to do, the President before had not even tried, but it took a President to get it done."[50]

Following the example set by several *New York Times* articles, Mr. Russert omitted her reference to President Kennedy.[51] He also quoted *New York Times* columnist Bob Herbert who accused Mrs.

Clinton of "taking cheap shots" at "Reverend Dr. Martin Luther King Jr."

Russert aired Bill Clinton's statement about Senator Obama:

> "Give me a break. This whole thing is the biggest fairy tale I've ever seen."[52]

Russert offered up a video of Democratic operative Donna Brazile's reaction:

> "As an African-American, I find his words and his tone to be very depressing."[53]

Mr. Russert again quoted Bob Herbert, who accused the Clinton camp of working to "undermine" Obama's message of "hope and healing." Tim Russert asserted he was showing viewers "exactly what President Clinton said," while omitting the bulk of the former President's statement. Clinton's comments referred specifically to Senator Obama's changing position on the Iraq war, not his candidacy.[54]

> "Second, it is wrong that Senator Obama got to go through 15 debates trumpeting his superior judgment and how he had been against the war in every year, enumerating the years and never got asked one time, not once, "Well, how could you say that when you said in 2004 you didn't know how you would have voted on the resolution? You said in 2004 there was no difference between you and George Bush on the war and you took that speech you're now running on off your Web site in 2004 and there's no difference in your voting record and Hillary's ever since."

> "Give me a break. This whole thing is the biggest fairy tale I've ever seen."[55]

This was a critical moment in the campaign. President Clinton's "fairy tale" comments, taken out of context, were the beginning of his being referred to as racist and created a schism between the Clintons and the African American community with whom they had always been so popular.

The bombardment by the media and the blogosphere continued. Senator Clinton's supporters were called racist, bitter, Archie Bunkers, low-information, over-the-hill, rednecks, uneducated, dried-up, shoulder-pad feminists, sweeties, Hillary hags, and much worse. If one was an African American Hillary supporter, the slurs were vile beyond measure.

There was scant coverage of the heckler at a New Hampshire campaign stop who held up a placard yelling "Iron my shirt"[56] in his attempt to embarrass Senator Clinton.

> "Oh, the remnants of sexism are alive and well," Mrs. Clinton said. ...."As I think has just been abundantly demonstrated, I am also running to break through the highest and hardest glass ceiling."[57]

Feminist author Robin Morgan wondered what if heaven forbid someone said to Obama, "Senator, shine my shoes?"

I got into a debate with a black friend of mine because in her view you cannot even compare the ills of racism with misogyny. "Don't even go there," she said. I argued that while racism is abhorrent it is unacceptable in polite society, yet many do not take hate speech against women seriously. Women of every race are on the receiving end of violence, both in this country and around the world, every minute of every day. Many of their abusers are not called to account, or get a slap on the wrist in lieu of a punishment befitting their acts. Hateful speech and attitudes can lead to violent crimes. There is no separation. She relented and said, "Okay, they're both bad."

> "I've always met more discrimination being a woman than being black."
>
> -- Shirley Chisholm

Chris Matthews famously confessed he got "a tingle up his leg" upon hearing one of Senator Obama's speeches. Given his tingle, it was odd that Matthews referred to men who backed Hillary Clinton as "castratos in the eunuch chorus."[58]

I looked at a few of her strong supporters: Mayor Michael Nutter, General Wesley Clark, Governor Ed Rendell, Robert Kennedy, Jr., Governor Ted Strickland, Senator Evan Bayh, General John M. Shalikashvili, Magic Johnson, Jack Nicholson, Congressman Joe Sestak, Rob Reiner, General Henry Hugh Shelton and Bill. Not a castrato in the bunch.

"She's everyone's first wife standing outside a probate court." "McCain is likable. She's not"[59]

-- Mike Barnicle, MSNBC

"She's never going to get out of our faces. ... She's like some hellish housewife who has seen something that she really, really wants and won't stop nagging you about it until finally you say, fine, take it, be the damn President, just leave me alone."[60]

-- Leon Wieseltier,
literary editor, *The New Republic*,
as quoted by Maureen Dowd of *The New York Times*

Pundits hissed, "She's so ambitious." Hillary was called "ego driven and power hungry," yet a man in the Senate less than two years before running for President was not described as ego driven or power hungry.

Los Angeles Times columnist Meghan Daum stated that voters were "freaked out by Clinton's aching need for the presidency" and that "we want her to pursue the nomination without looking like a pursuer."[61] It strained credulity that a woman campaigning for the toughest job in the world should have to play hard to get in order to be appealing.

I was reminded of the documentary "Every Little Step," chronicling the casting process for the revival of "A Chorus Line." While coaching auditioning dancers on the attitude required for the routine she had just taught them, choreographer Bayoork Lee looked at them pointedly and said "eat nails." Maybe we don't want to see a woman, any woman, eat nails.

Hillary Clinton was graded less on her candidacy or policies than her womanhood. She was cast as the attacking female while a protective cocoon was spun around her opponent. I didn't want a president I had to protect. I wanted one who was going to protect me.

The media found fault with all things Hillary since they viewed the candidates through the prism of their own desire. Joan Walsh, editor-in-chief of *Salon.com*, made that clear:

> "I was struck when I got to Iowa and New Hampshire in January by how our media colleagues

were just swooning over Barack Obama. That is not too strong a word. They were swooning.... the biggest names in our business were there, and they were, they could repeat some of his speech lines to one another. It was like a Bruce Springsteen concert where the fans sing along. And, you know, I respected it to some extent."

"He's a towering political figure. Of our generation, he's probably the best politician, he's inspiring. And, reporters, white reporters, black reporters, we want to get beyond racism in America. So he was, he was inspiring. The downside, though, is that they hate, hate Hillary Clinton, most of them."[62]

Hatred had no place in the equation. The old baggage of those who purported to be professionals should not have been a concern. I expected objective coverage. This contest was too important for swooning.

"When Sen. Hillary Clinton... raises her voice, and when a lot of women do, you know, it's -- as I say -- it reaches a point ... where every husband in America ... has heard at one time or another."

"Look, the famous Dr. Johnson, ...and I hate to repeat it, said, you know, 'To see a woman speaking is to watch a dog walking on its hind legs ... Sure, he said you're surprised not to see it done -- not that it's not done well, but to see it done at all."[63]

-- Pat Buchanan, MSNBC

When Hillary opened her mouth, she was called harsh, "shrewish" and shrill. Perhaps it was less her voice and more the idea of a woman giving the orders with which they took issue. I was reminded how I'd have to modulate my own voice at times so as not to sound too commanding. *Bloomberg* columnist Margaret Carlson referred to Senator Clinton as a "domineering mother." How could she be saddled with the burden of embodying the perfect mother in addition to the other hoops she had to jump through?

The domineering male is acceptable. We expect men to be in charge and are not supposed to bristle at being ordered about or lectured by them. Many male politicians actually wag a finger, almost admonishing the crowd, when offering up their talking points. Imagine a female politician attempting that trick.

A man seeking high office would also never be criticized for being absent from his children's lives. That would not be an effective way of attacking him – but for a woman? You betcha.

I had heard some say, "I have no problem electing a woman, just not *that* woman!" A closer look at how we judge powerful women illustrated that was neither a realistic nor truthful statement.

The New Agenda, an organization formed in reaction to the sexism visited by 2008's election coverage featured a video "Where's The Line," revealing the ways in which Hillary and Chelsea Clinton, Sarah Palin, Michelle Obama, Cindy McCain and Elizabeth Edwards were dissected and insulted: "Schizophrenic, bitch, Stepford wife, multiple personality disorder, angry black woman, emasculating, caribou Barbie, soppy and bitchy, Sybil, diva, 'he might be attracted to a woman who used her mouth for something besides talking…'"

Then there were creative campaign T-shirts:

Bros Before Hoes

Stay Out Of My Village Bitch

Wanna See Hillary Run? Throw Rocks At Her

If You Can't Satisfy Your Husband, You Can't Satisfy America

Life's A Bitch Don't Vote For One

Pillory Hillary '08

Drill Baby Drill (featuring Governor Palin being penetrated from behind)

Sarah Palin Is A Cunt

Fuck Hillary -- God Knows, She Needs It

Hillary Nutcracker Dolls featuring inner thighs of spiked steel that were displayed in store windows felt like a warning to all women.

Columnist Connie Schultz reported meeting with women at a college campus who were given this "gift" by their boyfriends if they dared vote for her. A girl stood horrified, the doll clenched in her hand, tears burning her face. There was no comedy in such a gesture.

When the blogger boyz called Hillary a "filthy sow," it hit home on a cellular level and I had to respond. A group that put up a billboard saying "I Wish Hillary Had Married O.J." was likewise a shock to the system.

What were these ladies' crimes, aside from being female? The preoccupation with identity politics, bowling scores and bourbon shots, was odd given our nation's economic and foreign policy difficulties in 2008. I thought we would be better served with a sober discussion of who was best able to lead our country.

Seeing women trashed for sport was even more disturbing because there was an appetite for it. I felt like a captive audience, no matter which TV station I watched, which radio station I listened to, or which newspaper I read. I may as well have been tied to a chair, forced to watch this coverage as a loop, so furious I wanted to chew through the furniture.

Hillary had long fought for issues that mattered to me. Finally, I had someone I wanted to fight for. I was so proud I wanted to shout it daily but increasingly felt I'd better keep that joy under wraps.

When a producer friend called, we held our breath, wary of asking who the other supported. We both blurted out Hillary! Relieved to be in the same camp with me, she confided that she had already lost friendships arguing over the candidates. Another friend said talking to my husband and me about this topic was like being sucked into a deep hole. I didn't tell him of the sharp ache in my throat after hearing his words.

Whatever sexism or disrespect I'd dealt with in my life, I found a way to handle it in the moment; brush it aside and move on. That this was still bubbling just under the surface in our culture made me think I was living in a parallel universe. My childhood habit of toughing it out and saying nothing was still with me until New Hampshire made the dam burst. We say the sky's the limit for a woman in this country. The response was different when we were presented with a test case.

I saw it on the TV screen happening to someone else. Observing from a distance made it all the more obvious. I was no longer that numb little kid, captive and powerless to stop my father abusing my mother, or a young woman dealing with some lawyer staring at my breasts when I handed him a memo. The more they told Hillary to shut up and sit down, the more I said "How about you sit down and let the lady have her say -- since I think what she has to say makes more sense."

Senator Clinton was navigating uncharted territory. The bottomless disrespect on the airwaves denied me the pleasure of enjoying her accomplishments, win or lose. The vitriol from various corners made me afraid to put a Hillary bumper sticker on my car. I started having nightmares about being cut up into little bits.

The media firestorm in New Hampshire was representative of every contest. I am not the only one who's greater involvement was prompted in reaction to efforts to demoralize her supporters. I may not have bought a bumper sticker, but I found other ways to advertise. I didn't know I was already a year too late.

6 QUESTIONING THE HOPE/CHANGE EXPRESS

The last three-way debate with Hillary Clinton, Barack Obama and John Edwards took place on January 21, 2008 before the South Carolina Primary. Senator Clinton was booed for daring to mention Senator Obama's involvement with the "slumlord Rezko."

Senator Obama said he had done five hours of pro-bono work for Rezko years before and barely knew him. I didn't know who Tony Rezko was at the time. I sensed from Senator Obama's body English he was not being truthful. By the expression on Hillary's face, she knew it, too. The audience continued to be hostile. She let it go with a knowing smirk.

I made it my business to find out about "Rezko." Senator Obama had received a total of $250,000 in campaign contributions from him (he eventually refunded a large portion under pressure). They were closely associated for seventeen years, with Obama recommending Rezko for lucrative housing development contracts in his district as a State Senator.[64] *The Boston Globe*[65] had a series of articles on this which never got traction.

Under indictment at the time, Mr. Rezko along with his wife, had helped the Obamas to purchase their home. "A few months after Obama became a U.S. senator, he and Rezko's wife, Rita, bought adjacent pieces of property from a doctor in Chicago's Kenwood neighborhood." Mrs. Rezko paid $625,000, buying the vacant lot at full price, whereas the Obamas bought their home at $300,000 below market value.[66] It was later disclosed that Tony Rezko had toured the house with Mr. Obama before the fact.

When the full extent of their relationship was revealed regarding the house purchase, Senator Obama responded, "It was boneheaded." That was regarded as an acceptable explanation by the press. The story died.

Tony Rezko was convicted on 16 out of 24 counts of wire and mail fraud, money laundering and aiding and abetting bribery on June 4th, 2008, the morning after the Primary was decided.

I had never imagined politicians were boy scouts. But Mr. Obama was basing his campaign on the fact that he was above questionable activity. His claim to be "a new way of doing business in Washington" was advertised as one of his best selling points.

At that same debate, John Edwards, instead of his typical practice of tag-teaming with Senator Obama to carp at Hillary, questioned Obama about his State Senate votes. Obama had voted "present" 129 times (including a number of women's "choice" issues) and voted "wrong" 6 times, meaning he had "hit the wrong button" on 6 different occasions.

This was never explained or justified and I couldn't get past it. It felt like political expediency. Hillary took some grief for her comment that "in the White House, you can't just vote present," but I sensed much of Senator Obama's career up to this point had been about protecting his future rather than his constituents. He seemed allergic to criticism and slightly disconnected from the gravity of the job he was vying for. I suspected his arrogance would be his undoing.

His actions in the U.S. Senate reflected that he had a habit of avoiding risky votes. All Senators miss a certain percentage of their votes. Senator Obama missed about 40% of his. I was curious as to why a newbie Senator would not be more conscientious.

Senator Obama was charged with heading a subcommittee in the Senate on European Affairs and Afghanistan but never held one meeting. Since we were at war with Afghanistan and he was billed as the anti-war candidate, I found that curious. At a debate he said he'd been busy campaigning and that was why he hadn't held a meeting in fourteen months. After being called on that lapse, he did not correct the situation.

Contrary to popular belief, the bulk of Senator Obama's campaign contributions came from large donors.[67] Many of his advisors were corporatists, including Austan Goolsbee and Jeffrey Liebman, who both favored privatizing social security. He had only been in Senate session 143 days before running for President. He had no foreign policy experience nor was he an economist.

Early on in their primary battle, Senator Barack Obama boasted, "I am confident I will get [Hillary's] votes if I'm the nominee. It's not clear she would get the votes I got if she were the nominee."[68] Cocky and inexperienced were ingredients that made for a troubling cocktail.

Adding this together, it was not logical that this gentleman would know how to govern at this most difficult time in our nation's history, speeches or charisma notwithstanding. Even then-Senator Joe Biden made much the same comment about Senator Obama at the time: "The Presidency does not lend itself to on the job training."

There was no doubt that David Axelrod ran a great campaign for Senator Obama. There were super-sized rallies complete with women fainting in the aisles, people screaming "I love you, Barack" from the throngs in the audience.

Having been an actor for thirty years, I was distrustful of glitz and hoopla. I knew what happened when the camera zoomed out past the range of flats masquerading as solid walls. I could see the two-by-fours holding up what to the untrained eye had looked like a real house. One should never buy the cover art. I can feel the difference between the real thing and a carefully crafted façade. I should know. I had one.

Pundits referred to Hillary as "inauthentic" or "overproduced" yet somehow did not assume that Mr. Obama's events were likewise political theatre.

While I agreed that Obama's campaign was prettier than Hillary's, I shouted to anyone who would listen – campaigning is not governing. The campaign manager is not going to be running the country. At least, I would hope not.

While the Senator claimed to be progressive on Gay Rights, he campaigned down south with Donnie McClurkin, an "ex-gay man reformed through prayer." As reported by *The New York Times*:

> "Senator Barack Obama is drawing criticism for signing up a gospel singer with controversial views about gay men and lesbians for his campaign in South Carolina... Mr. McClurkin, a black preacher who sang at the Republican National Convention in 2004, has gained notoriety for his view that homosexuality is a choice and can be "cured" through prayer, a view ridiculed by gay people.
>
> Critics on the Internet say Mr. Obama is trying to appeal to conservative blacks at the expense of gay people. Surveys have found that blacks are less supportive than whites are of legalizing gay relationships.
>
> Mr. Obama said through a spokesman that he "strongly disagrees" with Mr. McClurkin's views."[69]

Senator Obama's was interviewed by the editorial board of the *Reno Gazette Journal*. Sam Stein of *The Huffington Post* quoted Mr. Obama's statements praising Ronald Reagan. He had also compared himself to both Reagan and JFK:

> "I don't want to present myself as some sort of singular figure. I think part of what is different is the times. I do think that, for example, the 1980 election was different. I think Ronald Reagan changed the trajectory of America in a way that Richard Nixon did not and in a way that Bill Clinton did not. He put us on a fundamentally different path because the country was ready for it. They felt like with all the excesses of the 60s and the 70s and government had grown and grown but there wasn't much sense of accountability in terms of how it was operating. I think he tapped into what people were already feeling. Which is we want clarity, we want optimism, we want a return to that sense of dynamism and entrepreneurship that had been missing."[70]

In 1996, it was President Clinton who said, "The era of big government is over." President Clinton's centrism and ability to work with Republicans to balance the budget was ignored in Senator Obama's apparent outreach to crossover voters. Since his name was Clinton, he could not be praised.

Strategically, I understood why Mr. Obama did this, but lauding a Republican seemed an odd way for a Democrat to behave. He was not taken to task for this by his left-leaning supporters.

As to Mr. Edwards, I made my decision about him a long time ago and had been referring to him, perhaps unkindly, as a "hairdo" since 2003. It could have been because of his supercilious smile. Something about him never rang true to me, and while I put up with his being in second position on Kerry's ticket in 2004, I never sensed he had the gravitas to be President.

When he dropped out of the race after a disappointing finish in South Carolina, Edwards made reference to stepping aside "so history could blaze its path."[71] The media helped in this regard, allowing Edwards to fade away so they could sell the WWE Smackdown pitting Hillary and Barack against each other.

Although Senator Obama was supported by much of the old guard of the Democratic Party, he was advertised as the candidate of "change" – and the underdog. All we heard in the run-up to Super Tuesday was "Will Obama have *time* to catch up?" "Can he *beat* her?" "Can he *knock her down*?" People tend to root for the underdog.

Questions regarding Senator Obama's political and personal associations, the logic behind his contradictory campaign promises and voting behavior went unanswered.

Comparing the two candidates, one had only to ask whether Senator Clinton would have been excoriated for that which Senator Obama was excused.

7 A VIEW FROM THE GROUND

My dad used to say "If you can make it through February, you can make it through the entire year."

He died February 3, 1978.

Senator Clinton's campaign had everything riding on a big win Super Tuesday, February 5th. On that night, Tim Russert stared at the camera, agape. He could not bring himself to utter the words that Hillary Clinton had just beaten Barack Obama in the Massachusetts primary by 15 points. Her victory came despite Senator Obama having the endorsements of the state's most powerful political figures, Senators Teddy Kennedy and John Kerry, and Governor Duval Patrick.

Obama's campaign manager, David Axelrod, also ran the campaign that got Mr. Patrick elected Governor. There was some brouhaha that Obama and Patrick traded speeches using similar verbiage. Governor Patrick wasn't polling well and it would appear Massachusetts voters opted not to choose a similar message when they heard it a second time.

Mr. Russert's pause seemed interminable. Hillary was gonna be a thorn in some people's sides a while longer.

Hillary won New York, California, New Jersey, Massachusetts, Oklahoma, Arkansas, Tennessee, New Mexico and Arizona. Chris Matthews said "She held serve."

While Hillary did well, it was short of a big enough win to end the game.

Missouri Senator Claire McCaskill declared, "At the fierce urging of my 18-year-old daughter, I could not sit in the bleachers any longer."[72] She had endorsed and campaigned for Senator Obama.

Hillary lost Missouri by less than one point.

The next morning, it was reported that Senator Clinton had loaned her campaign $5 million in January so that she could remain competitive with Senator Obama's huge war chest. She was not a solitary tower after all. She needed our help. She got it.

The rest of the month sent a chill wind of eleven caucuses and smaller states that all went Senator Obama's way. Hillary replaced Patti Solis Doyle with longtime ally, the stalwart Maggie Williams, as campaign manager. Her back to the wall, Texas and Ohio became must win states for her. Her faithful supporters braced against the cold, praying for March to get here as quickly as possible.

"Hillary should get out now."

-- Jonathan Alter, *Newsweek*, 2/23/2008

"Time for Hillary to drop out."

-- Jack Cafferty, CNN, 2/25/2008

"There is dissension in the Hillary Clinton camp. Top aides have been in arguments, shouting back and forth about differences in strategy. Should Clinton come on strong? Should she go negative? Should she be upbeat and positive? Here's my answer: Stop campaigning.

The evidence is overwhelming that since Super Tuesday, the minute that Clinton steps foot in a state, her numbers start to plummet.[73]

-- Richard Cohen, *Washington Post*, 2/26/2008

I first worked the phone banks the weekend before the Texas and Ohio primaries. Every volunteer at that center spoke fluently about her policies. "Low information voters" my ass. My friends and I huddled near each other, bolstering each other's confidence. Unbelievable the nerve it takes to disturb unsuspecting strangers in their homes.

I recalled an article in the *New York Times* about city and state representatives who refused to abandon Senator Clinton for Senator Obama despite great pressure to do so. When they needed help in their districts, she showed up. I had a conversation with a gruff guy in Texas who planned to vote for Senator Obama. I kept him talking...

"Sir, I'm an ex-New Yorker and when Hillary first got elected, firemen thought she was a carpetbagger and were booing her. But they changed their tune because when Hillary saw how many of them were getting sick after 9/11, she showed up after the cameras stopped rolling to make sure that they had the care they needed. And 25,000 New York firemen came out to endorse her."

His response was silence. For five seconds. Then he blurted, "I got some rice fryin' on the stove." He hung up. My throat tightened and I could feel my face getting hot. I just stared at my papers. My buddy John put his hand over his cell phone, "You made the guy think." I don't flatter myself I changed the man's mind. I didn't want anyone to write Hillary off on the basis of propaganda. Decide this one on the issues, damn it.

Sixty year-old Caroline was my favorite volunteer: "I strongly urge you to vote for Hillary, she represents change – with *substance*." We giggled quietly, raising our eyebrows in agreement and incorporated her mantra into our next calls.

On March 4th, Hillary won Texas, Rhode Island and took the crucial bellwether state of Ohio by 10 points.

Senator Obama took Vermont.

Taking the stage, Senator Clinton made her victory speech:

> "For everyone who's been counted out, but refused to be knocked out; for everyone who has stumbled and stood right back up; for everyone who works hard and never gives up — this one is for you!"

There were six whole weeks until the Pennsylvania primary. Anything could happen – maybe even some vetting of her opponent. The Clinton campaign had new life. And so did her supporters.

Yet the Democratic leadership fretted all too early that the "drawn out, divisive" primary must end. Considering their worry-fest began nine months before Election Day, this was code for

"Drop out, Hillary." Democratic voter registrations were way up. So was Party excitement as evidenced by the DNC's burgeoning coffers. What was the harm in letting the entire country participate in the most exciting primary we had had in many years?

Otherwise painfully silent, Al Gore said in mid-March we had plenty of time to contest the general election and to let the Primaries play out. Speaker Pelosi's subtle complaints and strong arming sent a clear message. Twenty-three heavy hitter campaign donors sent a letter telling Ms. Pelosi in not so polite terms to back off. She did – for a while, anyway. Nancy Pelosi was a disappointment to me as Speaker. I had heard too much double talk from her on policy since she had assumed that post. The bulldog was gone. She was the last person I wanted steering the ship of the Democratic Party.

Perhaps the DNC leadership succumbed to fears of the "divisive and polarizing" label that had been pinned on Hillary, thinking Senator Obama would put an end to partisan bickering. Senator Clinton pointed out the naïveté of such a notion. To assume anyone, by virtue of their charm, would make those entrenched in their own belief systems give up the fight indicates one is not paying attention to the reality that is Washington.

Senator Clinton was not the face the DNC wanted on the spaghetti jar they were selling to the American people and the world. And that was that.

The liberals in the Senators boys' club were among the worst of Hillary's detractors:

> "There is no way that Senator Clinton is going to win enough delegates to get the nomination. She ought to withdraw and she ought to be backing Senator Obama. Now, obviously that's a decision that only she can make frankly I feel that she would have a tremendous career in the Senate…I think that her criticism is hurting him more than anything John McCain has said."[74]

-- Senator Pat Leahy, 3/28/2008
chair, Judiciary Committee

It was kind of Senator Leahy to pontificate about where her career should start and end. He had also complained that John

McCain was getting a "free ride" since Senators Obama and Clinton were fighting with each other.

> "There was a poll the other day that said 22 percent of democrats want me to drop out and 22 percent want Senator Obama to drop out and 62 percent said let people vote. One thing you know about me when I tell you I will fight for you I will get up every day and that's exactly what I will do. I believe going to work for you is what I am called to do."[75]
>
> -- Senator Hillary Clinton,
> campaign rally, Mishawaka, Indiana

My friends and I redoubled our efforts.

I had spoken with voters in Texas, Ohio, Pennsylvania, Mississippi, Kentucky, North Carolina, Indiana, Wisconsin, Oregon and West Virginia. Many volunteers logged in thousands more calls than I. Calling Oregon, one woman said, "God bless you for all your hard work." When I asked another if she would be supporting Hillary, she said "Absolutely not!" and hung up. I wanted to ask her why she supported Obama, since he voted "yes" on the unpopular Bush/Cheney Energy Bill which directly affected Oregon, whereas Hillary (and McCain) voted "no."

No matter how many cogent arguments we presented for not supporting a man with elastic policies and little experience, big media intimated we must be racist. How do you prove you are *not* something? I wanted to shame them for their false words but had no way to do so. As a kid, nothing angered me more than being accused of something I didn't do.

There were valid reasons for not believing the myth of Barack Obama enough to vote for him, none of which had anything to do with his ethnicity. I made at least five hundred campaign phone calls. I only spoke with one woman who said anything racist to me. She said, "Confidentially I don't know how any black man is going to do anything for a white man in this country." I had nothing more to say to her so I hung up. Anyone else who engaged me talked about the issues, not skin color.

A woman in North Carolina said she and her husband were both Republicans and long distance truckers. "We vote our conscience in this house, we don't vote party." She gave me an earful about China, off shore drilling, taxing oil companies, pension plans and more. She was well informed and we found common ground on a couple of issues. She asked me to tell Hillary "the next time I spoke to her," that "*she* should run things at the White House and just tell Bill to stay in New York." I said, "I'll be sure to pass the word along..."

Speaking with her reminded me of a four-month tour I had done with a small theatre company soon after college. Traveling throughout the south I felt alien, very much a New Yorker and not of anywhere else. My calls during the Primary changed that. An acquaintance said "those people living in red states are less educated and informed." His bias betrayed his ignorance. At one time, maybe I was just as bad, referring to everyone else as the "flyover people." For that I am sorry. I was wrong.

I have in-laws sprinkled half way around the U.S., sophisticated in their knowledge and understanding of political affairs, some more than their coastal counterparts. The nonsense spewed by people I thought knew better made me take a second look at what I'd been thinking all this time. I know many informed, caring people in LA. I also know a few who are clueless. No one gets a pass by virtue of geography or party.

In addition to breaking out my credit card for campaign donations more often than I cared to admit, I was crazy-glued to the computer. My husband, championing Hillary as much as I did, was getting so sick of my tunnel vision at times I thought he'd pitch our brand new monitor out the window, and the CPU after it. Thankfully, he stuck with it, and me. I could not have hoped for a better partner.

Knowing how many were divided in their households in 2008, I considered myself lucky I didn't have to deal with my mate disparaging my efforts. I knew a few who gave up the fight in frustration for that reason. Many relationships and friendships ended over this election. If I had it to do all over again, I would do the same thing, but sooner. And louder.

"She is a monster."[76]

-- Samantha Power,
foreign policy advisor to Senator Obama

As voters got to know and hear Hillary on the stump, many scratched their heads about her reputation, bearing witness to her approachable nature. Hillary hit her stride and emerged as a politician no longer in anyone's shadow, winning a grudging respect from some Republicans who had been her detractors. Once she just let Hillary be Hillary out on the campaign trail, she was formidable.

There was a stink about Hillary not releasing her tax returns. David Plouffe, one of Obama's campaign architects, called Clinton "the most secretive politician in America today." We saw none of Senator Obama's academic records, not one article he had written while President of the *Harvard Law Review*, no thesis, the entirety of eight years' worth of his Illinois State Senate records had evaporated and he released a one-page 276 word 'summary' from a doctor in lieu of medical records covering twenty-two years of care. President Obama gave Hillary a run for her money in the secretive department.

When the Clintons' tax returns were offered up shortly thereafter, they reflected paying fully 33% of their large income to taxes and showed donations of 10% of their income to charity. No retractions of suspicious insults were forthcoming. The release of eight years of her schedules as First Lady revealed Hillary never stopped working. Yet Tim Russert and his guest panels "...repeatedly discussed what the schedules say, or do not say, about where Hillary Clinton was during Monica Lewinsky's encounters with President Clinton, in many cases teasing segments or leading them with that information."[77] According to MSNBC anchor Contessa Brewer:

> "We want to talk about the 11,000 pages of documents released by Bill Clinton's presidential library that provide the most comprehensive insight into Senator Hillary Clinton's tenure as first lady. Among the revelations, that Mrs. Clinton was at the White House on at least seven occasions when her husband was engaging in sexual encounters with Monica Lewinsky."[78]

The Fourth Estate indeed.

Along with his wife Valerie Plame Wilson, Ambassador Joe Wilson was a staunch Hillary supporter who had written several editorials touting her qualifications. One such *Huffington Post* piece stated in part:

"...In response to Hillary's detailed, substantive speech on Iraq, Obama replied with ad hominem insults. Instead of presenting his own plan, his campaign indulged in character assassination.

David Axelrod, the top Obama political strategist, for one, knows better. After all, he and his wife were direct beneficiaries of Hillary Clinton's personal kindness and public policy experience when, in the midst of the impeachment trial of her husband, she travelled to Chicago to support Susan Axelrod's efforts to raise money for her foundation, Citizens United for Research on Epilepsy (CURE), established by her after one of the Axelrod children was afflicted with the malady." [79]

Ambassador Wilson shared excerpts from two Ben Wallace-Wells articles that appeared in the *New York Times*:[80]

"It was January 1999, President Clinton's impeachment trial was just beginning in the Senate and Hillary Clinton was scheduled to speak at the foundation's fund-raiser in Chicago. Despite all the fuss back in Washington, Clinton kept the appointment. She spent hours that day in the epilepsy ward at Rush Presbyterian hospital, visiting children hooked up to machines by electrodes so that doctors might diagram their seizure activity and decide which portion of the brain to remove. [81]

At the hospital, a local reporter pressed her about the trial in Washington, asked her about that woman. At the organization's reception at the Drake Hotel that evening, Clinton stood backstage looking over her remarks, figuring out where to insert anecdotes about the kids. "She couldn't stop talking about what she had seen," Susan Axelrod recalled.[82]

Later, at Hillary Clinton's behest, the National Institutes of Health convened a conference on finding a cure for epilepsy. Susan Axelrod told me it was "one of the most important things anyone has done for epilepsy." And this is how politics works:

David Axelrod is now dedicated to derailing this woman's career."[83]

David Axelrod knew better. It was against his candidate's interests to admit it. David Axelrod officially became the anti-Christ.

When I was once blindsided by someone close to me, a girlfriend had consoled me by saying, "Don't take it personally. He would have done it to Buddha."

The phrase, "It's not personal" reinforces the dirty business that is politics. Nothing is off limits. As Hillary pointed out in her writing, and later repeated on "Late Night With David Letterman", her early summer job of "sliming fish was the best preparation she could ever have for living in Washington."[84]

On April 3rd, I attended a fundraiser in LA for Hillary, a first for me. Contrary to the way the media painted her supporters, the audience looked like the rainbow coalition. They were also educated, informed and responded enthusiastically to her specific answers on policy. She must have received twenty standing ovations from the sold-out crowd.

Moved by the electricity in the large theatre, I gawked in amazement. Here was a qualified woman who had a chance to become President. I couldn't hold back my emotions. She was warm and funny, answering questions that were fished out of a bowl for ninety minutes. I was comforted by the way she was showing off, 'Ask me anything, I'm ready,' she seemed to say.

At dinner with two friends the following week, I told them about my work on behalf of the campaign. When I started my compare and contrast spiel about the candidates, one of them said "It's bullshit, it's all bullshit. They'll all break your heart in the end. They've all sold their souls."

I reasoned to myself that she'd had her heart broken the same way. Still, I started to pay a little too much attention to my salad, cutting my mixed greens into much smaller pieces while the rest of the discussion played out between my two friends.

After dinner, we walked into Anthropologie for some shopping therapy, a colorful store stinking with overpriced tee shirts and misshapen urban and urbane clothing. I looked at the cherry wood floor, wishing it would open up and swallow me.

I drifted off so my friend's stinging words wouldn't penetrate. I was adept at making up another world to leave the discomfort of this one. I often hid away growing up, sitting in a movie theatre by myself to watch a favorite film over and over or walking for hours through New York City, enjoying a calming silence navigating through endless human traffic. It was a peaceful retreat I longed for again.

I felt an odd sense of separation pursuing a course with more passion than most others in my circle. It was embarrassing to broadcast how hard I was working to get Hillary Clinton elected. But why should it have been? Some of my other friends must have wondered what was happening to me.

Terrified or not, I was starting to make noise, in person, by mail, by phone. I cared less and less who heard me or whether or not they approved. Noise is a relative thing. In the past I had a double life, loud, but not visible, smart, but never making an indelible mark. Now even if I'm told "it's all bullshit," I like making a noise that leaves a mark.

As Hillary fought on, news correspondent Andrea Mitchell commented how terrible it would be if Hillary "stole" this nomination from Obama. More spin. I got louder nonetheless: letters, calls, donations.

I made impassioned calls to Nancy Pelosi, Harry Reid, my Congressman and my Senators. I lost track of how many times I called Howard Dean's office. I wrote to reporters and sent encouraging letters to Hillary's website. I did it without shaking. I wanted to be on the record. She's the best you've got and I want to make sure you all know I think so. I wasn't giving up.

I liked watching Hillary not give up. Talk about grit.

Pennsylvania was a crucial swing state and the Obama campaign was throwing everything they had at the primary to deliver the knockout blow, spending $11.24 million on ad buys in Pennsylvania. Hillary's campaign spent $4.85 million.[85]

The afternoon of the Pennsylvania Primary, at the end of a TV shoot I was doing, I had turned on CNN in my dressing room to watch Wolf Blitzer and John King cover the election returns. Listening to them spin the exit polls, you would have thought

Senator Clinton was getting clobbered. Demoralized after ten minutes of their negative posturing, I had to turn off the television. Once at home, I watched the election returns on a website where I couldn't hear any talking heads.

Hillary took the primary by a near even ten points.

Her team played the theme from "Rocky" to march her into the auditorium after she won. The media and Obama supporters alike said, "Yeah, but Rocky lost." Yes, he lost by decision, but there were five sequels – and he won them all.

> "The clamor for Hillary Clinton to drop out of the presidential race has reached new levels of intensity since the Pennsylvania primary. Of all the things Hillary has done, Obama supporters find her tendency to win large elections in swing states as by far the most irritating. If she beats him in Indiana, they'll be surrounding her house with torches."[86]
>
> -- Gail Collins, *New York Times*

Former presidential candidate George McGovern was another Democratic stalwart pressuring Hillary to drop out "for the good of the party" – while she was still winning primaries. My answer: For the good of the party – keep going.

She won nine of the last fifteen contests.

It was early May when I'd made outreach calls to North Carolina. I still had my heart in my mouth. I read a comment posted on *Taylor Marsh*, a pro-Hillary blog, from a man describing himself as a white, educated thirtyish North Carolina male, "clearly Obama's demographic":

> "I voted for Hillary because some nice lady cold-called me and was willing to talk to me about the issues for fifteen minutes, otherwise I probably wouldn't have voted at all or would have voted Obama. For anyone who is afraid to make these calls, it didn't matter that the lady tripped over her words or that I could tell she was a little nervous. It mattered to *me* that it mattered to *her* enough to pick up the phone and make her case. That said a lot to me."

Given the anonymity of the Internet, he could have been a Hillary operative encouraging people to work the phone banks, but I'd like to think he was sincere. Many on both sides were participating in a way they never had before. For those who maintained a civil tongue in their heads, I was grateful they were getting involved whomever they supported. I no longer wished to leave the driving to our elected officials. I knew I annoyed the hell out of them when I called, yet I remembered an old commercial slogan: "An educated consumer is our best customer..."

I called my Congressman's office after sending several pointed letters urging him to withdraw his endorsement of Senator Obama and go with Hillary. In fairness, my Congressman's staff was always polite and took the time to talk with me – whether or not I liked what they had to say. I told his assistant of Senator Obama's many contradictory statements on policy and that I was worried about his stand on Israel.

"We know all of that. We are looking at the bigger picture," she said.

I could only guess she meant the DNC was looking to fill their coffers through his fundraising juggernaut and add new college-aged voters to build the party for the 21st century. I asked that she tell the Congressman my husband and I would not vote for him this time out. She was not concerned. He was running unopposed.

Dear God, that whole conversation was for nothing. Who was going to unseat him after twenty-five years in office? Nice as that lady was, I may as well have been talking to a wall.

On May 6th, despite being outspent by a large margin yet again, Hillary pulled out a win in Indiana. Obama was supposed to take Indiana comfortably since it was his neighboring state. He won North Carolina by 12 points. The next morning, the headline in the *Los Angeles Times* read, "Obama Cruises, Clinton Clings." The drumbeat kept getting louder.

Nothing was as painful as seeing economist Paul Krugman get into the act, likewise hanging his head that Clinton had little hope and should give up the ghost. Calling him "the last reasonable man at *The New York Times*," I emailed Krugman to inform him that very little in the delegate numbers had shifted and he shouldn't refer to Senator Obama as the "overwhelming favorite." I couldn't bear him deserting us too since he had pointed out the superiority of her policy positions, particularly on health care and the economy.

Then came the coup de grace. Hillary had done much good work with Senator Kennedy on SCHIP over the years, and both Clintons had helped to save Senator Kennedy's Senate seat years before. Nixing the possibility that she be Senator Obama's running mate, Senator Kennedy said the following:

> 'Obama should choose a running mate who "is in tune with his appeal for the nobler aspirations of the American people. If we had real leadership — as we do with Barack Obama — in the No. 2 spot as well, it'd be enormously helpful."'[87]

On May 14th, the day after Hillary beat Obama in the West Virginia primary by 41 points, John Edwards chose to endorse Senator Obama, thereby stealing her news cycle. Politically it was very smart of the Obama campaign. Whenever he had a bad news day, his campaign would announce another super delegate coming over to his camp.

The following week, Hillary lost Oregon to Obama by 10 points but in the Kentucky primary, Hillary beat Obama by 36 points. Mr. Edwards' endorsement was supposed to help Senator Obama with working class voters in Kentucky. It didn't.

The Edwards campaign was hopeless from the start. *The National Enquirer* was the only publication that had for months been reporting on the story of his infidelity and the possibility that he was funneling campaign funds to support his mistress and their baby. It was later discovered many in the media knew and kept silent as Edwards remained in the primary, possibly siphoning off Hillary's votes in the Iowa caucus.

A huge scandal that might have brought down the Democratic Party if Edwards secured the nomination got no coverage when it counted. Rank and file Americans had no idea at the time of Edwards' endorsement that his disgrace would be made public a couple of months later. Instead of kingmaker to Senator Obama, I could only see him as an intended spoiler. A man with his baggage had no hope of winning.

I tired of complaining to *MSNBC* and *CNN* about their bias. I was banging my head against a very hard wall. I submitted letters to the editors of many newspapers around the country. None were ever published. The exception was a brief editorial I sent to a newspaper in Guam promoting Hillary in advance of their primary. Guam! A gentleman responded and said they'd be happy to publish my piece – after the vote.

* * *

Needing respite from the Hillary hate that had become de rigueur on the news, I became addicted to Taylor Marsh's website and checked in daily. I got myself a login and password and dared to "blog" rather than just "lurk". What to call myself? My mother's nickname for me, Ani (Aah-Nee), seemed fitting under the circumstances.

I remember the first tentative comment I posted. I felt like a doofus. There it was; my lame comment with my name "ani" next to it. Ugh. Can I hit the undo button? Now it's out there for the world to see. But I kept at it, attempting to participate in a discussion on the thread. A few folks started responding, encouraging me to get more involved.

Surfing various sites, I was both fascinated and appalled by the drive-by nature of the Internet crowd. The commentary ranged from spot-on brilliant and bitingly funny to misinformed, incendiary and occasionally obscene. The lack of a face-to-face confrontation encouraged brazen discourse. It's been an education. There was also a reactive quality and people would post information not yet verified only to correct it with an "oops" a few hours later.

I will never forget the first few bloggers who made me feel welcome. Sisterdo is a wonderful, caring person who often blogged in capital letters. While typing in all caps is considered yelling and is generally frowned upon, (all this weird etiquette I've learned) coming from her, it was welcome. Her missives were refreshing and her passion exceeded my own. Sometimes her comments were ALL CAPS AND BOLD!!!!!!! Damn. I'd better pay attention! She's a great lady and we picked one another up off the floor more than once. There are many wonderful names to go with supportive people. Their kindness, smarts and even rage helped to get me through the year.

Taylor Marsh's website was not a protected blog. Anyone could register and post comments, though the site was administered carefully, banning ad hominem attacks. By mid-May, more "trolls" crept in, insulting Hillary supporters and working to sway people to Obama.

I posted a comment on a popular political website that Hillary was happy to "wear out her shoe leather to do the hard work required." Someone responded with a comment about my "cunt leather." This was not an anomaly during the campaign. I couldn't help but feel some men found being hateful to a woman an extra perk. Unless this commenter was a test tube baby, he was borne of a woman just like the rest of us.

The level of contempt not only for women but for any woman he deemed no longer "juicy" was as appalling as it was inaccurate. While this seemed like someone at an adolescent stage of development, mad at Mommy for making him clean his room, I knew I was being optimistic. Many dispatched themselves to hand out just these kinds of insults to women not supporting who they felt was the right candidate.

Dirty words. The slang had changed. The meaning and purpose had not – to objectify and degrade.

We were not budging.

News sites like CNN, MSNBC, ABC and *The Los Angeles Times* allowed many demeaning blog comments about Senator Clinton without moderation. Pictures of Hillary with the nose of a pig, as a witch on a broomstick, or with her head poking out of a toilet were also circulated around the Internet.

As detailed in Bill Moyers' PBS interview with Kathleen Hall Jamieson[88], highly trafficked Facebook sites were also used as a destructive influence, some describing sex acts that should be performed on Hillary by animals.

Huffington Post and *Daily Kos* were powerful websites that had little positive to say about Hillary Clinton. MSNBC's Keith Olbermann regularly offered guest posts at *Daily Kos*. His vile attitude toward Hillary Clinton found a welcoming audience. *The Huffington Post* offered headlines such as:

"Why Hillary Clinton's Slash-and-Burn Politics May Hurt Her More Than Obama."

"John McCain Should Go on Vacation, Hillary Clinton is Doing His Job for Him."

"Holding Up a Mirror To the Clinton Cult."

"Sister Frigidaire Tries To Ice MSNBC."

"Clinton's Very Bad Day."

"Clinton Camp Considering Nuclear Option."

"The Hillary Hatred Equation."

"Why It's Time for Hillary Clinton To Go."

"Worst Person In The World."

"Even The Racists Are Deserting Hillary."

I noticed that when I posted blogger comments that were Hillary-positive on certain websites, they were moderated out. Many blogger friends reported the same experiences.

Lentinela, one of HuffPo's regular commenters offered the most accurate assessment:[89]

> "I see daily articles on HuffPost that savage Hillary Clinton. I see no comparable vitriol leveled at any of the other candidates. I think she can rightfully be faulted for her vote on the Iraq war resolution. But Edwards can be equally faulted and yet received no similar condemnation. Obama cared so little about ending the Iraq war that he actively campaigned for [Senator] Lieberman's re-election. Lieberman has been a continuing impediment to peace and an active supporter of war. Yet Obama receives daily gushes of idolatry on HuffPost. I think it has to do with gender more than anything else because the level is so irrational."

As bad as the titles or articles were, the blog comments were worse. Their Hillary-hate was frightening, some blogger entries encouraging violence against her.

> "...if you ever saw the language, the vulgarity, the vitriol that is hauled at Hillary Clinton by liberal Democrats, by the liberal blogs, largely by, frankly,

Obama supporters, you'd be appalled. I mean, you'd punish your children for this."[90]

--Marie Cocco, as interviewed by
Howard Kurtz on CNN

It would have been simple for a magnetic personality such as Senator Obama to make clear he would not tolerate supporters who behaved this way. Threats of rape and other physical violence have long been used as tools to keep women in their places. As Ms. Cocco noted, it was another rude awakening to see people claiming to be Democrats engaging in these attacks.

I didn't appreciate those who voted to re-elect George Bush saying they didn't like his policies, but were happy he lowered their taxes. When I heard sex-based hate spewed toward Senator Clinton by someone who claimed to be on my side otherwise, that kind of cherry picking didn't work for me any better.

Hillary's campaign website/blog was moderated and no negative comments about Barack Obama were allowed. On the other pro-Hillary blogs I visited, no one was kind to him. The comments were that he was inexperienced, arrogant, lying about his past and record, and that he was lost without his TelePrompTer. The most familiar comment was the he was "an empty suit." I was never on any website that advocated violence against him. However "slitting her throat and throwing her in the trunk of a car and driving it into the river" was written about Hillary. I saw it myself.

8 WOMEN WHO RAN FROM HILLARY

In the summer of 2005, I had a conversation with two friends about Hillary running for President. They rhapsodized about how great she would be. While I agreed, I was cynical about her chances. I said, "In the privacy of the voting booth, it is not men who will take her down. It is women. Not enough women will vote for her." Almost three years later, I made myself forget what I knew in my gut to be true and campaigned for her anyway.

Robin Abcarian's *Los Angeles Times* article, *Drift Away From Clinton Frustrates Many Women,*[91] quoted Texas Democratic activist, Darlene Ewing, who was confounded by women 'arbitrarily' drifting toward Obama's candidacy: "They're running to the rock star, to the momentum, to the excitement." She quoted feminist writer Robin Morgan who expressed anger that women were "wringing their hands because Hillary isn't as likable as they've been warned they must be," and *Saturday Night Live's* Tina Fey who said, in typical ironic fashion:

> "We have our first serious female presidential candidate in Hillary Clinton. And yet women have come so far as feminists that they don't feel obligated to vote for a candidate just because she is a woman. Women today feel perfectly free to make whatever choice Oprah tells them to."

Oprah Winfrey was referred to as "arguably the world's most powerful woman" by CNN and *Time.com* and "…the most influential woman in the world" by the *American Spectator*. Two economists estimated her endorsement of Barack Obama translated into over a million votes.[92, 93]

Coming to prominence with the help of women, Oprah Winfrey's decision not to invite the first viable woman candidate for President on her show was painful. Since she was convinced that Mr. Obama was "The One," it was curious she wasn't confident her audience would come to the same conclusion.

Why not put both Clinton and Obama on her show on different days, so that her audience could do a side-by-side comparison and arrive at the decision on their own? She did not do so. Her ratings took a dip after that.

On March 14, 2008, Speaker Pelosi answered ABC's George Stephanopoulos who had a concern that women might be upset Hillary was being pushed aside. Ms. Pelosi said he shouldn't worry, that women will fall in line.[94] The first female Speaker of the House discussing other women as though we were sheep did not sit well with me. But I guessed she was reiterating historical fact. Women seemed willing to follow a party that gave them comparatively little for the effort. I included myself in that category.

Every four years the party trotted out the same threats about the other guys sending women back to the Stone Age regarding their reproductive rights and that seemed to do the trick. Women are still earning 80 cents on the dollar but have not yet moved as a block to force a correction to that inequity.

Bill Maher said some women wouldn't vote for Hillary in adherence to the religious belief that "a man shall lead them."

Around that time, I was invited to be a witness at a small wedding ceremony in Las Vegas. I didn't know the denomination of the preacher. Paraphrasing his sermon, he said the man is strong, but is a dog and is innately bad. It is the woman's job to clean him up and deal with it. The preacher then said the woman is the vessel of the church, but is weak and must lean on the man for support. My husband and I looked at each other. I dug my nails into my palms.

Women had complained Hill didn't leave Bill after his affair with Monica Lewinsky. Some said she was "sanctimonious" about her decision and chose not to vote for her. If I had just been humiliated on the largest stage imaginable and was working to hold it together, I might be a bit defensive myself. There were public figures who threw stones at Hillary for the choice she made to stay in her marriage. Some have now discovered, painfully and publicly, they too live in a glass house.

Ms. Abcarian pointed out some women used Hillary Clinton's Iraq War Resolution vote as a reason not to vote for her. Branding Barack Obama as the anti-war candidate who had the "good judgment" to say no on going into Iraq struck me as a hollow argument.

A colleague said "she couldn't forgive Hillary" for her decision. While I understood her sentiments, I pointed out that Hillary stood on the Senate floor and urged President Bush in the strongest language to act cautiously. She made it clear this authorization was meant as a tool for forced diplomacy, not war.

Perhaps Senator Clinton did not believe President Bush would recklessly countermand Congress. Perhaps she suspected he might. She and Senator Robert Byrd proposed legislation the next day to try to restrict Bush's options further and let the inspections finish. We all know how that turned out.

On Dec. 26, 2007, Chris Matthews interviewed Congressman and former Admiral Joe Sestak, who offered arguments in support of Hillary Clinton's candidacy. Rep. Sestak pointed out that Senator Clinton understood the processes of Washington, that she was a woman of vision:

> "She's ahead of her time. Think of where she went as First Lady. She went to India, soon to be the number two economic power in the world...She went to China and spoke about human rights and women's rights. And most importantly, I think, she went to Africa. She recognized before others did that poverty is where terrorists go. They hide. Finally, this past year, the military woke up and actually established, Chris, as you know, what's called the Africa Command. She was there talking about security—poverty being a security issue well before others. ...We need a president with vision, but [also]

someone who can go to the boiler room and fix Washington, that's broken..."

Mr. Matthews responded, "Hillary voted for the Iraq War Resolution, Obama opposed it." He gave no further clarification of that statement. The implication by the media went far beyond Senator Obama merely voicing an opinion on the subject.

I had told my colleague that Hillary's IWR vote was an unfair litmus test, since her rival for the nomination never had that vote to make. Many well educated and otherwise informed people didn't realize he was not yet elected to the U.S. Senate at that time.

"Yes, he was," she argued. "He voted against the war."

"Um, no, actually, he couldn't have. The vote took place in October of 2002 when he was only in the Illinois state legislature. He was not sworn in as a Senator until 2005. In fact, he voted to fund the war two more times once he became a Senator."

She looked at me. That was the end of that discussion.

She echoed a widespread misperception that the media did little to correct. The Obama campaign did not correct it either. They used the same verbiage Matthews had and kept touting Senator Obama's "good judgment." According to ABC News:

> "Clinton's steadfast refusal to say she regretted her vote to authorize use of force in Iraq -- unlike Obama, who always opposed the war, and Edwards, who said his vote for war was a mistake -- turned off many anti-war liberals in Iowa, who make up a disproportionate number of caucus goers." [95]

ABC News put Obama on a par with Edwards and Clinton in this regard, giving the impression that his opposition came from the Senate floor. They wrote he "had always opposed the war." [96] But from where had he opposed it?

Much was made of the speech Mr. Obama made at an anti-war rally in 2002. It was given in the ultra-liberal Hyde Park district of Illinois, where he was speaking to a crowd that surely agreed with his sentiments. There was no news coverage of it; Mr. Obama later went into a studio to record the speech for posterity.

Americans well remember how dangerous it was for anyone to speak out in 2002. George Clooney was interviewed by Charlie Rose during this period. He felt the administration was determined to go into Iraq and was against it. He confided that for his trouble, he was referred to as a traitor and was being lambasted on the airwaves regularly.[97] But he is an actor, not a politician.

Toward the end of 2004, Whoopi Goldberg returned to Broadway to perform an updated version of her one woman show. It was very critical of President Bush. As I recall, she was Public Enemy Number One for a while, though President Bush's poll numbers had already dropped to 55% by that point.

Clearly 2002 was a much more heated period, yet Mr. Obama had never received any of the "unpatriotic" or "traitorous" branding foisted upon anyone who dared to voice a dissenting opinion. He was not ostracized then or thereafter, nor did he come under the Bush Administration's microscope. He had nothing on the line. There was no expenditure of political capital, no risk. How public could his remarks have been?

Were he actually in the Senate, his vote, and his voice in opposition to the war, would have been another story. That is a side-by-side comparison I would have liked to see.

While campaigning for Senator Kerry in 2004, Senator Obama acknowledged:

> "But, I'm not privy to Senate intelligence reports...What would I have done? I don't know."
> ... "What I know is that from my vantage point the case was not made."
>
> --Barack Obama, "Meet the Press," July 2004[98]

As President Clinton pointed out, while running for Senate in 2004, Senator Obama removed his 2002 anti-war speech from his campaign website, calling it "dated."

> "On Iraq, on paper, there's not as much difference, I think, between the Bush administration and a Kerry administration as there would have been a year ago.
> [...] There's not much of a difference between my position and George Bush's position at this stage."
>
> -- Barack Obama,
> speaking with the *Chicago Tribune*, 07/27/04

Once he arrived in the Senate in 2005, he did not use his good judgment to move us to change course on Iraq:

> "Obama's Senate voting record on Iraq is nearly identical to Clinton's. Over the two years Obama has been in the Senate, the only Iraq-related vote on which they differed was the confirmation earlier this year of General George Casey to be Chief of Staff of the Army, which Obama voted for and Clinton voted against."

-- ABC News, 5/17/07

The stakes and pressure were very different for Hillary Clinton as the junior Senator from the state on the receiving end of the worst attack in our nation's history. How can we assess whether to forgive one candidate when another had no possibility of being judged by the same criteria?

Speeches are one thing, actions are quite another. It is easier to hold someone's record against them when they've been around a while. Many party elders encouraged Barack Obama to run for this reason -- he didn't have a record to haunt him. Senate Majority Leader Harry Reid shared in his 2009 book that he was just such a person, pushing Senator Obama to run for President after only a year in the Senate.

By this logic, I should have run for President in 2008, since I have far less of a record than Mr. Obama. There would have been nothing whatsoever to hold against me, except for the unfortunate fact that I'm a woman.

A female acquaintance, a teacher, praised General Colin Powell for his endorsement of Barack Obama. She excused General Powell for telling the tale before the U.N. Security Council that got us into a war she despised, yet she refused to forgive Hillary for believing the testimony of one of our most respected military officers.

* * *

Robin Abcarian also reported that Ellen Malcolm of Emily's List, a political action group that supports pro-choice women for office, called a news conference to support Clinton in her presidential bid.

Malcolm criticized Obama's lack of leadership on the issue of reproductive rights, and noted though Senator Obama appeared at an Emily's List fundraiser, there was a big difference between that and Senator Clinton taking on the President of the United States to pass RU486, making the morning after pill available over the counter. Yet author and columnist for The Nation, Katha Pollitt, signed on to the following petition during the primary:

> "Choosing to support Senator Obama was not an easy decision because electing a woman president would be a cause for celebration in itself and because we deplore the sexist attacks against Senator Clinton that have circulated in the media. However, we also recognize that the election of Barack Obama would be another historic achievement and that his support for gender equality has been unwavering."

I then reviewed some of the comments Senator Obama had directed toward Senator Clinton:

> "You challenge the status quo and suddenly the claws come out."

> "I understand that Senator Clinton, periodically...when she's feeling down, launches attacks as a way of trying to boost her appeal,"[99]

> "You know, over the last several weeks since she fell behind, she's resorted to what's called 'kitchen sink' strategies,"..."She's got the kitchen sink flying, and the china flying, and the, you know, the buffet is coming at me.[100]

Senator Obama called both a female reporter and female factory worker "sweetie"[101] on the trail and then asked her, "What do I need to do? Do you want me on my knees?" ... "I'll give you a kiss."[102]

Katha Pollitt did not object.

My husband spoke to a woman, fifty-five, who said she voted for Obama because "I like him. He's just nice." I had a forty-two year old female Obama supporter say to my face that she thought "Hillary is smarter, but Obama is for change." A politically savvy girl friend said "Hillary's too brilliant to be President." Did that mean nobody likes a smarty-pants?

Essayist, author and cultural commentator Camille Paglia wrote a number of anti-Hillary screeds that were as contradictory as they were dismissive. Excerpted from *Why Women Shouldn't Vote For Hillary Clinton*:

> "This symbol of raw female ambition has never comfortably fitted into a conventional sex role. As the first child of a hard-working and authoritarian father, Hillary absorbed his willfulness, competitive drive and suspicion. Excelling academically, Hillary felt ill at ease with the feminine persona so deftly deployed by pretty, popular girls in that era. Frumpy, stumpy and myopic, she identified with the new idolatry of shiny careerism promulgated by the second-wave feminism of the late 1960s, when she emerged from posh Wellesley College."[103]

Shiny careerism? To my knowledge, Ms. Paglia was and is a very accomplished woman in her own right.

According to this essay, part of the reason one shouldn't vote for Hillary was because she was "frumpy, stumpy and myopic." It would appear Paglia theorized that because Senator Clinton was not a beauty queen, achievement was her fallback position. Ms. Paglia gave ample evidence that Senator Clinton's drive was somehow threatening or inappropriate for a woman. That, more than the Hillary-bashing, was disturbing. Again, a woman was trying to fit another woman into a cramped container.

In Ms. Paglia's other columns for *Salon.com*, there was never a sense that the good deeds noted on Senator Clinton's very long resume were done for anything other than political gain, to the extent her accomplishments were acknowledged at all. That ambitious women were still being categorized as duplicitous indicated that perhaps it was not Hillary Clinton who had the "suspicious" nature.

Paglia stated "Hillary's disdain for masculinity fits right into the classic feminazi package..."[104] and "She is a brittle, relentless manipulator with few stable core values who shuffles through useful personalities like a card shark."[105] Yet reading the rest of her commentary during the primaries, the otherwise cynical Paglia applauded Barack Obama with the wholesome faith and naïveté of a young schoolgirl. Why was it so easy to arrive at the conclusion that a female politician was evil but the male was saintly when they both had to jump through the same hoops, offering up their sales pitches on the way to the election?

Even my mom was a tough sell.

My mother likewise had a suspicious attitude toward women in charge. This may also have explained why she harped on any negative story she heard about Hillary while classifying Obama as a "nice young man." His smile was enough for her. She likely voted for Senator Clinton in the primary after all my pestering and research but it was a long slog. It surprised me that I had to work so hard to convince her. She was still dubious about a woman's qualifications because she had never trusted her own.

Clinton's unfailing commitment to women didn't seem to matter to Nancy Keenan, president of NARAL. Keenan likewise abandoned Hillary for Obama during the Primaries even though Hillary helped to put NARAL on the map, always receiving a 100% pro-choice rating from them.

Many of NARAL's district offices voiced opposition to Ms. Keenan's executive decision. It did no good, but I was relieved to see everyone had not forgotten Senator Clinton's battles on their behalf.

> "I see my whole life going down the drain. A cute young guy comes in and sweeps away all the hard work that the older woman has done."
>
> -- Billie Jean King,
> speaking to Cokie Roberts[106]

Soon after, the *New York Times* reported on a Bush administration plan to define several widely used contraception methods as abortion.[107] Hillary Clinton held a press conference and called this a "gratuitous, unnecessary insult" to women and "joined family planning groups to condemn the proposal that defines abortion to include contraception such as birth control pills and intrauterine devices."

The plan would have cut off federal funds to hospitals and states where medical providers are obligated to offer legal abortion and contraception to women.

> "We will not put up with this radical, ideological agenda to turn the clock back on women's rights …

Women would watch their contraceptive coverage disappear overnight," said Clinton.[108]

Senator Clinton and Senator Patty Murray made a big noise to ensure this did not happen.

* * *

Rebecca Traister's April 2008 *Salon.com* article, *Hey Obama Boys, Back Off Already*, discussed younger women's growing discomfort with a new shock wave of misogyny. She noted how many male Obama supporters came on like bulldozers when pushing their candidate. Thirtyish men who called female friends to "talk some sense into them" about their decision to vote for Hillary offered an unexpected symbolic slap to a new generation who thought we were past all that. Her essay was one of a lonely few on the subject and I was grateful she had bravely chosen to cover it.

Yet at the same time, it appeared she had mischaracterized older women who supported Senator Clinton. While I appreciated the importance of Ms. Traister's observations, I didn't want to get thrown under the bus, being stereotyped with the same verbiage the media had been using for months.

She identified herself as a thirty-two year old woman who, along with her contemporaries, felt alienated by the "second wave feminist" writings of "old warhorses" like Gloria Steinem and Robin Morgan. She also made an implicit assumption that older women must be enamored of these writings or a more militant style of expressing the sentiments they espoused:

> "This riveting Democratic Primary campaign has provided us with its own stock characters: There are the young "Daily Show" watching Obama-maniacs getting over their irony addiction by falling earnestly in love with the Senator from Illinois. There are the pissed-off second-wave feminists, uptight and out of touch, howling as their dream of seeing a woman in the Oval Office fades. And then there are the young women caught between them."

Though I was forty-nine at the time, I felt "caught between," too. My experiences prior to 2008 were more like Ms. Traister's. Fortunate to have supportive men in my life, I was at first rendered frozen witnessing the media spew its daily bile. Under the circumstances, I was irritated to be dismissed as "out of touch," "uptight" or "howling." The anger of Hillary supporters was justified. No woman of any age deserved to be derided with those words.

It was possible Traister was being ironic or expressing a younger woman's need to differentiate from an older generation. Perhaps she felt the idea of women's equality and all the rights and privileges that went with it could be trusted in today's society but left unspoken.

While I was not part of the second wave, I wasn't "horrified" by it either. The writings of feminists who came to prominence in the sixties and seventies may seem militant now but such work was reactive out of necessity. I hadn't sought those voices out, but found myself becoming more militant throughout the primary when making my case.

I had never fought as hard for anything or anyone. I would stop dead at the end of a sentence, almost shocked at the strength and passion behind my own words. On her own journey, it appeared Ms. Traister had realized why. Doing battle against an avalanche of negativity, one had to get louder to penetrate the belligerent rhetoric flying in the other direction. A young man who Ms. Traister noted had an "irresistible urge to punch Hillary in the face" would also tend to put one on the defensive.

Her report echoed my own experiences with some men who had dismissed Hillary without bothering to veil their contempt, or explain themselves.

Some college-aged women had told Ms. Traister they turned away from Hillary just so they wouldn't be verbally attacked. To run from a candidate due to peer pressure, or a fear of being ostracized, makes clear we are not done with old battles on behalf of women's rights.

A colleague of mine said she was in a supermarket and had encountered other Hillary supporters who spoke in whispers. "What happened to free speech?" she asked. I'd had the same experience in the workplace. I whispered my support so as not to "offend" opposing democrats. Yet they felt no need to whisper.

It could also be argued that even women who voted for Hillary were running from her, because they felt uncomfortable voicing full throated support.   Feeling cowed about one's passion for a candidate, at the very least, a woman might be less likely to encourage others to support Hillary, despite sticking with her in the privacy of the voting booth.

I knew a number of women who were afraid to wear their Hillary buttons. They kept their votes quiet. Living in California, where Hillary took the primary by a convincing margin, I saw tons of Obama bumper stickers. I don't remember seeing any for Hillary though she clearly had many ardent supporters in the state.

I had encountered a twenty-three year old woman who said she "hated that Hillary bitch!" It was as though Hillary's very existence was revolting. Her reaction was unnerving to the extent that she gave me no underlying reason for her feelings. I was more disturbed by what appeared to be a knee-jerk response.

Robin Morgan revised her celebrated seventies essay, *Goodbye To All That*, on behalf of Hillary. Her words went viral on the Internet during the Primary. A few excerpts follow:

> "Goodbye, goodbye to . . .
>
> blaming anything Bill Clinton does on Hillary (even including his womanizing like the Kennedy guys–though unlike them, he got reported on)...
>
> Enough of Bill and Teddy Kennedy locking their alpha male horns while Hillary pays for it.
>
> an era when parts of the populace feel so disaffected by politics that a comparative lack of knowledge, experience, and skill is actually seen as attractive, when celebrity-culture mania now infects our elections so that it's "cooler" to glow with marquee charisma than to understand the vast global complexities of power on a nuclear, wounded planet.
>
> the notion that it's fun to elect a handsome, cocky president who feels he can learn on the job...
>
> ...Goodbye to the accusation that HRC acts "entitled" when she's worked intensely at everything she's done—including being a nose-to-the-grindstone, first-rate senator from my state.

Goodbye to her being exploited as a Rorschach test by women who reduce her to a blank screen on which they project their own fears, failures, fantasies.

Goodbye to the phrase "polarizing figure" to describe someone who embodies the transitions women have made in the last century and are poised to make in this one..."

As if in response, Ms. Traister discussed what her contemporaries regarded as the "retro tone of the pro-Clinton feminist whine." It was as if younger women felt they must defensively insult the concept of feminism in order to be considered acceptable in today's society.

I witnessed that many younger women felt the notion of "feminism" was passé and had no desire to be associated with it. That may also have driven women from Hillary. It is also desirable to be considered "cool" and Hillary was not cool.

Women who supported Hillary were accused of "vagina voting." A concept and statement I found repugnant. Whatever my outrage at media mistreatment, my support of Senator Clinton was about logic, not feminism or vaginal identification.

Although no woman was under any obligation to support her, it was ironic that a new generation who chose to reject the "old warhorses" were loath to acknowledge that part of their current opportunities were earned for them by ladies who spoke out in years past, risking more than ridicule for doing so. Wasn't it possible to reject one's predecessor without spitting on her?

The negative associations attached to the very word feminism were disconcerting. According to Merriam-Webster's dictionary, feminism is 1) the theory of the political, economic, and social equality of the sexes; and 2) organized activity on behalf of women's rights and interests. If I could add a third meaning, it would be the pursuit of an end to violence against women. I saw nothing in the definition itself that was inherently offensive or diminishing to the male of the species.

The dismissive attitude toward "feminism" harkened back to my memory of women becoming managers in the work place in the early eighties, wearing boxy suits with foulard bow ties. As Harrison

Ford's character noted in the film *Working Girl* – "dressing how a man would dress if he were a woman."

Washington Post columnist Kathleen Parker had a term for feminists: "the hirsute Birkenstock wearing sisterhood."[109] It wasn't hard to imagine why many women would run away from such a caricature.

Still, Rebecca Traister's conclusions led her to a watering hole not far from mine – that we had regressed forty years, but with insidious, sophisticated verbiage and methodology that was much more challenging to identify.

In her *Huffington Post* diary, Jessica Wakeman wrote that she eventually felt protective of Hillary Clinton, though she did not support her candidacy. She quoted radio host Laura Flanders:

> "The post-feminist line is that feminism isn't needed anymore -- in fact, wealthy white women have the luxury of rejecting feminism's advances -- and therefore the mainstream media acts like it's over in America. We're not allowed to talk about it anymore...We're not allowed to say there's a connection between what the pundits say and what society does.
>
> It is Hillary's problem, not our problem."[110]

It is not feminism that is out of date, but the lie that independent, or outspoken women, are "ball crushers." I had hoped there was no one who rejected Hillary out of a need to reject a stereotype they found distasteful.

I had never labeled myself a feminist though clearly, I am one. I still walk fast, like the New Yorker I've always been. As far as I'm concerned, whoever gets to the maitre d' first asks for the table. It means nothing. We're all in this together, male and female.

Why were women still being defined in black and white terms?

Feminism is not the antithesis of femininity, although in the presidential race, there was certainly a sense that a woman had to down a shot of bourbon, and have "testicular fortitude," as a male Hillary supporter so affectionately put it.

Hillary's "cackle" or all around demeanor were meaningless. I maintain that any woman who reached as high as Hillary did would have gotten what Hillary got.

Perhaps a woman being Commander in Chief represented too much of an upset to the status quo and we were still uncomfortable with that concept, although many did not admit that out loud.

Ms. Magazine later featured Barack Obama on their cover.

The photo showed him pulling his shirt open to reveal a t-shirt underneath that said, "This is what a feminist looks like."

In the year 2008, a magazine founded on the principal of women's empowerment and advancement sent out a message that said "Daddy will save me."

9 THE MEDIA AS ABUSIVE HUSBAND, THE DNC AS ENABLER

"You may write me down in history
With your bitter, twisted lies,
You may trod me in the very dirt
But still, like dust, I'll rise."

-- Maya Angelou,
reading to Hillary Clinton at
Wake Forest University

In my family, we had an unfortunate practice of trashing each other at dinner and by breakfast we'd just say, "Pass the juice." Normal behavior resumed, happy and chirpy as a day at Disneyland. No apology was forthcoming. Whatever the incident, it had evaporated. I marveled how the needle could drop back to zero with no discernible effort.

Children find a way to thrive, like grass growing through cracks in the concrete, hungry for a ray of sun. I had made my home life the new normal. Not understanding the cumulative effect of suppressing my reaction to my environment, it took many years being away from such stimulus to allow myself to detox. Only recently had those sensations faded to a soft focus, supplanted by happier memories. As a kid, I knew once I was old enough to move away, there would be consequences for such abusive conduct outside the walls of our new normal.

Imagine my surprise in discovering that both the media and the Democratic leadership functioned alternatively as abuser and enabler in the 2008 election cycle without repercussion.

The Double Standard

Discussing Hillary's campaign on February 26, 2008, Pete Snyder of FOX News said, "Someone is going to have to go out there and take her behind the barn."[111] I closed my eyes and tried to picture him saying the same thing about Senator Obama. "Someone needs to take him out behind the barn." And do what to him? Would Mr. Snyder still have his job?

Referencing Chelsea Clinton's choice to hit the campaign trail for her mother, MSNBC's David Shuster made the comment:

> "Doesn't it feel like the Clintons are 'pimping' their daughter out in some weird way?"[112]

What if Mr. Shuster had made Mrs. Obama, or the Obamas' lovely children, Sasha and Malia, the subject of such an inappropriate statement?

Chris Matthews called the Clinton press shop "knee cappers"[113] for complaining. The *Huffington Post* likewise derided Senator Clinton for protecting her daughter.[114] Mr. Shuster received a brief suspension for his remarks about the Clintons. What penalty would have been exacted had he dared to make such a comment about the Obamas?

After David Shuster resumed his on-air duties, he also resumed his old antics, presenting Tucker Carlson with a Hillary "laughing pen."[115] This way, he could continue to deride her voice and laugh at her "cackle." Where was his evaluation of her policies?

MSNBC's Keith Olbermann was without peer playing the role of abusive spouse with his baseless Hillary bashing and rabid pronouncements from the mount. For him to mention the Clinton campaign in the same breath as the racist David Duke was shameful. Nothing made Hillary supporters angrier than his comment that "a super delegate should take Hillary into a room and only he comes out."[116]

Why were these men addicted to using violent metaphors?

His apology after the outrage that comment inspired was that "he used the wrong pronoun."[117]

When asked if it was appropriate to call Hillary Clinton a "White Bitch," Alex Castellanos of CNN said "...she thinks her problem is she's a woman; her problem is she's Hillary Clinton. And some women, by the way, are named that and it's accurate."

Almost as one, the media spit out the same talking points: Hillary is attacking Barack!! "She is making him unelectable." Bad Hillary! Mean Hillary.

Former presidential candidate Gary Hart published an opinion piece in the *Huffington Post* decrying Hillary's negative tactics[118] – meanwhile his comments during his 1984 primary run against Walter Mondale were at least as harsh.[119]

Why would Hillary not be permitted to fight for the nomination as hard as any man?

Senator Clinton was criticized for her remark that she and Senator McCain "brought a lifetime of experience to the job and Senator Obama brought a speech he gave in 2002." How was that worse than Senator Obama besmirching her character or belittling her record?

Senator Obama also said he would be more willing than Clinton to work with Republicans: "Her natural inclination is to draw a picture of Republicans as people who need to be crushed and defeated." And "I'm not a person who believes any one party has a monopoly on wisdom."[120] Yet she had the reputation of working with Republicans to pass bi-partisan legislation.

The Obama campaign sent out deceptive "Harry and Louise" mailers misrepresenting her healthcare policy, prompting the famous Hillary quote: "Meet Me in Ohio!" She was the one accused of "going negative."

Jake Tapper of ABC News reported that an unnamed Democratic Party official said Hillary's campaign was "pursuing the Tonya Harding option"[121], otherwise known as kneecapping:

> "The delegate math is difficult for Sen. Hillary Clinton, D-NY, the official said. But it's not a question of CAN she achieve it. Of course she can...
>
> ...She will have to "break his back," the official said. She will have to destroy Obama, make Obama completely unacceptable."

Yet the media did not have a problem with Senator Clinton being painted as "completely unacceptable." If she burped, the press was all over it. Unfounded charges went unanswered. Neither the media nor the DNC corrected the record.

Debates were another adventure altogether.

Saturday Night Live famously lampooned CNN commentator Campbell Brown for mooning over Senator Obama as she moderated one of Clinton and Obama's February match-ups.

If a good looking man pays me a compliment, I might not be immune from walking around with a goofy grin on my face for a minute. Okay. Two minutes. This being true, I understood Ms. Brown wanting to "fluff Senator Obama's pillows." He smiled his lovely smile at her, turned on the charm and she got a little goofy, too. I get it. Well, I *would* get it if she weren't supposed to be an educated journalist well paid to have some objectivity.

One would think it was understood that as a politician, he was working the room. To see someone in her position lob softballs in his direction and show favoritism embarrassed me. On another occasion, Hillary asked if Senator Obama wanted a pillow.

Don't you dare complain, Hillary! Cowboy up!

At debates, Hillary would typically get the tough questions first, and the rough treatment. Senator Obama would say "I agree with Senator Clinton." Commentators would say "brilliant!" I thought I was watching the Marx Brothers.

At their match-up ahead of the Ohio Primary, moderator Tim Russert had barked questions at Senator Clinton so ferociously, I worried he would leap across the table at her. It appeared he was attempting to throw her off her rhythm or intimidate her. He addressed Senator Obama in more respectful tones.

Hillary received a great deal of criticism for "going negative" in her "3:00 a.m. ad." The ad asked who we wanted to pick up the White House phone during a crisis.

Saturday Night Live had its own take on that call. Their skit featured Obama sitting in the oval office looking stressed and disheveled, hungrily dragging on a cigarette in the middle of the night, calling Hillary in her bedroom. The talented Amy Poehler played Hillary, in curlers and a robe, a ton of cold cream on her face.

She calmly answered the President's questions, telling him what he needed to do next.

Dana Milbank of the *Washington Post* noted in his March 4th column that the only grilling the media chose to give Senator Obama came as a direct result of *SNL* making fun of their warm and fuzzy coverage.[122]

After the news of Senator Obama's close relationship with Reverend Wright flooded the airwaves in mid-March, no one bothered to challenge Senator Obama's daily flip flopping on what he knew or didn't know about the Reverend's incendiary diatribes from the pulpit during his admitted twenty-year attendance. He had contradicted himself on this matter on national television at least four times in one week. I waited in vain for ABC, CBS, NBC or CNN to take two pieces of videotape and play his statements side by side.

The Senator repeatedly called the Reverend his mentor and spiritual advisor, named a book after one of his speeches and averred regular attendance at his church, yet claimed he never knew Reverend Wright said "God damn America" five days after 9/11, nor had he any knowledge of Wright's other inflammatory sermons: "Bill Clinton's "ridin' dirty," "Barack knows what it means to be a black man living in a country and a culture that is controlled by rich, white people. Hillary ain't never been called a n——," "the US of KKK A," his theory that AIDS was invented by the US government to kill black people, and more.[123]

Either Mr. Obama slept in church, heard the sermons and sympathized with some of them, agreed with none of it but sat there with his family for political street cred for twenty years, or only pretended regular church attendance to attract other churchgoing voters. There was no good way to spin it.

Fair or not, this would have sunk any other politician. Had this information been revealed a month before Super Tuesday instead of six weeks after, it would have done just that, even to someone as charismatic as Senator Obama. This story was known nearly a year before the Primaries began, yet no major news station besides the conservative leaning FOX News would touch it.[124]

Three days later, Senator Obama made his now famous speech on race. Lovely as it was, it was meant to distract from the issue at hand. Judging by the press headlines that lauded his efforts, the Obama campaign had achieved the desired result. He had weathered the storm and the media's attitude was "nothing to see here folks." Hillary remained silent, refusing to comment until she was asked a direct question on the matter. She said, "He wouldn't have been my pastor."

And then came her statements about Bosnia, referring to a trip she had made to the region as First Lady in 1996.

> "I remember landing under sniper fire. There was supposed to be some kind of a greeting ceremony at the airport, but instead we just ran with our heads down to get into the vehicles to get to our base."

> --Hillary Clinton, speech at
> George Washington University, March 17, 2008.

No! Why bother? You don't need to sound like a combat veteran!

She corrected herself when called on it, and said she had "misspoken" but apparently she had made these comments more than once.[125]

Oh, Hillary. I was so irritated that she had behaved like other politicians by telling a fish story. They all do it. But they were men. That was different. Somehow that was not considered as serious a breach of morality.

Senator Clinton making this statement felt reactive, as if she thought she needed to beef herself up on foreign policy. Senator Obama had claimed her visits to eighty countries as First Lady were no more than a succession of tea parties. He had also declared that because he lived in Indonesia as a child that qualified as foreign policy experience.[126] Yet no one laughed. As Senator, Hillary had spent six years on the Foreign Armed Services Committee. She did not have to compete with her opponent in this arena.

Hillary had good reason for her trip to Bosnia as detailed by Tod Robberson of *Dallas Morning News*:

> "In addition to showing support for our troops and for the Peace Accords in Bosnia, Mrs. Clinton met with Bosnian religious leaders, women and community activists and, when she returned to

Washington, was able to give administration officials her firsthand assessment of the nascent reconstruction effort.

After leaving Bosnia, she met with leaders of Turkey and Greece and in those countries promoted efforts on behalf of international development and democracy. In Istanbul, five years before 9/11, Mrs. Clinton presciently convened representatives of some of the world's major religions to advance a dialogue about religious reconciliation and ways to counter religious extremism."[127]

I wished she had shared this information rather than worrying about sounding macho. She didn't need to prove she had a spine of steel. As the always colorful Democratic strategist James Carville later pointed out, "If she gave [Obama] one of her cojones, they'd both have two."[128]

I cringed hearing her remarks about sniper fire but in truth, I was angrier about the fact that she had no margin for error. No matter what foolishness came out of the other side, it was not being scrutinized in the same way by the press. Damn it, Hillary, don't you make a misstep. Not a single one!

Hillary was ripped to shreds for her statements on Bosnia. As a result, polls showed there was an increase in the number of voters who perceived her as dishonest.[129]

I couldn't imagine why she would try to get away with it. The press never gave her a break, and she knew it. In April, she had shared an anecdote about a supporter's healthcare nightmare at several campaign fund raisers. The major papers got a hold of it and again called her a liar. When it was investigated and found to be true,[130] the corrections were much quieter than the accusations.

On April 11, 2008, Mayhill Fowler of the *Huffington Post* shared a revealing sound bite from Senator Obama, recorded at a private fund raiser in San Francisco. This, I gathered, was in response to a question about his inability to make better inroads with small town voters:

> "You go into some of these small towns in Pennsylvania, and like a lot of small towns in the

Midwest, the jobs have been gone now for 25 years and nothing's replaced them," Obama said. "And they fell through the Clinton Administration, and the Bush Administration, and each successive administration has said that somehow these communities are gonna regenerate and they have not.

And it's not surprising then they get bitter, they cling to guns or religion or antipathy to people who aren't like them or anti-immigrant sentiment or anti-trade sentiment as a way to explain their frustrations."[131]

Senator Obama's comments went viral.

Though unemployment was cut in half during President Clinton's administration, with 22 million new jobs created, the Clinton name was trashed once again. But it was only the "bitter voters" comment anyone cared about. Mr. Obama later characterized his remarks about Pennsylvanians as "boneheaded."[132] No matter how elitist his statements, another storm had been weathered.

Senator Obama likewise got little flack for saying his uncle had liberated Auschwitz,[133] a falsehood unless his uncle served with the Red Army, or making himself head of the Banking Committee when he was not on the Banking Committee,[134] or saying he was the product of the marches in Selma, Alabama though he was already four years old at the time. There were more, but the press was in a forgiving mood when it came to parsing the statements and campaign contradictions of a candidate they found so appealing.

On April 16, 2008, at the debate in advance of the Pennsylvania primary before a television audience of eleven million, Senator Obama made an effort to explain his "bitter" comments. He found a more tactful way to make the same remarks.[135]

Then Hillary apologized for her statements on Bosnia:

"On a couple of occasions in the last weeks, I just said some things that weren't in keeping with what I knew to be the case and what I had written about in my book. And you know, I'm embarrassed by it. I'm very sorry I said it. I have said that, you know, it just didn't jive with what I had written about and knew to be the truth."[136]

I moved on. The media did not.

However, ABC hosts George Stephanopoulos and Charles Gibson made this particular debate a departure from the rest. They put Senator Obama on the hot seat, asking some tough questions. News outlets admitted it was Senator Obama's weakest performance:

> "Mr. Obama does not look as thrilled to be still standing there."
>
> -- *New York Times*, The Caucus, 4/16/08

> Hillary ..."certainly seems more self-assured on the Iran question than Obama did..."
>
> -- Josh Marshall, *Talking Points Memo*, 4/16/08

> "Obama 'did not have a good night.'"
>
> --Chuck Todd, MSNBC Post-Debate Analysis, 4/16/08

> "[T]here's no way Obama could have fared worse."
>
> -- Marc Ambinder, *The Atlantic*, 4/16/08

The complaints came in loud and hard from Obama supporters to ABC – unfair! Unlike all us dames complaining about bias, the network actually listened on this occasion. Messrs. Gibson and Stephanopoulos backed off in their subsequent coverage.

A mentor of mine said, "Even when she wins, she loses." It galled me, but she was right. Hillary was accused of attacking at the debate. I sighed at the stereotype of the catty female.

We had expected another meet-up between the candidates before the Indiana and North Carolina primaries in May, but Howard Dean cancelled any further debates between them saying it was "too divisive" for the party. The DNC was in essence providing cover for their favored candidate.

In debates and at press conferences, journalists repeatedly asked Hillary if she would support and campaign for Senator Obama and if she felt he was qualified for the position. She was cornered into defending the candidate she was running against. Yet I had few recollections of Senator Obama being pushed in the same way to say he would "campaign his heart out" for the eventual nominee if it were to be Hillary.

George Stephanopoulos later hosted a town hall style interview before a live audience with Hillary. He stuck his chin out at her, playing gotcha wherever possible. He questioned whether she would back off her previous statement that if Iran turned aggressive and attacked Israel, she would "obliterate" them. Without pausing, she said, "No."

Instead of sitting in a chair as blocked, she stood up, took command of the proceeding, turning it into a real town hall. The cameras zoomed out, struggling to find her in the frame. With no choice in the matter, they adjusted to the new format. Mr. Stephanopoulos was forced to stand alongside, looking up at her. She showed him who was Commander-in-Chief that day.

A number of Hillary supporters had taken to watching FOX News during the primary in desperation. Since the conservative leaning network didn't have a dog in the Democratic primary hunt, one could on occasion get more well balanced coverage of the two candidates, as long as one didn't watch Sean Hannity or Glenn Beck. Anchor Bret Baier, for example, was balanced, civil and just reported the news.

In my view, FOX's Greta Van Susteren and CNN's Lou Dobbs likewise stood apart as the only other fair reporters of the entire election season.

* * *

The rest of the media was still out for blood. According to ABC News, while campaigning in South Dakota, Hillary was interviewed by the *Argus Leader*. Responding to reports she called "flatly untrue" that she had made overtures to the Obama campaign about either being VP or exiting the race, she said:

> "This is part of an ongoing effort to end this before it's over..." Clinton said that perhaps people are forgetting that there were other candidates in the past who were finishing a distant second and who went all the way to the convention. "I remember very well 1980, 1984, 1988, 1992," she said.

"People have been trying to push me out of this ever since Iowa."

"Why?" the reporter asked. "I don't know. I don't know. I find it curious. Because it is unprecedented in history. I don't understand it. Between my opponent and some in the media there has been this urgency to end this. And historically, that makes no sense. So I find it a bit of a mystery," Clinton responded.

The reporter asked if she buys the argument that Democrats are seeking party unity.

"I don't because I've been around long enough. My husband did not wrap up the nomination in 1992 until he won the California primary somewhere in the middle of June, right? We all remember Bobby Kennedy was assassinated in June in California. I don't understand it," Clinton said.[137]

Responding to this unfortunate sound bite, every news outlet jumped on the bandwagon accusing Clinton of invoking Robert Kennedy's assassination as a reason to stay in the race... On May 23rd, the *Huffington Post* ran a huge red masthead with an angry picture of Hillary with the headline:

"WHY WOULD I DROP OUT? MY HUSBAND DID NOT WRAP UP THE NOMINATION" UNTIL JUNE "BOBBY KENNEDY WAS ASSASSINATED IN JUNE"

The Reaction

TIME Magazine: Strange and Tasteless,

Washington Post: At Best A Poorly Chosen Example

Andrew Sullivan: Clinton Just Imploded

Howard Fineman: a Campaign that Probably Needs To Be Put Out Of Its Misery Real Soon

Olbermann: She Just Invoked a Nightmare"

The same day on *HuffPo*, David Rees posted his article, "Why Would I Drop Out Before Barack Obama Is Assassinated." Then, in parentheses, in tiny letters below the huge article title: (The title of this post is satirical. It is not a direct quote from Senator Clinton.)

The tiny disclaimer notwithstanding, Mr. Rees' title in itself was damaging.

Rees repeated her damning quote and while he pointed out that she apologized, he only included part of her remarks, without the words that made sense of her original statement. She was quoted correctly and in full context by ABC News:

> "Earlier today I was discussing the democratic primary history and in the course of that discussion mentioned the campaigns that both my husband and Senator Kennedy waged in California in June in 1992 and 1968. And I was referencing those to make the point that we have had nomination primary contests that go into June that's a historic fact. The Kennedy's have been much on my mind for the last days because of Senator Kennedy."

> "I regret that if my referencing that moment of trauma for our entire nation - particularly for that family - was in any way offensive," Clinton continued. "I certainly had no intention of that whatsoever. My view is that we have to look to the past and to our leaders who have inspired us and give us a lot to live up to and I'm honored to hold Senator Kennedy's seat in the United States Senate in the state of New York. And have the highest regard for the entire Kennedy family."

She phrased her initial remarks badly but they were in no way a call for Mr. Obama's assassination. For the *Huffington Post* to report this without the full and reasonable explanation contained in her entire statement was disingenuous at best and continued the practice of painting everything Senator Clinton did in the worst possible light.

Other major news major news organizations blew this gaffe out of all proportion. In response Senator Clinton offered another statement:

> "I pointed out, as I have before, that both my husband's primary campaign, and Sen. Robert Kennedy's, had continued into June," she wrote. "Almost immediately, some took my comments entirely out of context and interpreted them to mean

something completely different — and completely unthinkable."[138]

The *New York Times* reported that "the Obama campaign sent the entire political press corps the transcript of a "searing commentary" about Mrs. Clinton by Keith Olbermann on MSNBC."

George Stephanopoulos, the host of ABC's "This Week," asked David Axelrod, Mr. Obama's top strategist, about the e-mail:

> Mr. Stephanopoulos: You say you're not trying to stir the issue up. But a member of your press staff yesterday was sending around to an entire press list — I have the e-mail here — Keith Olbermann's searing commentary against Hillary Clinton. So that is stirring this up, isn't it?"
>
> Mr. Axelrod: "Well, Mr. Olbermann did his commentary and he had his opinion. But as far as we're concerned, this issue is done…"
>
> Mr. Stephanopoulos: "But your campaign was sending it around." [139]

Hillary was raked over the coals as "the Worst Person in the World," only the darkest motives attributed to her actions.

* * *

The Visuals

Major news outlets would go out of their way to find any and all unflattering photos of Hillary – mouth open, looking angry, aged, or sullen, eyes half closed. As Marshall McLuhan famously said, "the medium is the message."

> "Take a look at the pictures news outlets run. Typically, Hillary looks like a crazy person, her mouth agape, her eyes as bug-eyed as the runaway bride's. Meanwhile, Barack Obama typically looks cool, calm, collected - or, better yet, pensive and reflective."[140]
>
> -- Margery Eagan, *Boston Herald*

These unflattering photos of Hillary were another dog whistle, hinting Senator Clinton must be hysterical, not in control. I could hear familiar words buzzing in my head. "She must be on the rag."

We can't trust a woman with the nuclear codes because "you never know when her emotions might get the better of her" and she'll blow us to kingdom come.

The Drudge Report, a conservative news clearinghouse with an enormous reader base, featured a photo of Hillary with the caption "the Toll of a Campaign." Drudge ran the photo two weeks before the Iowa caucuses. Her face was so wrinkled, the photo looked as though it had been doctored to make her look ancient. Rush Limbaugh pounced on the image, discussing it on his radio program. His listening audience numbered at least twenty million.

Drudge linked the photo to Mr. Limbaugh's website as he asked a vital question:

> "Does Our Looks-Obsessed Culture Want to Stare at
> an Aging Woman?"

Media Matters reported on a spate of articles and pundit gabfests from here to Australia that worried over her "aged" appearance and what that meant for our country:

> "Later, during the December 17 edition of Fox
> News' The Big Story, right-wing pundit and
> nationally syndicated columnist Michelle Malkin
> asserted, "You all saw the famous photo from the
> weekend of Hillary looking so haggard and, what,
> looking like 92 years old. If that's the face of
> experience, I think it's going to scare away a lot of
> those independent voters that are on the fence."[141]

Having stood in close proximity to the Senator, I knew she looked nothing like that photo. Sexism combined with ageism made for quite the double whammy.

Regarding her "haggard" appearance, the reality out on the trail during the endless primary battle was quite different. As the campaign wore on, reporters noted Mr. Obama was looking visibly frayed while Hillary was fresh as a daisy. Must have been all those hot peppers she ate every day to stay healthy. Once again, spin had trumped truth.

> "When Barack Obama speaks, men hear, 'Take off
> for the future.' And when Hillary Clinton speaks,
> men hear, 'Take out the garbage.'" Clinton "does

register with married men, like a small worm boring through the brain."

-- Marc Rudov, FOX News

The *New York Times* featured a photograph from the point of view of Senator Clinton's shoes. She was on stage giving a campaign speech, with President Clinton in the background looking up at her as though she were the fifty-foot woman and he was a henpecked husband worshipping at her feet.[142]

The *Huffington Post* was one of many news sites that likewise offered up every sputtering, aggressive picture of Senator Clinton they could find. There were thousands of photos of the candidates, many taken in a matter of seconds. Snapping a picture in the middle of an exclamatory statement does an effective job of making an otherwise sensible person look like a whacko.

Prof. Kathleen Jamieson discussed the psychological effect on voters of these visual depictions:

> "...[P]eople who are producing them are trying to attach what scholars call *negative affect* to Hillary Clinton. ...To the extent that you have negative feelings, have basic *affect* when you see something. If I can attach that to something, I can make you feel uneasy about it. I can increase the likelihood that you're going to vote against Hillary Clinton.

> So we know, for example, that if I show you a picture of someone who's smiling and feels comfortable...you think more positively of the person, even if you don't know who the person is. Then I show you a scary picture, an off-putting picture. You react negatively. You respond negatively. I can increase the likelihood that you'll say you'll vote against that person even if you know nothing about them."

> "[S]ome of this is what we used to call visual vilification. But it's also attaching an emotional response to the picture to say feel uneasy, feel uncomfortable. And as a result, keep that emotional tag tied as you hear her explaining positions on issue.

Keep that discomfort. Hold onto it till you go into the voting booth.[143]

* * *

The Tricks

On Primary days, if there was any margin between the candidates and Barack Obama was projected to win, TV networks would put the "winner" check next to his name with no actual votes recorded. However, if the exit polling was in favor of Hillary, they would not call the state for her until well into the evening, after 65%-75% of the votes were tabulated, even when she won by a decisive margin. It was a signal to voters that Barack was "cruising" while Hillary was "struggling" for each win. Psychological warfare, make no mistake.

On May 19th, *Time Magazine* featured Senator Obama on the cover. The caption read "And the winner is…" with an asterisk below that said "*this time we're fairly sure." How far in advance of the release date did the magazine plan that cover? The primaries did not end until June 3rd and there were several states yet to vote. Didn't they carry *Time Magazine* in South Dakota and Montana? Couldn't such a cover influence the outcome?

At that time, *Time Magazine* also featured a picture of Hillary tied to the railroad tracks.

I came across a damning and apt description of the situation in an article, *Hating Hillary*, by British journalist Andrew Stephen, published on May 22, 2008. He noted that Ronald Reagan (in his unsuccessful 1976 bid), Ted Kennedy, Gary Hart, Jesse Jackson and Jerry Brown "continued their campaigns until the end of the primary season and, in most cases, all the way to the party convention" but

> "…[n]one of these male candidates had a premature political obituary written in the way that Hillary Clinton's has been, or was subjected to such righteous outrage over refusing to [ac]quiesce and withdraw obediently from what, in this case, has always been a knife-edge race. Nor was any of them anything like as close to his rivals as Clinton now is to Obama.
>
> …[P]robably the worst offender is the *NBC/MSNBC* network, which has what one prominent Clinton

activist describes as "its nightly horror shows". Tim Russert, the network's chief political sage, was dancing on Clinton's political grave before the votes in North Carolina and Indiana had even been fully counted - let alone those of the six contests to come, the undeclared super-delegates, or the disputed states of Florida and Michigan....

...never before have the US media taken it upon themselves to proclaim the victor before the primary contests are over or the choice of all the super-delegates is known, and the result was that the media's tidal wave of sexism became self-fulfilling: Americans like to back winners, and polls immediately showed dramatic surges of support for Obama."[144]

Most of the media had been declaring her dead since January 3rd. Driving home the same message night after night, month after month – even if it didn't start as true, the majority of the mainstream media would not rest until they made it so.

Mr. Stephen felt that history would "look back on the past six months as an example of America going through one of its collectively deranged episodes" much like "Prohibition" or "McCarthyism" and that "gloating, unshackled sexism of the ugliest kind" ..."has been shamelessly peddled by the US media."[145] He was one of a few men, though "no particular fan of Hillary's" (it seemed they all needed to make sure we knew that), who at least had the decency to put these words to paper.

The respected Mr. Russert was not alone in declaring Hillary Clinton politically dead. While voters were headed to the polls during one of the early May primaries, I watched George Stephanopoulos state that "the contest is basically over." Did any of these gentlemen demoralize any of her voters enough that they stayed at home? Wouldn't that fall outside their purview?

I contributed to a group identifying themselves as WomenCount PAC. They were raising money to take out full page ads in influential newspapers in response to continued efforts to get Hillary to drop out.

Their *New York Times* ad featured a picture of Senator Clinton, campaigning at night in the rain, microphone in hand, the other hand reaching out to the crowd. That magnificent photograph should have been her campaign poster from the beginning. This was Hillary -- determined and fierce.

The caption read, "NOT SO FAST!"

> "...Hillary's voice is OUR voice, and she's speaking for all of us." "We stand united in our unwavering support for Hillary Clinton."
>
> "We know that when women vote, Democrats win. Now it is the responsibility of our party to hear our voices and count all of our votes. We want Hillary to stay in this race until every vote is cast, every vote is counted, and we know that our voices are heard."[146]

There was no way I wanted her to quit. She had the courage of a lion. We needed her. Her ability to stand up in the face of her detractors was something I had not yet seen from another politician.

Fighting for her was a gift to me. I did my homework. I made a solid argument. I didn't back down. The way she stood up taught me to stand up. Beyond her depth on policy, it was her guts, tenacity and diligence that I thought would make her a great president.

Obstructionism would not stop her. She knew how to reach across the aisle. She also knew how to fight. Foreign leaders would not intimidate her. She'd been in rooms with many of them for years. The pressure cooker that is the White House would not tire her. She understood the rigors of the job.

As Pennsylvania Governor Ed Rendell had pointed out, the work of governing is less contained in a speech than in the value of competence, slogging it out daily to get effective legislation passed, offering guidance and leadership to Congress, putting out fires, and yes, dealing with the 3 a.m. phone call.

Hillary had also blossomed on the campaign trail, striking a more populist tone, having transformed into a "happy warrior,"[147] relaxed and enthusiastic with every voter. After her victory in Pennsylvania, even MSNBC's Tucker Carlson who had called her "castrating, overbearing and scary" exclaimed that he was "in awe."

But no matter how good a politician Hillary had become, I never thought she was going to solve all my problems. Hillary Clinton was human; an imperfect person in an imperfect world who just happened to be a knowledgeable, caring policy wonk who liked to roll her sleeves up and get to work.

Even big media had to admit it was embarrassing that the frontrunner for the nomination had amassed the majority of his delegates from caucuses and red states and couldn't seem to score a big win, apart from his home state of Illinois. They were quoted as saying "he was limping toward the finish line."[148,149] These same media outlets had carped for months that Hillary had no hope.

Hillary Clinton wound up winning more votes than any candidate in Primary history, yet if you listened to the news or the DNC, widespread support for her was America's best kept secret.

Senator Obama was by no means the prime culprit here. Just as Hillary Clinton was the constant on her side of the equation, Barack Obama likewise was the constant of his: his voting record, his personal and professional associations, his oratory, his policies or reversals. If the media chose not to report the information or to minimize it, what politician wouldn't take advantage of such great good fortune?

I had called the DNC so many times I lost count, begging them to be fair, to keep the party leadership out of it, and stop the pressure to shut this thing down. Just let all the states have their voices and their votes. Chairman Dean had appeared on network TV to decry race baiting yet made no mention of sexist bias in the media. I spoke with his rather brusque assistant to point out this inequity. She denied his television appearance. "But it's on videotape!" I said.

The Goal

When one pretends a bad event is not happening, the objective is to make the accuser feel like she's crazy. I was familiar with this game. No one was willing to acknowledge the broken family system.

If the abusers ever did acknowledge it, then the false world they had created would come crashing down. The alcoholic does not want to give up drink and will rarely admit to the abuse he or she levels at others. Presumably, then they'd have to do something about it. The façade of purity and perfection would disintegrate.

This was evidenced by the immobile smile Speaker Pelosi wore when asked about the misogyny in the campaign. She did not admit it existed until after the fact.

Newsweek editor Evan Thomas stated in a radio interview[150] that no sexism existed in the campaign coverage.

Carl Bernstein intimated the media's behavior may have been a small factor, but no more. These comments came from a serious journalist who complained that Hillary was "inauthentic," defining her as a "celebrity." His book on Hillary, *A Woman in Charge*, had acknowledged her achievements and was more charitable towards the Senator than his sound bites for television, which reached a far wider audience.

Perhaps if they had set Hillary dolls on fire in front of the camera that would have met his criteria for outrageous bias.

NBC President Phil Griffin later addressed efforts to "repair a fractured audience base, a portion of which saw sexism in his network's Clinton coverage and vowed to boycott MSNBC." In particular he addressed, and agreed with, the negative assessment of Keith Olbermann's behavior while in the same breath excusing it:

> "It was, like, you meet a guy and you fall in love with him, and he's funny and he's clever and he's witty, and he's all these great things," Griffin said of the relationship between Olbermann and the Clinton supporters among his viewers. "And then you commit yourself to him, and he turns out to be a jerk and difficult and brutal. And that is how the Hillary viewers see him. It's true. But I do think they're going to come back. There's nowhere else to go."[151]

I emailed a note to Mr. Griffin:

> "Do you have any daughters, sir? If they were ever to be treated badly by a man would you likewise advise them to return to the abuse because they had nowhere else to go?"

Some of my women friends who had volunteered their time for Hillary were getting physically ill, unable to sleep, contracting stomach ailments, having nightmares, feeling depressed and enraged with no outlet for those feelings. A few male Hillary supporters I knew were no less angry, ready to throw their TVs out the window.

Not long before, I'd performed before a group of kids from Covenant House, a center for troubled teens working to kick substance abuse problems. One of the characters in my solo piece was cruel beyond measure. Though other audiences were amused by this person's wit, the kids from Covenant House sat in hostile silence. They were protective, angry, waiting for the moment "he" exited the stage. Their reaction was visceral and cut to the bone.

I had never experienced such a sensation. You could feel the tension in the theatre abate as "the heroine" re-emerged. These kids, having come from abusive households as I did, could smell cruelty a mile away. Once you've been on the receiving end of such behavior, denials or justifications are meaningless.

Hillary claimed she was "impervious" to this abuse. I was not. My friends were not. *Washington Post* columnist Marie Cocco echoed our sentiments in her column, *Misogyny I Won't Miss*:

> "I will not miss the deafening, depressing silence of Democratic National Committee Chairman Howard Dean or other leading Democrats, who to my knowledge (with the exception of Sen. Barbara Mikulski of Maryland) haven't uttered a word of public outrage at the unrelenting, sex-based hate that has been hurled at a former first lady and two-term senator from New York. Among those holding their tongues are hundreds of Democrats for whom Clinton has campaigned and raised millions of dollars...

> "Would the silence prevail if Obama's likeness were put on a tap-dancing doll that was sold at airports? Would the media figures who dole out precious face time to these politicians be such pals if they'd compared Obama with a character in a blaxploitation film? And how would crude references to Obama's sex organs play?

"...[F]or all Clinton's political blemishes, the darker stain that has been exposed is the hatred of women that is accepted as a part of our culture."[152]

We found that out when not one, but two women on different sides of the aisle threatened the status quo for different reasons.

How much of a factor sexism was in determining the outcome of the Primary may be up for debate but the true injustice is that it happened at all. Too many in the media applied their own convenient yardstick to measure causation and vindicated themselves.

In a contest this close – and it was very close – who is to say even 10% didn't matter?

10 MICHIGAN, FLORIDA AND THE CAUCUS CHAOS

On May 31, 2008, the Rules and By Laws Committee of the DNC met in Washington, D.C. to decide what to do about a gnawing disenfranchisement issue that could conceivably drive voters from Michigan and Florida into Republican arms in the general election.

At the start of the campaign calendar, five states moved their Primaries up, opting to hold them earlier than the legal limit in violation of Rule 11 as set forth by the Rules and Bylaws Committee. South Carolina, Iowa and New Hampshire were granted a "waiver" to do so with no penalty. For the same "crime," the Committee gave the "death penalty" to Michigan and Florida.

Florida had 211 delegates at stake and Michigan had 157, both offering a proportionate share of huge prizes to each Primary's winner. Because of their "crime," none of the delegates from these two states would be seated at the Convention. Some believed Michigan and Florida should have been thus disqualified, unaware of the irregular circumstances that disenfranchised them in the first place.

While many Hillary supporters were furious at the outcome of the delegate distribution decision at the RBC's May 31st meeting, that was not the reason for my frustration. As far as I was concerned, there was only one argument to be made and Florida Democratic State Senator Ted Deutch (later a Congressman), had made it.

Mr. Deutch offered a much needed clarification to confusion about Party rules in the Palm Beach Post[153] on April 6th, *Democrats' ballyhooed rules offer fix*, sharing that argument with anyone who had cared to pay attention. The article is reprinted here, in pertinent part, with Mr. Deutch's express permission:

> "…Let's be clear that the rules that we have been discussing are the delegate selection rules for the 2008 Democratic National Convention. The rules cannot tell a state or its voters whether the results of a legal election are valid; they only govern the selection of delegates to the national convention.
>
> A record number of Florida Democrats, more than 1.7 million voters, went to the polls for the Jan. 29 Florida Primary, and not one of them broke any rules by exercising his or her right to vote. But the DNC has said that they don't count.
>
> …[T]he focus of this debate should be the language of the actual rules, the states that violated them and the penalties imposed (or waived) because of those violations.
>
> Rule 11 clearly prohibits primaries or caucuses from being held prior to the first Tuesday in February, except in Iowa, New Hampshire, Nevada and South Carolina, each of which is assigned very specific limits on when they may hold their contests. Florida Democrats were penalized for violating Rule 11 when our state moved the primary seven days too early. Michigan Democrats, whose state moved 21 days early, were penalized, too. Oddly, Democrats in three other states that violated the rules were not.
>
> Iowa, permitted to go "no earlier than 22 days before the first Tuesday in February" (Jan. 14), moved its caucuses to Jan. 3 - a clear-cut violation. New Hampshire, granted the freedom to hold its primary "no earlier than 14 days" (Jan. 22) ahead of the pack, also broke Rule 11 by moving to January 8. And, of course, South Carolina, "no earlier than seven days" (Jan. 29), defied the DNC and moved to Jan. 26.

So what penalties, if any, should the rule-breaking states be subject to? According to Rule 20.C: "The number of pledged delegates elected ... shall be reduced by 50 percent." The rules do not say that the votes of Florida Democrats do not count. Indeed, the penalty established by the DNC's own rules is based upon the results of the primary; therefore, the results of the primary must be valid.

It's clear that Iowa, New Hampshire, South Carolina, Michigan and Florida all violated the same rule and should be treated the same. But that's not what happened. While the rules designate a 50 percent delegate reduction, the DNC imposed the death penalty - a 100 percent reduction - on Florida and Michigan. Amazingly, the other "rule-breakers" got no penalty at all.

The DNC has chosen to waive the rules when it believes that it suits the DNC's purposes. If the DNC insists on treating Florida differently, then it should be reminded that its own rules establish a 50 percent penalty rather than the death penalty given to Florida Democrats. ...Rather than continue this divisive debate, the DNC should simply return to the rules that it drafted.

...[T]he rules require that the votes are counted... the DNC must count Florida's 1.75 million votes and seat no less than half of our delegates based upon those votes."

Mr. Deutch's argument was aimed at his own state of Florida, but it applied equally to Michigan, if only insofar as addressing the arbitrary enforcement of the DNC party "rules" for delegate disenfranchisement.

It was both frustrating and infuriating to realize that had the RBC obeyed their own rules from the beginning, instead of making an arbitrary decision, the debacle of Michigan and Florida would likely not have occurred in the first place. *If* the 50% penalty were imposed on Michigan and Florida from at the start of the calendar, *then*:

Requests for later revotes in either state would have been unnecessary.

Whoever won those two primaries in January would have proceeding to Super Duper Tuesday with their proportional slate of pledged delegates at half strength.

Obama, Edwards, Biden and Richardson would never have removed their names from the Michigan ballot. Since half is better than none – everyone's name would have remained, while still adhering to the pledge they all signed not to campaign in either state. The pertinent portion of their signed pledge follows:

> "THEREFORE, I _____, Democratic Candidate for President, pledge I shall not campaign or participate in any state which schedules a presidential election primary or caucus before Feb. 5, 2008, except for the states of Iowa, Nevada, New Hampshire and South Carolina, as "campaigning" is defined by rules and regulations of the DNC."

"We're honoring the pledge and we won't campaign or spend money in states that aren't in compliance with the DNC calendar," Clinton spokesman Jay Carson said.

No muss. No fuss. No drama.

The Republican contests also penalized the states half their respective delegates for betraying the calendar in those states – not all of them.

I had not come across any justification for the Rules and By Laws Committee to give Michigan and Florida the death penalty in the first place, apart from what I could only assume was their desire to unreasonably punish these two states. Why were the states not penalized 50% in January per the RBC's own rules?

Regardless of what Hillary or any of the other candidates consented to, that did not explain the mystery of the RBC's unfathomable decision many months earlier. Unfortunately for Senator Clinton, both the states of Michigan and Florida had demographics that heavily favored her.

The candidates' signed pledges were also unrelated to the actual votes. The elections were ratified by the State Board of Electors, meaning the popular vote totals would count. Obviously, Florida was an easier situation to deal with, since all the candidates names were on the ballot.

Senator Obama was also not penalized any delegates in Florida for breaking his pledge not to advertise there, though he had run $1.3 million worth of ads.[154] An accident, he later said. He was lucky it was considered an accident, because the RBC rules stated that any candidate breaking the pledge to campaign in such a state would forever lose any right to any delegates awarded from that state.

As to Michigan, Senators Obama and Edwards, seeing they were way behind in the polls there, removed their names from the ballot and had asked their supporters to vote "uncommitted" instead.

Local Party websites, in Washtenaw County, Michigan, for example, explained that "If enough voters cast uncommitted votes, the party will send delegates to the national nominating convention who are not committed to a specific candidate."

CNN's Bill Schneider offered an explanation for the motives of the candidates who had removed their names in the first place. He had suggested the Democrats who withdrew may have calculated "that it was simply in their best political interest to do so."

> "If there's no campaign, the candidate most likely to win Michigan is Hillary Clinton," Schneider said. "Her Democratic rivals don't want a Clinton victory in Michigan to count. They want Iowa and New Hampshire, where they have a better chance of stopping Clinton, to count more."[155]

Obama, Edwards, Biden and Richardson later attempted to restore their names to the ballot in advance of the primary, but were blocked by the Michigan legislature.[156] In mid-March however, when the Clinton campaign offered to raise private funds for a revote, a Democratic source stated that "the Obama people are blocking it in the Legislature."[157]

Senator Clinton won both the Michigan and Florida Primaries by twenty-point margins. Even with a fifty percent allotment credited to her in those delegate rich states, she would have marched into Super Duper Tuesday with the "Big Mo" having officially won four out of six Primaries, New Hampshire, Nevada, Michigan and

Florida. Michigan and Florida would not have been demoted to "beauty contests."

No one can speculate or predict to a certainty what would have happened. Yet by denying half those delegates to her back in January when they would have made a difference, in violation of what seemed to be the Democratic Party's own stated rules, it could be argued that had blunted her momentum.

A look at the numbers reveals that adding these totals to Hillary's huge super delegate lead and her wins on Super Duper Tuesday might very well have sewn the nomination up for her then and there.

The situation was growing into a bigger and bigger mess. Every time I'd read some hopeful information in the news about a solution, it amounted to nothing. Dozens of options were floated. None were accepted. Voters from both those states, coming out to participate in record numbers, were incensed at being disenfranchised.

Anyone who doubts why Hillary supporters were furious at Howard Dean and select members of the RBC need look no further than these two states to clarify the butter. As the months ticked by, it appeared Chairman Dean was hoping the situation would go away. The popular ABC show *Boston Legal* even poked fun at the contest in one of their episodes. They implied the DNC was not neutral, but a private club and could do as they pleased.

* * *

Surely, it was a mistake for Hillary not to focus more attention on the caucuses. Caucuses may be unconstitutional, but they are still the law of Primary land. The process is by its very nature disenfranchising, excluding shift workers of all sorts, nurses, police, firefighters, restaurant workers, single parents, poor voters, older voters, and the military. Again, those groups tended to be a stronger part of Hillary's voting bloc. It was no wonder the Clintons had a less than stellar regard for caucuses.

In some circles, there was also an assumption that caucuses involved voters who were better informed, as though only wealthy or highly educated voters understood the issues. As someone so involved in the campaign, I had spoken with too many people of all social strata to believe such an elitist statement.

Two groups standing on either side of the room to yell about their respective candidates seemed to favor the younger and louder among us.

Dr. Lynette Long[158] prepared a comprehensive report on the caucus process and delegate apportionment, easily viewed on the internet. "Caucus states made up 1.1 million or 3% of all democratic votes, yet they had the power to choose 626, or 15% of the delegates."[159] When one sees how few caucus voters represented a large amount of delegates, wielding disproportionate power to choose our nominee, it became clear how the concept of one person one vote was ignored. ABC commentator Cokie Roberts and her husband Steve Roberts[160] discussed "the party's stupid, self-destructive nominating system" that we would do better to change:

> "...First, it was designed to anoint a nominee by early February, far too early in the process. The result: Obama built up an insurmountable lead at a time when he was still largely unblemished, untested and unscrutinized. The past six weeks have brought tougher media coverage, the Rev. Jeremiah Wright's tapes, the candidate's ill-considered comments about "bitter" voters and a wave of second thoughts among key groups like union members and white Catholics.

Mr. and Mrs. Roberts pointed out that the 2008 nominating system in place could not reflect those shifts, since the Democratic Party's "rules of proportional representation made it almost impossible for Clinton to catch up." Unlike Democrats, Republicans used a winner take all delegate rule per each state contested.

Their next statement floored me:

> "Since Feb. 19, seven states have voted. Clinton has won four — Pennsylvania, Texas, Ohio and Rhode Island —building up a popular-vote margin of 483,000. Yet her total gain in delegates was exactly 5. In Texas, she won by more than 100,000 votes, but because of that state's ridiculous rules, she actually came out 5 delegates behind."

As the Roberts' article detailed, Hillary won the Texas Primary by 4 points, 51-47, yet she lost the Texas caucus by 12 points, 56-44.

Caucus voters were a small subset of the total, yet her popular vote win was rendered meaningless.

Similarly in Washington state, citizens both caucus and vote – but only the caucus counts toward awarding delegates to the candidates. In the Washington caucus, the result was Obama 68, Clinton 31. However, in the Primary, which had more than double the turnout of the caucus, the result was Obama 51, Clinton 46.

The Roberts stated:

> "His delegate advantage in Idaho, Kansas and Louisiana — three states that will never vote Democratic — was a total of 38. By contrast, Clinton handily won three large swing states — Pennsylvania, New Jersey and Ohio. And yet, because of party rules, her combined marginal gain amounted to 28 delegates."

Cokie and Steve Roberts seemed as incredulous as I that three Republican states with few electoral votes had a larger say in determining the Democratic nominee than Pennsylvania, New Jersey and Ohio, three states that were critical to carrying a Democrat to victory in any Presidential election.

* * *

Starting with the first caucuses, word was also spreading on the internet of irregularities occurring in Iowa, Nevada and Texas, where people were being bussed into the caucuses from other areas, sign-in lists thrown away, participants diverted to wrong locations, locked out, or bullied out of their votes.

Not living in a caucus state, I knew nothing of this, but had heard some version of the same information from fellow campaigners in different states. It was but a blip in the media, but *Newsweek*, and *National Review Online* reported on a letter Clinton Campaign counsel Lyn Utrecht had filed reporting specific complaints of caucus irregularities occurring at different precincts in Texas that she had listed by name .[161,162]

Gigi Gaston, lifelong Democrat and granddaughter of a Massachusetts Governor, directed a documentary, "We Will Not Be Silenced," that offered corroboration of these occurrences.[163] I viewed video testimony and commentary from those participating in the caucuses detailing their experiences.[164] There were over 2,000 documented complaints of caucus fraud in Texas alone.

In a most heated environment, men and women went on the record to share their experiences. At the least, they deserved to have a fair hearing before those in authority in the DNC. I had no idea if the DNC had ever investigated. If they did, their findings were not made public. If there was nothing to them, what would have been the harm in publishing a report verifying the same?

The familiar sensation of powerlessness overtook me. I channeled my frustration by making more campaign calls and writing to super delegates.

On May 30th, the day prior to the meeting of the dreaded Rules and Bylaws Committee of the DNC, I attended a visibility rally at The Laugh Factory in LA.

The location seemed apropos.

I made my first campaign speech of sorts, participating in a video to be FedExed to the Committee offering our reasons for giving the delegates a voice at the Convention.

Dear Lord, I'm not only on talk radio, the internet and the phone – I'm on video declaring myself! A few people told me I should run for Congress. Run for the hills seemed more like it. I joked with some of the other attendees, picking lightly at my wrist. "See this? This is the world's thinnest skin." I'd need another three lifetimes to grow a hide thick enough to put myself in that particular lion's den.

Many of us were interviewed after the rally by a young freelance reporter doing an article for the *Huffington Post*. She scribbled notes furiously, and I'm sure, tried her best to tell our story. Reading it soon after, the hodge-podge that was reported was not representative of our main concerns. My statements were misquoted.

On May 31st, I was glued to the TV and the blogs, watching thousands of protesters who had traveled to Washington, D.C. for the RBC meeting to be watchdogs and show their support. It was our last hope to get some good news.

Howard Dean, in an attempt to placate furious Hillary supporters, said he'd had no knowledge of media gender bias because "he didn't watch cable television."

Time Magazine then reported "...after heated arguments from both sides...the panel's lunch turned into a three-hour closed-door session." It was my understanding that such a private session was also against Committee rules.

The RBC arrived at a solution that awarded Florida's delegates at half strength per the popular vote, yielding Clinton a net gain of 19 delegates.

Michigan was trickier:

> "Following a plan endorsed by the Michigan Democratic Party, the committee voted to allot Clinton, who won 55% of the vote, 69 delegates, and Obama, who most believed was the overwhelming choice of the 40% of Michigan primary voters who chose "uncommitted", 59. If the delegates had been meted out based strictly on the actual vote Clinton should've gotten 73 delegates, and her supporters claimed, Obama should have gotten no delegates, at least until the convention when the uncommitted could state their preference."

Obama was awarded an additional four of Hillary's delegates, which gave Hillary a net loss of eight. Many didn't understand how the RBC had arrived at their delegate distribution. After their decision was announced, Harold Ickes, a longtime Hillary operative said:

> "Mrs. Clinton has instructed me to reserve her rights to take this to the Credentials Committee. There's been a lot of talk about party unity let's all come together and put our arms around each other. I submit to you, ladies and gentlemen, that hijacking four delegates ... is not a good way to start down the path of party unity."

Hillary supporters who attended the meeting were outraged at the RBC's decision, shouting "Denver!" and "Take It to the Floor!"

Mr. Obama was awarded all of Michigan's uncommitted delegates plus four of hers, even though Messrs. Biden, Richardson and Edwards were still in contention at the time. The gift of those four delegates infuriated hard line Hillary supporters more than any other action of the RBC. Her supporters also questioned why the RBC required three hours behind closed doors to come up with such a solution.

* * *

The only positive takeaway from the whole miserable weekend was a woman I met at the Laugh Factory the day before. She was statuesque and stunning with a biting wit and waist length ringlets. We shared magic markers with the other volunteers as we knelt on the floor making the large signs we would later wave before traffic on Sunset Blvd. at our visibility event. I said to her, "I can't imagine the pressure you've been under, supporting Hillary."

She laughed, "Yeah, my Mama wants to take away my Negro card but I told her she can't have it – it's under lock and key!" We shared our various campaign experiences. Whatever I'd had to listen to was nothing compared to what her family and friends put her through those past months and the disparaging comments she had heard from strangers. It was our only meeting but I still remember her beautiful face and humor in the face of all of it. I knew I still had a long way to go until I'd found that kind of courage.

11 DUELING NARRATIVES

"I am absolutely certain that generations from now, we will be able to look back and tell our children that this was the moment when we began to provide care for the sick and good jobs to the jobless; this was the moment when the rise of the oceans began to slow and our planet began to heal."

-- Senator Barack Obama, June 3, 2008

"Some find that she makes their skin crawl. Some run screaming from the room. And some want to drink a gallon of rat poison while lying across a railroad track." ..."[M]uch of the support she has comes from people who wish her husband could serve a third term."

--columnist Steve Chapman, *Chicago Tribune*[165]

"This is the moment . . . that the world is waiting for... I have become a symbol of the possibility of America returning to our best traditions."

-- Senator Barack Obama

"Change is just a word if you don't have the strength and experience to make it happen."

-- Senator Hillary Rodham Clinton

On, Sunday, June 1st Hillary won the Primary in Puerto Rico by 32 points.

On June 2nd, the night before the two final Primaries, the Clinton family campaigned at a town hall together in South Dakota. No one could have imagined the title of best surrogate would be claimed by Senator Clinton's soft spoken daughter Chelsea. She proved to be a heavy hitter, even better than her famous Dad.

After Chelsea witnessed Hillary's loss in Iowa, she said she "wasn't going to let her Mom go out like that." For months, she had hit the college crowd, sharing her mom's policy positions in great detail. Despite the appearance of being far more fragile than either of her parents, she was relaxed and in charge.

I can't imagine what it must have been like for Chelsea to be an awkward teenager growing up under the glare of the hottest lights, her every move scrutinized. Being on the receiving end of cruel jokes at such a vulnerable age can't have been easy.

On that night in South Dakota, Hillary was at the microphone explaining her healthcare plan. After campaigning around the clock, her voice gave out. She surrendered to a coughing fit. Chelsea walked center stage, took the microphone from her mother and, almost mid-sentence, picked up where Hillary had left off to drive the point home. Momma Clinton got some water as President Clinton proudly looked on. Then Hillary's throat would cooperate and she'd walk back on stage, take the mike and continue.

A few minutes later, her coughing fit resumed and they repeated the procedure. Passing the baton? Tag team wrestling? Whatever you called it, the symbolic message meant a great deal to me.

Tuesday, June 3rd, the final day of the Primaries, was an ugly one. Early in the morning, the Associated Press released a false story that Senator Clinton had already conceded while voters in Montana and South Dakota were just heading to the polls.

I had called the AP offices in New York, Los Angeles, and Washington to ask that they retract the story. They refused and said the situation was beyond their control. I had contacted the FCC to see if counter action was possible. A gentleman responded that there was no redress for someone putting out a falsehood in the press.

Far from conceding, Hillary was working the phones to super delegates asking them to hold their water and not come out to declare their allegiance under pressure.

Governor Bill Richardson, among others, was likewise pressing super delegates to jump ship and support Obama in advance of the last day, intimating their support would be worth more if it was declared prior to the end of the Primaries. That afternoon, a number of super delegates came out of the woodwork but when California Rep. Maxine Waters abandoned Hillary for Obama, I knew it was over.

Hillary was supposed to lose both states that night, yet she won South Dakota by a convincing margin. After Senator Obama won Montana, he took the stage and declared himself the nominee.

The media was euphoric, screaming that Hillary should shrivel up and disappear, for lack of a nicer way to say it.

> "The night before, as the results of the Montana and South Dakota Primaries rolled in, she'd delivered a speech in New York that the cable-news bloviators and even some of her supporters deemed an egregious, churlish attempt to stomp on Obama's buzz. She hadn't conceded, hadn't endorsed, hadn't so much as acknowledged her rival's historic triumph. Her audience chanted, "Denver! Denver! Denver!" She seemed to revel in it. Was Clinton engaged in an ill-conceived effort to strong-arm Obama into putting her on the ticket? Was she being supremely Machiavellian? Or had she simply lost her mind?"
>
> -- John Heilemann, *New York Magazine*[166]

The country was anxious to celebrate Barack Obama's historic moment.

Her historic moment was ignored.

Perhaps she knew what her supporters knew – that neither she nor Obama had enough pledged delegates to claim the nomination. Perhaps she was not crazy or Machiavellian after all. Or, at the least, she might have been savoring a final celebration with her supporters since she had won two out of three primaries that last week.

There would be plenty of time for Senator Obama to claim the news cycle, and everything that went with it, the following day. Why wouldn't big media be smart enough to graciously let her have one night to enjoy her great – and unprecedented – achievements with her supporters? It was foolish to alienate even a portion of her 18,000,000 voters, whose support the DNC would need to win the election in the fall.

Again, let us reverse their roles here. What if Hillary had claimed the nomination that night, with Obama being named by the media as the "loser." Imagine how pundits would have cast Hillary as the selfish egomaniac who wouldn't allow her opponent one night with his dedicated supporters to acknowledge what no black man had ever before accomplished.

There had never been a campaign like this one, and likely there would never be one again. They both deserved to be equally honored for breaking new ground. She was told to sit down and shut up.

When I awoke the morning of June 4, 2008, I thought I would be furious, or curled up in the fetal position crying my eyes out. But I was relieved, even serene. I thought since the race had been declared over, at least I wouldn't have to watch her get flogged that day. For the first time in six months, I wouldn't have to watch, or avoid watching, the frat-boy media hit squad trash her mercilessly, simply because they knew they could get away with it. With rare exception, no one, save her own husband, stood up to declare anything was wrong with that practice.

The beatings continued.

Several news articles mentioned how the New York delegation, including Rep. Charlie Rangel, was moving against her, making it known they had been instructed not to support her at the Convention should she decide to fight on.

That same week, CNN anchor Wolf Blitzer had interviewed Clinton's campaign manager Howard Wolfson. He asked why Senator Clinton did not concede immediately. With a straight face, Mr. Blitzer also asked why she did not focus on the "historic" nature of her candidacy. I had to write one of my letters to him in response. I'm pretty sure I wrote asking him how he slept at night.

In the eyes of the media, Barack Obama was the only one allowed to have a "historic" run. Race trumped gender in the choice of narrative. Her narrative was sacrificed. "Shrillary" was at every turn characterized as a scheming banshee standing in the way of an idealistic, charming young man.

> "The bias is usually against Republicans, but sometimes it's against, like, an Al Gore in 2000 or a Hillary Clinton in 2008, 'cause Hillary, too, was running against history."
>
> -- Joe Scarborough, MSNBC[167]

Mr. Scarborough's implication was that the first woman to be elected President after forty-three men would not make history. In a man's world, a woman making history was not regarded as significant, meaningful, or necessary. She was not considered equal in the realm of history.

> "When I started working on women's history about thirty years ago, the field did not exist. People didn't think women had a history worth knowing."[168]
>
> -- Gilda Lerner

Diminishing women's accomplishments is nothing new. To date, there is no site allotted for building a national museum dedicated solely to women's history. As of this writing, legislation to grant permission for such a museum is still pending in the Senate.

The media picks our Presidents. They adopt the narrative and drive the point home with each story they report. Both narratives could not coexist and get equal oxygen. The media trumpeted the historic aspect of the candidate they wanted: the man, the new guy, the rock star, the mystique, the African American male. The change mantra, coupled with the fact that much of the press still harbored animosity towards the Clintons made it even easier. Women were once again asked to step aside.

From the beginning, pundits claimed: "Her campaign is horrible." Yes, her campaign had problems and made mistakes. No doubt consultant Mark Penn and Patti Solis Doyle, vital parts of her campaign team, did not serve her well. However, Senator Obama's fundraising juggernaut, with the DNC riding shotgun and the media functioning as his de facto PR firm were formidable advantages. Senator Obama outspent her by a huge margin, in some states by as much as five to one,[169] yet this 'woman' still made it a virtual tie. How horrible could her campaign have been?

Perhaps some have a primal need to see the woman as caregiver and want her to take care of us rather than to govern us. Perhaps there is a resentment of the woman as authority figure and the very idea engages people's need to rebel: 'mommy isn't going to tell me what to do anymore. I'm not going to take out the garbage.' No matter how we may outwardly suppress this sentiment, too many still believe women exist in service of men and should get out of the way to let them excel.

I reminded myself that black men got the vote fifty years before women of any color in this country. Far fewer Americans are aware that women were jailed, beaten, starved and tortured just for peacefully protesting in front of the White House in pursuit of the right to vote, whereas we are well aware of civil rights struggles of black Americans. That may be part of the reason voters and the media were willing to embrace his historic narrative, yet reject hers.

After Senator Obama had secured the nomination, he found time to praise the Clintons and the very administration he saw fit to deride throughout the primary. Younger voters, his main demographic, were not old enough to remember the truth for themselves. The Clinton years may not have been perfect but as Hillary had said, "What didn't they like, the peace or the prosperity?" We had a balanced budget, an enormous surplus, lower unemployment and economic growth.

On Saturday, June 7th Senator Hillary Clinton appeared before a huge auditorium of supporters to suspend her campaign. Senator Obama informed the press he would be playing golf that day.

> "Always aim high, work hard, and care deeply about what you believe in. When you stumble, keep faith. When you're knocked down, get right back up. And never listen to anyone who says you can't or shouldn't go on."

> "Life is too short, time is too precious, and the stakes are too high to dwell on what might have been. We have to work together for what still can be."

"Although we weren't able to shatter that highest, hardest glass ceiling this time, thanks to you, it's got about 18 million cracks in it."

"You can be so proud that, from now on, it will be unremarkable for a woman to win primary state victories, unremarkable to have a woman in a close race to be our nominee, unremarkable to think that a woman can be the President of the United States. And that is truly remarkable."

Senator Hillary Clinton, Concession speech,
Washington D.C., June 7, 2008

Hillary was dressed in black.

My husband and I were mourning, too. That afternoon, we stood in line at the post office to hand in our new voter registration forms. Instead of "democrat" we checked "decline to state."

This was our protest, as small an action as it was. I felt foolish that tears were rolling down my face as we stood in line. I had always voted a straight party ticket. The Democratic Party voiced nary a complaint about her treatment throughout this nationwide nightmare. Regardless of the outcome, after the disrespect this woman received I didn't know what my party stood for anymore.

Hillary had said "I'll work my heart out for you." And yeah, it breaks my heart to this day more people didn't hear the message.

12 "ANI" FINDS A HOME ON THE WEB

Under normal circumstances after a Primary, all was forgiven in a few days. Everyone would shake hands and shake off any hard feelings, gather behind the nominee and go full steam ahead. CNN contributor Bill Schneider opined that because this contest had gone on for so long, Hillary voters would require a "30-day mourning period." Did he have actuarial tables to help him arrive at this figure? I surmised this was his way of telling us all to take a walk and go have a glass of wine.

> "In a CNN/Opinion Research Corp. survey completed in early June before the New York senator ended her White House bid, 60 percent of Clinton backers polled said they planned on voting for Obama. In the latest poll, that number has dropped to 54 percent. In early June, 22 percent of Clinton supporters polled said they would not vote at all if Obama were the party's nominee, now close to a third say they will stay home.
>
> In another sign the wounds of the heated primary race have yet to heal, 43 percent of registered Democrats polled still say they would prefer Clinton to be the party's presidential nominee. That number is significantly higher than it was in early June, when 35 percent of Democrats polled said they preferred Clinton to lead the party's presidential ticket."[170]

Big media feigned ignorance at our reasons for not falling in line. Out on the blogs, we were incredulous at Mr. Schneider's attitude. The media once again had its narrative, the facts notwithstanding. They had insisted we wanted to force Hillary onto Obama's ticket. They painted Senator Obama as a man of infinite patience having to "tolerate" bitter Hillary supporters who refused to go quietly.

No one I knew wanted Senator Clinton to be his angelic Dick Cheney. The majority of her supporters in the blogosphere felt she was more qualified and didn't want her in second position. Yet with the power of her 18,000,000 votes behind her, I could not imagine that Senator Obama wouldn't at least offer her the Vice Presidency—perhaps she had turned it down. Otherwise no one could understand an apparent show of disrespect that a woman of this caliber was not seriously vetted for the position when Senator Jim Webb, Governor Ted Strickland, Senator Evan Bayh and a number of others had already refused the opportunity.

Kenneth Walsh filed a story with *U.S. News*: *Despite Obama's Efforts, Clinton Supporters Won't Fade Away*.[171] Even the title was insulting. Where should 18,000,000 people fade away to? I felt like I was reading a copy of *Animal Farm*, where some votes are more equal than others.

> "[Clinton supporters] argue that she hasn't been given the respect she deserves even though Obama has apparently agreed to give her a coveted primetime speaking slot August 26 and he has been quite conciliatory."[172]

"Coveted?" I could almost smell their fear. It was as if they needed to characterize her as a scullery maid to keep convincing themselves she had no power. Mr. Walsh also quoted Obama operatives without question, not bothering to investigate the claims they made in his article:

> "They went negative on us (in the primaries)," he adds. "But we didn't fight fire with fire. It could've been scorched earth, but that's not where our guy is."[173]

I needed an outlet for my frustration. I tried my hand at writing a guest post for *BitterPoliticz*, the blog I had joined a couple of weeks before. Camille, the site owner, offered a supportive home for my work. My article appeared on June 14, 2008, amidst many bloggers informing the Bill Schneiders of the world what they could do with their glass of wine…

I had no idea what to expect in response. Tense, I watched as the comments piled up. A law professor with her own website encouraged me to forward my article to *NoQuarterUSA*, another pro-Hillary blog with a much wider audience. The site, run by Larry Johnson, an ex-CIA operative, security consultant and TV commentator had some great writers who backed up their work with plenty of research. Nobody there minced words. I took a shot.

My piece was published July 17th. I was thrilled. I had never done anything like that. But *NoQuarter*, true to its name was not a warm and fuzzy place. The writers were dolls, but the stories moved fast and the blog commenters had little patience for fol de rol, so it was another butt tingling moment seeing how it would be received.

An Open Letter to Vice President Gore

"When so many of us begged you to run for office again this year, you jokingly stated you were a 'recovering politician.' Certainly, you have more than earned the right to walk away from what you consider to be a toxic environment…

You of all people understand what it is like to be the more qualified candidate and be on the receiving end of ridicule by the drive-by hit squad media. You have stated that television is a one-way medium, not encouraging discourse, critical thought or active participation.

This year, we see even more clearly the influence and effect that favoritism of one and vilification and misogyny toward another has on the voting populace, as junk food is fed to a citizenry struggling to make ends meet, at points overwhelmed by their own responsibilities, without time to dig deeper for the truth of the story…."

I hit him with all the talking points. How Senator Clinton had won all the large states, save Obama's home state of Illinois, all the swing states, had the popular vote and electoral map victory in her pocket. She led in all the crucial demographics we needed to win this election in November. Even by Republican standards of "winner takes all" delegates in each state contested, she would have been our nominee.

I pointed out that Senator Obama's delegate lead was earned in February before any vetting, before we knew of Wright and Pfleger, Auchi, Ayers, Rezko, Bitter Gate, NAFTA Gate, even Sweetie Gate. I brought up the bizarre actions of the Rules and Bylaws Committee and reminded him what happened in the 2000 election when he did not stand up for the Congressional Black Caucus after they had demanded a full recount in Florida…I asked him to get past Clinton Derangement Syndrome to stand up for the best leadership.

My letter struck a nerve as it received hundreds of comments, many echoing agreement. I sent this letter to Mr. Gore via snail mail, fax and email, and was informed a number of other readers on *NoQuarter* sent the same or similar letters to him. Weeks later, I received a response from Vice President Gore on his personal stationery.

He thanked me for encouraging him to run for President. He asked me to stay involved in the debate on global warming and encouraged me to buy his book.

As Scooby Doo used to say: "Oourrlluughh???"

Perhaps his endless travel promoting his film "An Inconvenient Truth" had left him a little weary. I felt like I wrote him about my relative needing a kidney transplant and he told me to enjoy my stay in the Bahamas.

I would have preferred no response at all than having his assistant send a letter unrelated to words that took me hours to compose. His office was not alone in this. I've sent many email letters to Senators Boxer and Feinstein, but I think there must be something wrong with their websites. Half the time, I'd ask a question about national security and a week later, I'd get a response about environmental legislation. I'd write about sexism and get a missive about immigration.

This was part and parcel of the types of responses I had received from my Senators, my Congressman, super delegates, and news media, to the extent that I had received any response at all. Some would respond to something other than what I asked, or state they were not "ethically allowed" to answer to what I asked, and the worst of them told me in somewhat colorful language to sit down, shut up and not ask what I asked.

This had only exacerbated my impression that many of our elected officials lived in a rarified air, surrounded by wealth and influence. In 2009, *POLITICO.com* reported there were 237 millionaires in Congress.[174] Not unlike the news media, our representatives in both parties were busier pontificating to each other than listening to us.

Mr. Gore had once said "It is easy for a man to say he does not understand something when his livelihood depends upon him not understanding it." If the day arrives when our elected officials see they may lose their livelihoods, perhaps they too will awaken, finding it is in their best interests to be more respectful of the voting public and for once give an accurate answer to a question that is asked of them.

I questioned why accountability seemed to have diminished in recent years. In part, it was due to vertical ownership wherein corporate über-companies did and do their best to turn us into a TV-watching, SUV or hybrid driving, IMing, latté sucking crazed consumer class. So enamored of something glamorous and powerful outside ourselves, we no longer trust our own opinions, ask critical questions or expect to receive a meaningful answer. The 24-hour news cycle helps render us helpless, bombarded with so much new information, much of that junk news. There is always the next crisis, the next scandal or scare. Many times it was just easier to give up and go home. Or have a relaxing glass of wine.

My open letter to Mr. Gore was posted on *NoQuarter* on June 17th. That night, he endorsed Senator Obama in Michigan.

My letter to him was the first of over 100 web articles I wrote during the 2008 election season. They were impassioned and, I'm sure, repetitive. My posts were the Internet version of pundits or political operatives appearing on cable shows to drive home their talking points over and over. I made my argument for my favorite girl and gave candidate Obama plenty of grief for his flip flops on policy. My strength on *NoQuarter* and on other blogs was as a voice of conscience, fairness and no small amount of self-righteousness. I had raised my volume well past my comfort level.

"Ani," my blogger alter ego, might have found a more delicate way to make her points. But the sum and substance of my feelings remained the same. I did my best to keep it civil, however. If I'd lost that, I'd have had no argument.

Looking back at the primary season of 2008, I remembered how many news outlets savaged Al Gore back in 2000. Evgenia Peretz of *Vanity Fair* reported:

> "Eight years ago, in the bastions of the "liberal media" that were supposed to love Gore—the *New York Times*, the *Washington Post*, the *Boston Globe*, CNN—he was variously described as "repellent," "delusional," a vote-rigger, a man who "lies like a rug," "Pinocchio." Eric Pooley, who covered him for *Time* magazine, says, "He brought out the creative-writing student in so many reporters.... Everybody kind of let loose on the guy."[175]

Hillary got similar treatment from those same news outlets in 2008.

This led me to my new rule in picking Presidents. I vote for whoever the media doesn't want. So far the press has chosen our President the last three elections. Every week, I'd write to big media, asking that they help us make up our minds based on facts, not cheerleading.

I received no response.

The prattle on television networks was echoed in the blogosphere: "Get over it!" These were the words Hillary supporters heard more than any other. *NoQuarter*, for example, had some particularly nasty trolls who would get on the blog and write horrid things. The cruel words came from a righteous place, as though demeaning Hillary and her supporters was their right.

Jack Cafferty of CNN, wanted to know "Why Do Some Clinton Supporters Want To Derail Obama?" which was odd coming from a man who had said "[Obama] would probably prefer to run over [Hillary] with a flat-bed truck at this point."[176]

Commentator, RBC member and Gore campaign manager Donna Brazile appeared on CNN and said that the new Democratic Party was younger, hipper, more urban and urbane. I tried to parse her statement, seeing if she meant our votes were no longer needed.

Many of us who campaigned for Hillary were not surprised to find ourselves under the bus after the Primary. But some Democratic political operatives must have been dismayed to find themselves likewise chowing down on bitter burgers and arugula under the wheel hub with the rest of us.

Since I was hoping Wesley Clark would consider another run at the Presidency, his early endorsement of Hillary Clinton carried weight with me. Most do not. He was a strong surrogate for her on news networks and often stumped for her out on the trail. On June 5th, two days after the Primaries were shut down by super delegates and their pledges, General Clark posted a block of text on his website, WesPAC: "Barack Obama will make a great President. Let's all support Barack Obama."

Having read the General's memoir, his editorials and hearing his speeches over four years' time, I was surprised. He respected Hillary's abilities and was good friends with her. His putting this blog out so quickly struck me as his "et tu, Bruté?" moment. How could her surrogates give up before the Convention?

Most in the Party got on the unity pony right away. While this was business as usual, General Clark playing good Democrat didn't make the sting any less. This was not the typical primary but the closest one in history. It was as if everyone got their talking points from the party leadership and cast Hillary aside without a backward glance.

The following week, General Clark appeared on MSNBC's "Morning Joe with Joe Scarborough," advancing the position that Obama's good judgment trumped McCain's vast experience because "John McCain had never been in charge of policy formulation." I giggled.

When Scarborough pointed out that Obama hadn't either, Clark replied, "But he's not running on that. He's running on his good judgment."

I giggled louder.

General Clark must have chowed down on an extra bowl of Wheaties to come up with that one. The guy ain't a Rhodes Scholar for nothing. Clark, a senior fellow at the Burkle Foreign Policy Center, UCLA, mentioned in a lecture that foreign policy was one of the biggest stumbling blocks of rookie Presidents. He had to dig deep for a reason why a man with so brief a tenure in the Senate could compete with the smarts and know-how of Senator McCain, particularly on foreign policy. It was a circuitous, and most creative, argument.

Huffington Post contributor Cenk Uygur exclaimed, "I've never seen anybody go after McCain like that!" Those at the blog *Daily Kos* – also lovin' them some General Clark – were thrilled. I was hoping he'd be Hillary's VP pick, or Secretary of Defense when he became eligible for that position in 2010. It seemed obvious he had just thrown his hat into the ring to be Senator Obama's Vice President.

The steam was coming out of my ears, my scalp had just dislodged itself from the top of my head and my brain was on fire. I had written to him asking that he not attempt to get on Senator Obama's ticket.

The conniptions I put myself through! He *had* to get this letter. Watching General Clark, one of the few people courageous enough to speak out against President Bush's policies before Bush's poll numbers dropped was inspiring. Through his website, he daily encouraged us all to get more involved and join the debate. I was only doing what he told me to do...can't blame a girl for trying.

On June 29, 2008, General Clark went on "Face the Nation" and was more or less ensnared by Bob Scheiffer into the now infamous sound bite he made re Senator McCain that "being shot down in a plane does not qualify you to be President." The political freak show that followed saw Clark ostracized by both the Obama campaign and Republicans for that unfortunate remark. Senator John Kerry, for whom Clark campaigned tirelessly in 2004, kept bringing up the incident. I suspected Kerry didn't like competition from the brilliant Clark for either VP or a possible cabinet position, both of which Kerry had said he wanted.

I am not psychic, but I did attempt to warn the General. Call it intuition. It was tacky of the DNC and the Obama campaign to desert him, particularly since he had criss-crossed the country speaking on behalf of down-ticket Democrats for years.

> "The Obama campaign could have said they agreed with me. Go ask them why they didn't stand up for me."

-- Wes Clark, October, 2008,
as reported by student blogger Jason Plautz

I felt like Clark was part of the Impossible Mission Force: "...if you are caught, the IMF will disavow all knowledge of your actions."

Perhaps he allowed ambition to cloud his judgment or envisioned himself coming to the rescue, providing foreign policy smarts to the ticket. Perhaps he got caught in the crossfire of some of the old guard Democrats and their agendas. Since he was such a staunch Hillary supporter, he was late to Senator Obama's party and I doubt that was looked upon kindly.

There's plenty of room under our bus, General.

Welcome.

We serve French fries with our bitter burgers every Thursday.

B.Y.O. catsup.

13 WHY WE FOUGHT BACK

"I've never seen anybody treated so disrespectfully just for running."

-- President Bill Clinton

"He's so fresh!" "His inexperience is actually a plus."

-- Speaker Nancy Pelosi

"...I think there's almost more sexism than there is racism in this country. And frankly, as you know, she's not been my candidate, but I have to say that I have to really admire her ability to continue almost like a battering ram against her own party that has been the worst in trying to take her down and make her quit."

"And a lot of people are watching that and they're saying -- you know, they're secretly behind the scenes saying, you go for it, because you have a right as a candidate to run. And it's not your sex."[177]

-- Blanquita Cullum,
Radio Talk Show Host,
CNN interview

140

"He's clean. He's got the whole package."

-- Senator Joe Biden and
Senate Majority Leader Harry Reid

"It doesn't matter whether women in the United States have seen you in person, heard you in the debates or voted for you in the primaries or not. What matters is every woman who believes in America needs you to stay in the race all the way to the Democratic National Convention on Aug. 25-28 in Denver."

-- Lewis Diuguid, *Kansas City Star*

"I can't point to anything specific, I dunno, there's just something special about the guy."

-- Gov. Bill Richardson

On June 3rd, Hillary Clinton led in the popular vote and Barack Obama led in pledged delegates. Pledged delegates were elected at the state level, proportional to the popular vote. There were also 842 unpledged "super delegates" made up of current and former party leaders from all fifty states and were a phenomenon peculiar to the Democratic Party.

By the time Florida and Michigan were seated in full before the Convention, per Senator Obama's request, he and Hillary were separated by a handful of delegates out of 4,233. The required number of delegates to win the nomination was said to be 2118, but after all fifty states were seated the correct number was 2210. Neither candidate had enough pledged delegates to claim the nomination, even using the lower figure.

The declarations of the super delegates prior to the actual Convention were in truth worthless. Nothing meant anything until they had cast their votes on the Convention floor in August. This information was not well advertised to the American people by either the media or the DNC.

In 1980, the late Senator Teddy Kennedy was behind by 700 delegates in the primary and took his fight to the Convention floor.

Nobody would have dared to stop him. Senator Clinton had an excellent case to make in a much closer contest.

Five weeks after she was out of the race, Senator Clinton was still polling higher against Senator McCain. Senators McCain and Obama were running neck and neck.

In the blogosphere, some Hillary supporters had another concern. Remembering the "Swift Boating" of Kerry in 2004, we had thought Republicans were just keeping their powder dry until after the Convention, once they were 100% sure Hillary would not be the nominee. We had every expectation that they would let loose in the fall with all manner of negative ads on Senator Obama, once again raising the issues of his damaging associations, misstatements and policy reversals. Throughout the summer, he was never able to break the 50% mark in national polling, regardless of the great campaign he ran.

A senior Democratic strategist, who had played a prominent role in two presidential campaigns, told the *Sunday Telegraph*:

> "These guys are on the verge of blowing the greatest gimme in the history of American politics. They're the most arrogant bunch I've ever seen. They won't accept that they are losing and they won't listen."[178]

We had serious doubts that Senator Obama was going to win. And if not for the October surprise of the collapsing economy, he might not have.

With Hillary, any and all negatives were known. There was nothing left to vet and we knew in a debating situation, she would be formidable. Why shouldn't she fight for it?

Since Hillary was considered out of the race and no longer a media target, we thought it possible reporters might start vetting Senator Obama. Thousands of Hillary's supporters were feverishly calling super delegates, urging them to support her on the first ballot. We still held out hope that enough super delegates would change their minds by the time of the Convention, which was to be held the week of August 25th. There were a few super delegates switching support and trickling over to her as the weeks progressed.

Hillary and the rest in her inner circle knew something we didn't. She had been pressured to drop out, so our efforts became moot.

The media kept Hillary alive in the news cycle, many articles still covering her every move. We discovered the race was more exciting when she was in it. Mainstream media complained that Obama and McCain alone were getting kind of dull. However, Hillary vs. Barack sold a lot more copy.

In an interview with FOX's Greta Van Susteren,[179] Speaker Nancy Pelosi, offered a stiff smile, and pretended we had a united party. She would not allow so much as a nod to millions of disaffected Clinton voters as Ms. Van Susteren stared at her, incredulous.

"What do they want?" Ms. Pelosi said. I had to wonder in what environment she had sequestered herself that a reality of this magnitude escaped her. We wanted respect for our votes. Respect for all the delegates Hillary had legitimately earned. Respect for her.

An organization called The Denver Group was formed to ensure Hillary Clinton would be properly honored at the Convention. Knowing of my blog writing, I was asked to promote their cause at various Hillary-friendly websites. In the closest democratic primary in history, Senator Clinton had more than earned having her name put forth into nomination on the first ballot at the Democratic Convention. It was unheard of that a candidate with that many votes and delegates would be denied that right. She was entitled to a genuine roll call vote – not lip service paid by a mere symbolic gesture.

I felt the only just outcome under the circumstances would be to have both their names on the ballot. Super and pledged delegates would have voted legally at the Convention, per their rules. Let the chips fall where they may. Win or lose. I would have appreciated my Party for having the decency to accord both Senators equal respect. And I would have been happy to live with the outcome either way.

Marc Ambinder of *The Atlantic* reported that at a meeting of Hillary's fundraisers, Senator Obama was asked if he would accept a roll call vote at the Convention. According to a participant, he said:

> "Hillary and I are going to negotiate this thing and
> talk about it, and obviously we're going to do what is
> right for the party. We're all going to make sure we
> agree."

As far as we were concerned, there was nothing to negotiate. When Howard Dean ran for president in 2004, he had amassed a total of 130 delegates. He made sure he got his roll call. But a woman who had amassed nearly 2,000 pledged and super delegates should forget it?

In the run up to the Convention, two other troubling situations emerged that were diametrically opposed to Senator Obama's prior campaign promises.

First, FISA was coming to a vote: "[T]he bill under consideration gives telecommunication companies blanket retroactive immunity for their alleged cooperation in the administration's warrantless wiretapping program."

Senator Obama had campaigned on how disastrous it would be to consent to such a thing and promised a filibuster of the same. On July 9, 2008, he capitulated and voted for it. His supporters balked for a moment and then let it go. Senator Clinton kept to her word and was one of twenty-eight Senators to vote against this bill.

I worried that if Senator Obama was willing to do an about face on something important to so many Democrats, where else would he do the same? Someone with the skill set Senator Obama advertised could have staged the filibuster fight he promised us months before, had he the inclination to do so. Looking back, the romantic in me wonders what would have happened if he had kept his word.

A great orator would stand and speak on behalf of the American people and fight for a righteous cause, protecting the fourth amendment. He would look every Senator in the eye and make his case. Some of them might look at the clock, seeing lunchtime tick by as he spoke without a break. Late into the afternoon, he would not yield the floor. He'd talk himself hoarse. And then, a woman would stand up – Joan of Arc in a pantsuit. "Have some water, Senator, yield the floor to me. I'll keep going." He'd nod, and take a drink and she would continue the fight while he took a break.

I have no doubt that this lady, no matter their differences, would have stood side by side with Barack Obama to do this. She'd speak passionately until her voice caved. Maybe Senator Feingold would pick up the baton; how about Senator Patty Murray or any one of the other Senators who voted to protect our rights. I imagined the publicity if it went on for a couple of days. The Senate session heard around the world, a good old-fashioned filibuster. Right out of *Mr. Smith Goes to Washington*. A bunch of well-heeled Senators willing to put something on the line, talking till they had no more spit, standing there and sweating for the American people.

And when Barack Obama got his wind back – he would continue.

Would it even matter if he or they had convinced enough Senators to vote their way? Senator Obama, as one of a hard working team, would have shown that he was willing to go down fighting for a principle.

The great Rev. Martin Luther King once said "All labour that uplifts humanity has dignity and importance and should be undertaken with painstaking excellence."

Senator Obama would have illustrated something much more important about himself than any speech before the throngs ever could. He would have been exhibiting real leadership. That's a "uniter." Someone who does more than address a cause reading from a TelePrompTer, but a person who is willing to risk something for an ideal. For us.

If I had just once seen that guy, I would have taken a second look.

The following day I received a fund raising letter from the DNC – one of many. Stamped in block letters on the envelope was the following:

> "IT'S TIME TO UNITE BEHIND BARACK OBAMA"

I have received many fundraising letters over the years. It was the first time I had received a piece of mail telling me what "it is time" to do.

It felt kinda bossy for people who were asking for money. Even after sending notices that my husband and I had left the party, the DNC would not stop. I was bombarded with a letter a day from the DCCC, the DSCC, the DNC and the Obama campaign.

This brought me to another broken campaign promise. Senator Obama had earlier signed a statement pledging to limit himself to public financing in the general election. Senator McCain likewise made that promise and kept it. Senator Obama had changed his mind. Democratic Senator Russ Feingold of Wisconsin, who had partnered with Senator McCain on campaign finance reform said that this was "not a good decision."[180] That was that with that.

Don Fowler, DNC Member At-Large, South Carolina, Former Chair of the DNC, and Alice Germond, Secretary, DNC sent out two million fund raising letters soon thereafter. They were both members of the Rules and Bylaws Committee. Mr. Fowler was concerned that 'post-primary bitterness could imperil Barack Obama's chances':

> "...I must confess a bit of fatigue and irritation with people who continue to carp, complain, and criticize the results of the primary and lay down conditions for their support. The Los Angeles Lakers didn't establish conditions to recognize the Boston Celtics as NBA Champions; Roger Federer did not demand concessions before recognizing that Rafael Nadal defeated him at Wimbledon.
>
> It is time to act in a mature and resourceful fashion. It's time to put the primaries behind us. It's time to support Barack Obama without conditions or demands."

While it was unpleasant to be accused of immaturity, Fowler neglected to mention that in truth, no one was "defeated." It was telling that he wanted to secure support with condescension and ridicule.

I could relate to the sporting analogies Mr. Fowler used in his letter. I felt as though I had been beaten with a baseball bat, only to be told I should put on a turtleneck to cover my unsightly neck and bruised arms, wear a pair of dark glasses and pretend it didn't happen. He reminded me of a philandering husband who, caught in flagranté delicto, goes on the offensive, even though he is standing there with his drawers down around his ankles. He starts screaming that his wife is crazy, in order to cover his own, now exposed, behind.

Mr. Fowler needed to retire his baseball bat. It wasn't working.

At the same time, the Democratic leadership took to threatening women with the overturning of Roe vs. Wade, reactionary Supreme Court appointments, and a "100 year war in Iraq" in order to force our hands and get us to vote for Senator Obama. As a fellow traveler put it, "the beatings will continue until morale improves."

Never a fan of negative reinforcement, I had little desire to run toward a party that invited me with nothing, but threatened me with the loss of my reproductive rights. Even the ultra-conservative Justice Scalia had stated he would not overturn Roe v. Wade as it would fly in the face of *stare decisis*; well settled law.

After twenty years of Presidents Reagan and the Bushes, that law remained intact. Republicans knew overturning it would leave them without one of their favorite drums to beat at election time. Historically, Republican presidents have appointed conservative justices only to be disappointed by these judges' rulings once they ascended to the bench. There was no barometer for how they would vote. And I did not take kindly to being pushed around.

The DNC did not expect the kind of loyalty Hillary Clinton inspired. Democratic Party leaders didn't know how to handle the anger that erupted from 28% of her 18,000,000 voters who said under no circumstances would they support Senator Obama.[181] There were a number of voters nationwide who had changed their voter registration after the primary in protest of the actions of the Rules and Bylaws Committee on May 31st. The reasons for their actions were not reported.

The DNC's disrespect to women was glaring and created a deeper divide than anyone could have predicted. The resulting explosion led to the PUMA movement. This acronym stood for a group of Hillary supporters who called themselves People United Means Action. For insiders, the name meant Party Unity My Ass. Just Say No Deal and Hire Heels were other popular blog creations. Dozens of similar blog groups popped up everywhere.

PUMA's goal was to win over super delegates in advance of the Convention and to get Hillary's primary campaign debt paid off, feeling that would empower her case as a candidate. As with many grassroots movements, PUMA felt disjointed at best but it was also mischaracterized by the press and on the web. The rumor was that PUMAs were actually Republicans. This was nonsense. Whether one agreed with the actions of the resisters or not, the media's poor reporting record during the campaign was proof positive they could not be counted on to bear accurate witness as to PUMA's motives or membership.

Some prominent Democratic Hillary fund raisers jumped ship to campaign for Senator McCain, since he took the time to have town halls with Hillary supporters, listening to their concerns. I have no doubt he did this of political necessity. But his outreach worked nonetheless. Senator Obama's response to disaffected Hillary voters was not as adroit.

On June 20th, Obama met with the Congressional Black Caucus and apparently "nerves were still frayed" after the primary. Senator Obama then said:

> "I need to make a decision in the next few months as to how I manage that since I'm running against John McCain, which takes a lot of time. If women take a moment to realize that on every issue important to women, John McCain is not in their corner, that would help them get over it."

Rep. Diane Watson, D-Calif., a longtime Clinton supporter, did not like those last three words -- "Get over it." She found them dismissive, off-putting.

"Don't use that terminology," Watson told Obama."[182]

I gave the Senator the benefit of the doubt that he did not mean to be dismissive. Yet that was what Hillary supporters had been putting up with for the better part of a year. Not acknowledging the need for reconciliation was unwise.

A diary in the *Huffington Post*[183] later reflected the same condescending attitude. It advised Obama supporters to feign sympathy in order to get Hillary voters to support Obama:

> "....showing you've come around to respecting Hillary may ease their hurt enough to do the trick. (Even if you don't mean it. This is politics.)
>
> Eat crow.
>
> Let the HRC voter vent. You may have to draw on every bit of patience you have.
>
> Act empathic. Nod your head in agreement when the subject of Palin or Chris Matthews or Keith Olbermann's Hillary-bashing commentary is

mentioned. Learn these phrases and use them every so often: "I imagine it must be hard." "It must seem unfair." "I know, you wanted to see an accomplished woman as president in your lifetime." "I can understand your being hurt (sad, mad, furious, despondent, livid, resentful, apoplectic, intransigent, inconsolable, red-faced, nauseous, wretched, shit-faced"). Again, do not argue. Just listen.

Do not praise Obama. I know, this seems ridiculous...

Praise HRC. Never mention her flaws. Be gracious and do not bring up her vote for the war, or her "dirty campaign."

Yes. That was surely the way to bring us around.

The winner gets to write the history. Yet when one sees the actual numbers, the outrage of many of Hillary's supporters was understandable.

Final Popular Vote Tally:[184]

    Hillary Clinton 17,857,446 — 48.04%

    Barack Obama 17,584,649 — 47.31%

Final Pledged Delegate Count (after the seating of Michigan and Florida)[185]

    Barack Obama 1,747.5 — 39.55%

    Hillary Clinton 1,730.5 — 39.17%

There may be some disagreement as to how to tally the Florida and Michigan delegates. Conflicting reports say Hillary and Obama were separate by between 4 and 130 pledged delegates, or between ¼% to 2%.

Reports were circulating that Senator Obama and his operatives were pressuring elected delegates to switch their support prior to the Convention. According to the *Los Angeles Times*, throughout the summer, pledged delegates were being strong armed not to vote for the candidate they were elected by their states to support on the first ballot.[186]

    "Raymond Penko, a Clinton delegate from San Diego who campaigned door-to-door for her, said: "There was pressure all around to conform to what I would call the old boys' club. . . . As soon as Obama delegates heard that one was a Hillary supporter, they would shun you, tell you to get over it, say, 'Stop being a crybaby. What's your problem? Don't you want to win in November?'" [187]

"With the huge California delegation, lots of Clinton delegates got with the program."[188]

While super delegates were free to support whom they wished, pledged delegates were assigned. I didn't know "switching" was legal. What was the point of the primaries or winning the popular vote in a state if pledged delegates could arbitrarily choose to drop their candidate after the fact?

I was foolish to imagine anything I was doing throughout this campaign season made a difference. At the time, I thought how easy it would be to stick my head back in the sand. Just worry about where the next acting job was coming from, ink the dot for the guy with the (D) after his name and forget it. Man plans and God laughs.

God must have had a good guffaw that when I finally found my voice, it was to make statements many did not want to hear.

* * *

On Tuesday, August 26, 2008, Senator Clinton took the stage at the Democratic Convention. In her speech, she was in command and committed to the goals and values she campaigned on. Transcendent is the appropriate word. All that had gone before seemed to have no effect, although I knew in reality that could not be the case.

Someone the DNC pegged as a woman to be reviled had become an admired figure to many. How frustrating for the blogger boyz and media dogs like Keith Olbermann that couldn't keep her down. She looked radiant, composed and in charge. She did her job, gave a great speech on democratic values and urged support for Senator Obama.

Just prior to the vote the next night, Hillary had released her delegates.

Hillary had won California's primary by ten points. "[T]he California convention vote was Obama, 273; Clinton, 166."[189] Even Arkansas, which Hillary won to the tune of 70-30 in the primary, handed all their pledged delegates to Obama.

John Broder, reporting for the *New York Times*, spoke with members of the Florida delegation:

> "When Mrs. Clinton appeared on the screen they jumped up and waved Hillary placards – until instructed not to by floor marshals.
>
> "I'll vote for Obama, because I'm a Democrat," Ms. Larkin said. "But all my energy, all my support and all my money will go to local candidates."
>
> …They said the reinstatement of full voting rights just before the convention was too late.
>
> "If it had been done right the first time," Ms. Hoppe said, "Hillary would have been the nominee up there."[190]

At the Convention, the delegate tally from the first ballot was 3,188.5 for Obama; 1,010.5 for Clinton.

My party did not see fit to honor its obligations to its voters. Instead, they chose to stage a sham at their own Convention where Senator Obama's delegates outnumbered Senator Clinton's three to one. My stomach turned over when I took another look at the real numbers.

This qualified woman had achieved what no woman ever had. It would not be reflected in the books.

Senator Clinton's actions reminded me of the story of Solomon. To avoid a floor fight and pretend we had a unified party, Hillary chose not to fight on.

No matter the DNC's motives, how could I assume that sexism had nothing to do with it? Even if the DNC did not share the media's distaste for Senator Clinton, the effect was the same. I had grave doubts they could have behaved in this manner had the contest been between two men. I felt the DNC had been paying lip service to women and decided they could carry their own water.

It was crucial for the DNC not to admit to the American people that the nomination might have gone either way, otherwise some uncomfortable questions might have been asked.

During the primaries, Nancy Pelosi lamented that she didn't want to see the will of the voters overturned. If that were the case, super delegates in states that Hillary won by 10 to 41 points would have had no excuse for refusing to endorse her. Governor Manchin of West Virginia was just such a person. Senator Barbara Boxer had likewise promised to endorse the candidate who won her state of California back in February. She had previously held a fund raiser for Senator Obama and also withheld her endorsement until June 3rd, then ran to endorse him.

By withholding their endorsements, super delegates were overturning the will of voters in their respective states. Speaker Pelosi had no answer on that point.

My jaw dropped when I read an article in *The New York Times*[191] on December 9, 2009:

> "The Democratic Change Commission — established in the wake of the grueling 2008 nomination battle between President Obama and his now secretary of state, Hillary Rodham Clinton — has proposed that the elected officials and party higher-ups known as super delegates cast their votes based on state primary or caucus results. In recent battles for the Democratic nomination, super delegates, also called unpledged delegates, were not obligated to follow the primary or caucus result in their state.
>
> Openness, fairness, and accessibility are central to our ideals as Democrats, and the commission's recommendations to reform the delegate selection process will ensure that voters' voices and preferences are paramount to our process of nominating a Presidential candidate," Gov. Timothy M. Kaine of Virginia, the chairman of the Democratic National Committee."

Had each of the 842 super delegates been required to endorse the candidate who won their particular state, Hillary Clinton would have been our nominee, and likely our President today. Unfortunately for Hillary and her supporters, it was two years too late and a dollar short for the DNC to discuss changing their nominating rules.

PUMAs wanted Hillary to kiss her party goodbye and run as an Independent. My husband did as well and we argued about it through the summer. It was impossible. Her campaign was $22 million in debt. How could she run? Her campaign infrastructure was disbanding. If she took such an action, split the vote and caused Senator Obama to lose to Senator McCain, she would have been burned at the stake. That is a stone fact.

Hillary was and is a loyal Democrat to the core. She gave her word to fight for the eventual nominee and she kept it. At that time, I came across an article discussing Hillary's strategy session in 2000, in preparation for her first Senate run. President Clinton sat in. He said, "People are going to want to know why you stayed with me." She said, "I've been wondering that myself." He replied, "Because you're a sticker. You stick with things you care about."[192] She still cared about the Democratic Party.

Loyalty had been a double edged sword for me. I've been guilty of staying too long at the fair, and it has taken a team of mules to drag me away from something or someone I care about. Now one doesn't get that much rope.

In her speech, she offered a hat tip to her outraged supporters, "I want you to ask yourselves: Were you in this campaign just for me?" This was not about her. This was about capable leadership. It was also about respect. If I let the DNC get away with treating a woman in such a disgraceful manner, I would have been training them to do it again, not only to Hillary but to any candidate they chose to discard by not allowing that woman to exercise her full rights.

Senator Clinton was and is a much bigger person than I am to have risen above all of this. All I had was my vote and in protest, the DNC was not going to get it. I felt the Party didn't know what they were doing, or who they were throwing away. I am sure Hillary would not approve. Then again, her agenda is different than mine. Part of what I respect about her is her grace, evidenced by strict adherence to the chain of command. But the behavior of the DNC could not be papered over.

Giving them benefit of the doubt, at best they'd painted themselves into a corner with their idiotic contest rules, and comforted themselves that it would be easier for the country to accept if they pushed Hillary aside than if the reverse happened. Viewing our ingrained predisposition toward women in power, there was no overwhelming objection to their actions.

Though it would have been painful to hear, if Senator Clinton had expressed disappointment in my statements, it would not have altered my feelings. To borrow from President Obama's oft used line during the campaign, this is not the Democratic Party "I thought I knew."

Hillary Clinton was asked to fall on her sword in the name of a unified Democratic Party. In the end, she did so. Considering she was characterized as someone so "ego driven and power hungry," that was quite the gesture.

14 IS MAUREEN DOWD NECESSARY?

"Unfortunately for Hillary, there's no White Bitch Month."[193]

-- Maureen Dowd

The stinging slights offered by several women who had wielded the written word in an effort to cut Hillary Clinton off at the knees were in a class by themselves.

Sally Quinn of the *Washington Post* appeared on CBS' *The Early Show* with Harry Smith to say that Hillary is "a tortured person," "doesn't know who she really is or what she wants" and "maybe what she really needs is a wonderful, loving relationship with somebody instead of just going after power and being this ambitious person that I think she thinks she oughta be."[194] Newsweek's Eleanor Clift had referred to the Clintons as "the Corleones."

There were others. But none in the same orbit as Maureen Dowd of the *New York Times,* whose attacks against the Senator felt distinctly personal in tone. Dowd, along with her sister columnists, purported to know what was desirable – and acceptable – in a successful woman, yet they all imagined Hillary existed to be in service of a man, thereby telegraphing an addiction to a mindset that has been limiting women for eons. The woman does not, by definition of her sex, have to put her own goals aside.

While these ladies were paid by the column inch for opinion rather than fact, opinions infested by trash talk can penetrate the psyche over time, creating a convincing negative portrait of someone that is often disconnected from the facts of their record.

Such was the case with Ms. Dowd's pronouncements about Hillary Clinton:

> "After saying she found her "voice" in New Hampshire, she has turned into Sybil. We've had Experienced Hillary, Soft Hillary, Hard Hillary, Misty Hillary, Sarcastic Hillary, Joined-at-the-Hip-to-Bill Hillary, Her-Own-Person-Who-Just-Happens-to-Be-Married-to-a-Former-President Hillary, It's-My-Turn Hillary, Cuddly Hillary, Let's-Get-Down-in-the-Dirt-and-Fight-Like-Dogs Hillary."[195]

By painting Senator Clinton as a person with bi-polar disorder, Maureen Dowd officially joined the ranks of the sexists, hinting that "Sybil" Hillary might blow up the world from the Oval Office if she were having a bad hair day. Male politicians adjust and amend their message and narrative out on the campaign trail regularly. They are not referred to as mentally unstable.

Dowd also wrote that "experience does not beat excitement" and much to my chagrin and dismay, that was true. Obama's bedazzling branding and the celebratory press treatment he received were much better explanations for Hillary's difficulties in the primaries than Dowd implying she was some sort of psychopath. Her other declarations were likewise suspect:

> "The underlying rationale for her campaign is that she is owed. Owed for moving to Arkansas and giving up the name Rodham, owed for pretending to care about place settings and menus when she held the unappetizing title of first lady, owed for enduring one humiliation after another at the hands of her husband."[196]

Entitlement may have been the media's mantra, but it was not Clinton's. A woman who thinks she is owed does not bother with exhaustive preparation on every issue, nor would she have the will to campaign twenty hours a day without rest. Entitlement is allergic to hard work.

Dowd also proclaimed that many women chose Obama since they didn't care for Hillary's "shoulder-pad feminism." Who were these mysterious women she wrote about? She gave no example, only a sweeping generalization.

Her comments channeled Rush Limbaugh's term "Femi-Nazi." Dowd not only debased Hillary, but tended to classify women who supported her in the ball-buster category. In so doing, Ms. Dowd gave the impression she was attempting to ensure she was not thus characterized.

I was once told when you meet someone to whom you take an instant dislike, that person may echo a quality you yourself possess but would rather not own. A successful woman who came up in the male dominated world of journalism, Ms. Dowd must have needed those shoulder pads on a few occasions, yet she insisted these mysterious ladies felt…

> "[W]omen have moved past that men-are-pigs, woe-is-me, sisters-must-stick-together, pantsuits-are-powerful era that Hillary's campaign has lately revived with a vengeance.
>
> And they don't like Gloria Steinem and other old-school feminists trying to impose gender discipline and a call to order on the sisters.
>
> "…Hillary doesn't make it look like fun to be a woman…" [197]

I don't believe 'men are pigs, woe is me.' But when men, or women, in the media did behave badly, I said so. Chris Matthews calling Hillary "Nurse Ratched"[198] or Christopher Hitchens declaring "she's an aging, resentful female"[199] didn't sound like fun, but Hillary was courageous enough to be both trail blazer and lightning rod so Ms. Dowd wouldn't have to be.

I would have been less averse to the word bombs of Dowd and others if any of them devoted equal time taking Senator Obama to task for the fantastical fictions that comprised many of his campaign promises.

Whenever Dowd was interviewed, I found she exuded an aloof, lemon-sucking air. Smirking, tipping her head to and fro as she held forth, she was reminiscent of Lily Tomlin's Ernestine, the telephone operator. Snorting 'one ringy dingy, two ringy dingy,' Dowd was sure she had everyone's number.

Advertising a come hither expression in her New York Times by line photo, I wondered if Ms. Dowd worried that siding with a woman who possessed the ultimate ambition would forever deprive her of a date on Saturday night. Perhaps she feared she would be considered un-babe-like.

In her book, *Are Men Necessary*, Dowd theorized feminists of the seventies finally got what they wanted, equal rights and careers, and found out they didn't want what they got. Her oversimplification did not take into consideration that the lines were beginning to blur in the household. More married partners felt free to pursue their own goals and make their own rules about whether the man or the woman was best to make the dough or be the caregiver. Nothing was etched in stone.

Still, she concluded that men "would rather be with a woman who is in awe of them" and wrote that if you want to nab a man "you'd better have long hair and you'd better not be sarcastic."

My hubby, for one, thrills at the idea of a partner who is capable and has an opinion. He doesn't mind my edge. The length of my hair doesn't matter to him either. I mean, he's happy I have some but that's about it, and he "lurvs" Hillary. Ms. Dowd might have found a similar story had she spent time in some different circles.

Dowd wrote "Men are simply not biologically suited to hold higher office. The Bush administration has proved that once and for all." That statement made her behavior toward Hillary seem all the more peculiar.

Could Ms. Dowd conceive of a woman having the right skill set, daring to want the job without being guilty of overstepping herself? Giving her the benefit of the doubt, I had a yen to find out if there was any other woman on the horizon whom she thought might fit the bill.

Contrary to her assertions, no women I ran across thought Hillary portrayed herself as a victim, whether they voted for her or not. While I took it upon myself to shout sexism on her behalf, her campaign never asked me to do so. For a woman of Ms. Dowd's stature and experience to feign ignorance at the realities of this contest was the cruelest cut of all. Was it just business to her? Was she being trendy?

Senator Clinton handled the onslaught and was steadfast in the face of all of it. No matter how much big media threw at her, like the energizer bunny, she just kept going and going – and did it with a smile. Though I hated the daily drubbing she received, it made me feel better knowing she could handle it. For the latter half of the campaign in particular, Hillary hit the campaign trail with a gusto rarely seen. Still, I didn't expect her to break into a chorus of "I Enjoy Being a Girl."

I've never paid tax dollars so the President could have a good time. If I wanted the luxury of frolicking along the beach without worrying the country would fall down about my ears, I knew I had better elect a leader I thought would keep me safe at night. Having a beer with the Prez mattered less to me than looking under that person's hood to see that their engine actually worked.

Even as Dowd's fellow traveler, *New York Times* columnist Gail Collins was razzing Hillary, she acknowledged, "Her bond with the people isn't a passionate one, but when it works, it's a genuine connection that starts with the belief that she will work really, really hard on their behalf."[200]

The very qualities Dowd and others found problematic in the woman Hillary were the ones that would be applauded in President Hillary.

In her column, *The Hillary Waltz*,[201] Dowd compared Senator Clinton to the character Marschallin in the opera Der Rosenkavalier, who trained her young lover in the ways of love and ultimately set him free. Dowd posited the only use Hillary had in this campaign was to toughen Senator Obama up and make him a better candidate. Hillary arguably did so but to pretend that was her only purpose was to deny her historic accomplishment.

Dowd was also not alone in making the claim that Gloria Steinem was pushing women to vote for Hillary in the name of "sisters sticking together." By this logic, Steinem would have pushed women to later vote for Senator McCain's ticket because a woman was on it. She did the opposite and joined with the cadre who were deriding Governor Sarah Palin.

I didn't require the admonishments of girl power or sisterhood to urge me toward my decision to back Hillary, nor would I be seduced by cool to turn my back on my choice. Likewise, I didn't need Gloria Steinem to tell me when it was time to stand up and call foul.

Ms. Dowd also fibbed when she stated "[e]xit polls have showed that fans of Mrs. Clinton – who once said they would be happy with Mr. Obama if Hillary dropped out – were hardening in their opposition to him (while Obama voters are not so harsh about her)."[202] If anything, we were just as divided on both sides. A trip through the blog commentary in Ms. Dowd's own newspaper would have provided an enlightening education in all manner of woman-hate.

Her assertion that hardened Obama supporters were less averse to supporting Hillary was unreasonable, even cruel, given some of the hateful verbal attacks some of my friends endured just for having a Hillary '08 lawn sign.

At one point, Dowd stated President Clinton would need to drag Hillary across the finish line. She later intimated Senator Obama would not make it without Hillary doing the same for him in the general election.

It was confusing that Dowd would bestow so much power and influence on a woman she had spent years devaluing. This served to reinforce what I had witnessed from opinion makers throughout this journey – a need to stay au courant while having an allergic reaction to the truth.

Hillary's one hundred eighty campaign appearances on behalf of Barack Obama could hardly be what Dowd claimed was a "barely disguised desire to see him fail."[203] By her actions, Hillary Clinton showed she was the opposite of the vile harridan the Maureen Dowds of this world made her out to be. So fervent was Dowd's distaste, she would find every excuse to drag Hillary – and the Clinton name – into her columns, no matter the subject.

I had a theory that women who engaged in this sort of behavior did so either out of self-loathing, envy or self-preservation. They did not want to upset the status quo that had allowed them to succeed in a man's world. 'See – I will hate Hillary, just like you. I'm not that ambitious. I don't want to be *that* successful. I will help you degrade her so that you don't notice me standing here, successful, too.'

On February 28, 2008, Dowd wrote, "The fact that Obama is exceptionally easy in his skin has made Hillary almost jump out of hers."

On November 22, 2009, Maureen Dowd shared her new opinion of President Obama:

> "If we could see a Reduced Shakespeare summary of Obama's presidency so far, it would read: Dither, dither, speech. Foreign trip, bow, reassure. Seminar, summit. Shoot a jump shot with the guys, throw out the first pitch in mom jeans. Compromise, concede, close the deal. Dither, dither, water down, news conference."[204]

On June 11, 2010, Dowd's missive, *Isn't It Ironic*, went a step further in her characterization of him.

> "But he is an elitist, too, as well as thin-skinned and controlling."[205]

There was no making her happy.

I wondered if Ms. Dowd had at last come to missing Hillary's shoulder pads.

I was also reminded of the *Saturday Night Live's* "Weekend Update" sketch with Tina Fey and Amy Poehler. Fey turned sexism on its ear, proudly proclaiming that Hillary was a bitch (and so was she) – and that "Bitches get stuff done!"

There was something to be said for sisterhood after all.

15 SHE WHO MUST NOT BE NAMED –
A LOOK AT SARAH PALIN

Shortly before the election, a man in West Hollywood decided to hang Governor Sarah Palin in effigy outside of his home. A convincing lookalike doll was hung from a tree with a noose around its neck and was visible from the street. It was difficult for me to watch depictions of violence against women when the real thing was occurring every day. I was one of many who sent an email to the Mayor of West Hollywood asking that it be taken down. The Mayor wrote back that it was private property.

The Secret Service later got involved and the effigy was removed. An effigy of that kind of Barack Obama wouldn't have lasted two minutes, nor should it have. With all the violent rhetoric and many reports on the news of vandalism and worse that had been connected with the election, I found it terrifying that because of Palin's candidacy, or her anatomy, some found this acceptable. After a solid year as captive audience to woman bashing, I didn't think I could find a deeper well of anger. I was wrong.

I could not join in the daily lynching. If I rejoice that a woman I disagree with or dislike is on the receiving end of destructive treatment, I may look less seriously at sexist transgressions. If they abuse her, someday they may abuse me in the same manner if I become likewise inconvenient. I won't have redress against their tactics since I gave permission for their earlier bad behavior by my silence. The slippery slope slides both ways.

I found myself in the odd position of defending someone I wasn't planning on defending, but I could not make myself a hypocrite by only speaking up for a Democratic woman and ignoring a Republican one who, along with her children, was daily being vilified.

The amount of vitriol aimed at Governor Sarah Palin from the left was in direct proportion to the threat she represented to Democrats' hopes of electing Barack Obama. Even though she was the only candidate on either ticket who'd had executive and managerial experience, she was deemed unqualified. The crowds she drew were too large with the race being so close after the Republican Convention. She would have been ignored if, as the left intimated, she were merely irrelevant. Spending tons of copy smearing and discrediting Palin indicated they feared the opposite was true.

Thrust onto the national stage with only seven weeks to find her footing before the election was a tall order for anyone. Arguably Palin did well, energizing the ticket. She is no Hillary and can use more polish and more depth on policy, but the memo that she was a moron was a smear job.

Before Sarah Palin was chosen as Senator McCain's running mate, media outlets sang a different tune about her[206]:

> "In Alaska, Palin is challenging the dominant, sometimes corrupting role of oil companies in the state's political culture." ..."Palin, too, earns high marks from lawmakers on the other side of the aisle."[207]
>
> -- *Newsweek*

> "She's proceeding to shatter the political mold."
>
> -- *USA Today*

> "In her first year as governor of Alaska, Sarah Palin has plunged ahead with the fearlessness of a polar explorer."[208]
>
> -- *Associated Press*

> "Governor Palin stands out in a state that has seen few fresh faces in politics. She is untainted by

government scandal and unburdened by political debt."[209]

-- *New York Times*

Sarah Palin is an attractive woman with a hunky husband, five kids and an amazing career. She's managed to have it all. I'm sure that rubbed a few in the wrong way. She came from a hardscrabble background and achieved the American dream. She was a whistleblower who took on corruption in her own party, a popular Mayor who became the Governor of Alaska. When chosen as McCain's running mate, she was the most popular Governor in the country, with an 80%+ approval rating.

Because she had taken on Republican Party corruption, as well as the oil companies, Palin was a media darling and liberals had likewise cheered her on. These self-same news agencies decided Palin was a she-devil, worse even that Hillary, when she got in the way of The One.

One of the first acts of this "right wing" Governor was to veto anti-gay legislation on the grounds it was unconstitutional. She later appointed a pro-choice woman judge to the Alaska Supreme Court and received a great deal of flack from her own party for doing so. She said this judge was the best qualified for the position. She has also stated she is in favor of birth control and the morning after pill. Her position on gay marriage is identical to that of Messrs. Obama and Biden.

She was at all times painted as a reactionary and a loony.

Did I think she was ready to assume the Presidency? Maybe not, but she was not running to be President. I was not enthusiastic about Joe Biden assuming the Presidency either. Although I respected his many years of service, his penchant for gaffes, or as Mr. Obama called them "rhetorical flourishes," and his often wrongheaded notions on foreign policy (dividing Iraq into three states, for example) were not a comfort.

Before the Vice Presidential debate, the Boston Globe reported that voters were shouting to then-Senator Biden: "Take her down" and "Make her cry."

Watching the debate that evening all the feelings came back of the hateful Hillary horror show. It's not enough. You're not enough.

No matter how you do it, we will find something wrong with it. We will find something wrong with you: your pantsuits, your ass, your cackle, your statements, your voice, your unpleasant ankles, your family, your husband, your record, which we will pretend amounts to much less than the light briefcase of the man against whom you are running.

At the debate, "Sarah-cuda" gave as good as she got, considering she was debating a seasoned pol with thirty-six years in the Senate. Several news organizations documented Biden telling between ten and fourteen fibs during the debate. He got a pass.

According to Nancy Pelosi, Barack Obama was "fresh." According to Democratic Congressman Charlie Rangel, Governor Palin was "disabled."

Governor Palin's teleprompter operator got ahead of her during her first nationally televised speech, introducing her to the world at the Republican Convention. She continued from her notes, unfazed. President Obama's teleprompter operator got ahead of him during a speech a few months into his term. The President stopped in his tracks, needing to correct the prompter before he would continue. No one accused him of being incompetent.

The double standards were so predictable I had stopped listening.

Two male colleagues made demeaning remarks about Sarah Palin in my presence. They figured since I had been a lifelong Democrat, I would not find their insults to a Republican candidate of my gender upsetting:

> "She's only the Governor of Alaska – I mean, who lives there, like 50 people, you know, next to that bridge to nowhere. Does she shovel moose poop in front of the door of the shack she lives in with that husband of hers and five brats? God, she's stupid. Just because she can see Russia from her window, she thinks she knows something about foreign policy? She's a heartbeat away from the Presidency. I mean, McCain's on his last legs. He'll be dead two months after taking office. So she commands the Alaska National Guard – what are they, like, the boy scouts?"

Contrary to the memo put out by Obama's people that John McCain was doddering and "losing his bearings," as of this writing he is still alive and kicking and heading the loyal opposition out on the Senate floor, fiery as ever.

Howard Dean was Governor of Vermont, which is a small state. No one accused him of representing a "joke." If anyone wondered about the value of the Alaska National Guard, someone ought to have asked Palin. Her security clearance was likely higher than Senator Biden's, by virtue of her state's proximity to Russia.

Bearing an uncanny resemblance to Sarah Palin, it was actually Tina Fey who said "I can see Russia from my house." Sarah Palin never did. In the Bering Strait, the Russian island Big Diomede is located 2-1/2 miles from an island in Alaska. Per the *New York Times*, on a clear day, one can also actually see Siberia from a western vantage point in Alaska, as Palin correctly pointed out.

Certainly *SNL* had the right to satirize her, as they did with all the candidates. Palin, like Hillary, was a good sport about it. Both ladies gamely appeared on the show, happy to poke fun at themselves.

A peripheral friend emailed me an offensive piece of material on Palin by Eve Ensler. The article was to the effect that women in Wasilla, Alaska had to pay for their own rape kits while Palin was Mayor after they had been traumatized and "ripped open." This was found to be false. While the police chief of Wasilla at the time did not want taxpayers to "bear the burden," there was no evidence that anyone in Wasilla had been charged for a rape kit, nor was Palin responsible for instituting such a policy as Mayor, nor was there such a law on the books in Alaska while Palin was Governor.

This was a huge slam on Palin by many news sites, but further investigation revealed that a law on the Illinois books, 410 ILCS 70, the Sexual Assault Survivors Emergency Treatment Act, required that a hospital would bill a sexual assault survivor's insurance company for a rape kit. Ms. Ensler wrote no such condemning article about Illinois Senator Obama, however.

Alaska also has the 8th most liberal abortion policy in the nation.

This was not about defending one candidate over another – simply an example of media bias. It was clear that the search was on for any dirt available on Governor Palin, yet Senator Obama enjoyed no such scrutiny by the press.

Prior to receiving this email, this friend and I had not talked politics in 2008. I knew she was a big fan of Senator Obama's and out of respect for her views, I remained silent. After I received her Eve Ensler missive, I politely informed her that I was not an Obama supporter and had campaigned hard for Hillary. I did not say who I would support in the general election otherwise. There were third party candidates, after all. She responded that she was shocked! Shocked!! Oh, the humanity!! The self-righteous outrage of it all! My response to her message was thorough. She wrote to my husband as well. He responded, too.

For all the respect we had received from this woman, and all the times my husband and I had entertained her at our home, we were considered low information Neanderthals. Everything that came before had been wiped away. Interesting that she would trust the word of a politician she had never met over people she had for years known to be decent, sober and reliable. She wrote that my husband and I might be suffering from deep seated racial bias.

I was never so ashamed of having spent my life as a Democrat, whether I agreed with Palin's politics or not. Democrats taking up this abusive cause, hurling false accusations, were driving me and moderate people like me away.

On August 20, 2008, a Reuters/Zogby poll showed McCain with a five point lead. After the Republican Convention, the McCain/Palin ticket experienced a healthy bounce in the polls. Before the economy crashed in October, Senators Obama and McCain were nearly tied. Not coincidentally, there followed a huge spate of articles during this period in print media, with the accompanying speculation on networks and cable that Obama might not pull it off because "we were not ready as a nation to elect a black president."

Having failed to vet a candidate they so liked, the media had much invested in his winning and had to double down on their bets. Once more, they played the racial guilt card to remind voters if they chose not to vote for Senator Obama, it was probably because they were secretly racist.

Discrediting Palin was key. Every day a new media slam would be revealed about her. Pundits tried everything. *The Atlantic's* Andrew Sullivan implied that Palin's infant son Trig was actually the child of her eldest daughter, a product of incest with her father. Palin was crazy. Palin was a religious nut job. Palin was a diva. Palin's wardrobe expenditures were exorbitant.

Out of curiosity, did anyone think that male candidates wore the same suit every day on the campaign trail? Wouldn't their wardrobe cost money as well?

* * *

Whatever one might have said about Senator McCain and Governor Palin, it was also harder to argue with their positions on Iraq knowing they each had their most precious blood in military service. Unlike many of the right wing neo-cons before them, these were not chicken hawks. Due to his own experiences in Viet Nam as a POW for five years, Senator McCain understood the cost of war better than most.

Certainly I wanted us to bring our soldiers home from Iraq as quickly as possible, but as General Colin Powell once said, "You break it, you own it."[210] No President, regardless of party, would have been able to pack up the tent and go home from either Iraq or Afghanistan, as we later found out. Not Clinton, not Obama, not McCain. In and of itself, that was never a good argument to elect one over the other.

It also became harder to curse the Governor's pro-life position when she made the difficult decision to have her son Trig, who had Down Syndrome.

> "I've never seen anything this bad in my life, and, Greta, I was with Geraldine Ferraro in '84 -- and this is worse....I don't agree with Sarah Palin on the issues. I mean, she and I are very far apart, but I have never seen from some of my friends such vicious and mean-spirited attacks on her most personal choices, which is what they are. We ask that our choices be respected. Hers should be respected. And this questioning of whether she should as a mother of five be running for Vice President, I don't recall

anybody saying that Arnold Schwarzenegger shouldn't run for governor of California because he's got four kids. I think this is just really unfair, really sexist, and very likely to provoke a backlash."

-- Susan Estrich, former Democratic Party strategist
interviewed by Greta Van Susteren

"Rosario Marin, a former United States treasurer, said she was "absolutely incensed, offended, insulted" that stories had addressed Ms. Palin's infant son, Trig, and his Down Syndrome, suggesting, she said, that someone with a child with special needs should not seek the vice presidency. "Shame on them," she said of the media's portrait of Ms. Palin."

"Who better than her to understand the challenges we have as career women trying to balance career and family?" said Ms. Marin, who said she, too, was the parent of a child (now grown) with Downs Syndrome. "They would never dare to say that about a man."[211]

Jason Linkins of the *Huffington Post*[212] inferred that Sarah Palin was to blame for the horrid photos circulating the internet that cruelly manipulated images of her son Trig after Governor Palin's private email account had been hacked, the photos pilfered. Mr. Linkins stated that when Palin saw the first photos ridiculing him, she should have let it slide. By getting angry, and saying they had "desecrated" him, Linkins opined she made it a bigger problem, drawing more attention to the controversy, thereby encouraging others to jump on the bandwagon. But what mother would not have reacted the same way?

Children of politicians are off limits. Yet there was every indication that Sarah Palin's children were fair game because she had dared to show them at the Convention. There is no political candidate who wouldn't present their entire family to the country on such an occasion. Had she hidden her infant son from view, the media would have excoriated her for that as well.

Actor John C. McGinley has a son with Down Syndrome and is an outspoken advocate raising awareness about his son's condition.

He later penned a moving article in the *Huffington Post*, sharing the gifts his son Max bestows upon everyone in his vicinity. Mr. McGinley asked people to cease using the "R" word about Max and kids like him in his wish to foster better understanding.

While Sarah Palin and her family were not mentioned in his piece, I remembered *Huffington Post* spent much copy knocking Palin and her choice. Scanning responses to his article, I didn't notice anyone making the connection. The blog comments to Mr. McGinley about his article and his son were lovely, filled with compassion and compliments.

Palin chose to live her principles. While I would not have made the same choice, it was troubling to see women who had called themselves feminists intimate that she should somehow be ashamed of her decision to have her son.

I'd gotten irritated with Republicans who couldn't keep their noses out of our bedrooms while claiming to be the party of small government. How were those who passed judgment on the Palins for choosing to give their child a loving home any different?

I'm with Hillary on the abortion issue, safe, legal and rare. Since I am and always have been pro-choice, that means women have the right to choose, either way. Feminism, or the right to protest, is not just the province of the left.

Just as the neo-cons hijacked the Republican Party in 2000, I didn't see the far left hijacking the Democrats as leading to a better outcome. My dad used to say, "Always the golden middle way." The attacks on Sarah Palin were just as vile as any attack ever leveled at our side by Rush Limbaugh or Ann Coulter.

Knowing how heated I felt during the election season, I could only imagine how high the stakes felt for everyone on both sides. I'd had lunch with a friend who commented, "After the way the Republicans won the last two elections, who can blame us for doing whatever we have to do to win." Everybody went a little whacky, with lots of help from the rabble rousing media.

Contempt for Palin amounted to classism. She didn't talk right or attend the right schools. Perhaps I didn't attend the right schools or have the right pedigree either. I have known people with the best educations who couldn't navigate their way to the grocery store.

Schooling and credits are a nice insurance policy or justification for hiring someone, but are not always guarantees of performance.

A week prior to the election, Democratic speechwriter Wendy Button penned an article for *The Daily Beast* entitled *So Long, Democrats.* Ms. Button had written for Senators Edwards, Clinton, Kerry and Obama, as well as other national and international leaders. I found these excerpts telling and was amazed at her actions in so heated an atmosphere:

> "Since I started writing speeches more than ten years ago, I have always believed in the Democratic Party. Not anymore. Not after the election of 2008.
>
> "Not only has this party belittled working people in this campaign, it has also been part of tearing down two female candidates.

We found out more about Joe the Plumber in two days than we had about Mr. Obama in two years. Ms. Button continued...

> "Governor Palin and I don't agree on a lot of things, mostly social issues. But I have grown to appreciate the Governor. I was one of those initial skeptics and would laugh at the pictures. Not anymore. When someone takes on a corrupt political machine and a sitting governor, that is not done by someone with a low I.Q. or a moral core made of tissue paper.
>
> I can no longer justify what this party has done and can't dismiss the treatment of women and working people as just part of the new kind of politics. It's wrong and someone has to say that. And also say that the Democratic Party's talking points—that Senator John McCain is just four more years of the same and that he's President Bush—are now just hooker lines that fit a very effective and perhaps wave-winning political argument...doesn't mean they're true. After all, [McCain] is the only one who's worked in a bipartisan way on big challenges."

In a follow-up piece, Ms. Button shared she received death threats as a result of her statements. I reread her article and wondered if those who had such a vitriolic initial response to her views and frustrations with her old party would feel the same several years later.

I feared threats, too, for not singing Senator Obama's praises. I still hoped to work as an actor and the heated rhetoric coming from many in Hollywood made me feel I would be rejected – to the extent anyone knew or cared who I was in the first place.

I had no objection to anyone criticizing any politician on the issues and rejecting them on that basis. I just preferred we leave the personal out of it.

If someone decided Sarah Palin was unworthy of support, so be it. But the violent bile spewed by comics like Sarah Bernhardt who warned Palin she would be "gang raped if she dared set foot in Manhattan"[213] was horrifying and made anyone on my side who chimed in agreement look irrational.

* * *

While there were negative campaign ads on both sides, and rhetoric I did not care for, the Republican onslaught against Obama that my Hillary supporting buddies had expected did not quite materialize.

The conservative establishment was never keen on Senator McCain. In a rating of 49 'conservative' senators, he ranked 49th. The likely reason three million Democrats were able to cross party lines to vote for him was the reason he lost – he was not conservative enough. That coupled with six million Republicans who sat on their hands during the election to register their displeasure with George Bush, had all but sealed the deal.

In the final weeks before the election, both the Obama and Hillary wings of the Democratic Party wanted Hillary to carry their water. One side wanted her to push Obama to victory, in part by destroying Sarah Palin. Hillary Democrats demanded she loudly reject him and speak out against the poor treatment of women.

I had tried in vain to figure out why people couldn't resist beating on Hillary; even some of her supporters. After the longest and most grueling primary contest in history, anyone could agree that she and her family deserved time to recuperate. Hillary Clinton is a tough cookie and a professional politician, but the need to have her as all things to all people indicated that, perhaps unconsciously, we were relating to her as the archetypal mother. This association can unleash deep and powerful feelings which defy logic. I found a description on the internet:

> "The bountiful mother figure ... she swells with abundance – she promises fulfillment of need. The Great Mother, however, can frighten as well as sustain ...Mother Earth may sustain the crops, but Mother Earth can generate terrible forces – earthquakes, floods and volcanic eruptions. Our primitive psyches enshrine the ecstasy of hunger banished by mother's breast, but we also harbor dark shadows of her absence, of her inability to make everything better."[214]

In the world of politics, perhaps the concept of mother is too tough to erase from the collective psyche, accounting for the double standard foisted upon both Senator Clinton and Governor Palin. My wish to change the landscape required me to make note of this to whatever limited audience was reading my commentary, no matter how tiresome the debate may have been to some, instead of demanding that mommy make it all better.

In response to vitriol flooding the airwaves once Palin became a large part of the debate, Senator Clinton made a simple statement that sexism had no place in this contest, while campaigning to help Senator Obama get elected. That was the beginning and end of her job.

Hungry for ratings, the media would have liked nothing better than to cover a cat fight between these two ladies. To this day, big media tries to coax the same. Neither Clinton nor Palin have taken the bait and discuss each other in respectful terms. I was relieved to see both women make a conscious decision not to fall for the divide and conquer scenario.

> "Should Secretary Clinton and I ever sit down over a cup of coffee, I know that we will fundamentally disagree on many issues, but my hat is off to her hard work on the 2008 campaign trail. ...[A] lot of her supporters think she proved what Margaret Thatcher proclaimed: "If you want something said, ask a man. If you want something done, ask a woman."[215]

-- Sarah Palin

"Well you know, I've never met her, and I'd look forward to sit down and talk with her. Obviously we're going to hear a lot more from her in the upcoming week, with her book coming up and I would look forward to having a chance to get to meet her."[216]

-- Hillary Clinton

I still harbor hope that a woman will get up on the soapbox and encourage left and right leaning women to find common ground on reproductive rights. We would then be able to push for what else is of importance to us. Then the guys would never win another election until they did more than make empty promises and stop condescending to us as one-issue voters.

16 ACTORS ARE PEOPLE, TOO

As a blogger keeping my identity confidential, some readers on the Internet who stood in firm support of my commentary trashed the profession they had no idea I had been part of for many years. Some of their statements repeated the bad rap Hollywood has long held. Actors are vacuous, phony, amoral, and don't know what they are talking about.

To say that someone who lives in Hollywood is a brainless, lefty loony who hates America is just as unfair and baseless as saying those who live in red states are backward, uninformed hillbillies. These labels stop us from having a meaningful debate about much of anything. The behavior profits no one but politicians and special interests that pit us against one another, using our fears to fill their coffers, trotting out the same hot button issues every couple of years, never really intending to advance any cause beyond Election Day.

And where did I fall in this debate? My behavior wasn't the standard of what one would expect of a 'Hollywood type' in 2008.

Four days before the election, I was shooting a McDonald's commercial, playing the mother of a young groom. We stood around the three-tiered "McNuggets" cake in our wedding finery, waiting for the crew to set up the next shot. Probably no more than twenty-five years old, my "son" took a large cake knife and went straight for the brunette plastic bride atop the cake, gesturing as if to chop her head off while mouthing the word "Palin" with contempt. Most of the crew and the bride laughed along in agreement. His attitude most resembled the other young female Democrat who scowled "I hate that Hillary bitch" to me months earlier.

It was likewise difficult to watch and listen to those with whom I had worked in a town I loved offering up sound bites so dismissive of anyone not in agreement with their sentiments about the candidates. Yet there were those in Hollywood who had different views. With rare exception, they were a lot quieter about it.

Venturing timidly onto a few conservative websites during this frustrating period, I would sometimes offer a comment, telling them I was a Hillary supporter and felt for the first time what it must be like to be a conservative – often mischaracterized by many in the mainstream media, derided or otherwise ignored.

Some sites were welcoming, some let my comments pass without answer, still others didn't post my entries. A few blogs, like their liberal mirror images, were fairly uniform in blanket condemnations of the other side. Effective communication has at points been a frustrating endeavor.

The stereotyping I witnessed in 2008, not only toward actors, but toward any and all defined groups, made clear how easy it was to practice contempt prior to examination. I felt a growing need to expand beyond my own circle, pushing back against those who would use demagoguery to keep otherwise likeminded people divided.

I thought of the many hours my parents had spent demonizing each other for their respective religions, and how much they might have accomplished had they not used that issue as an excuse to tear each other down.

I was later invited to audition for an independent film dealing with the great divide caused by voters choosing between Hillary Clinton and Barack Obama. My agent forwarded the character breakdown to me so I might glean what approach the filmmakers wanted for the part. They described "a woman, fiftyish, a Hillary supporter, an activist pushing to get Hillary's name into nomination, might be racist."

I stared at the page, shaking my head. I did something I would never do. I went to the audition, and via my work in front of the casting director, tried my best to counter these notions. She was lovely and open to hearing what I had to offer but so many thoughts and feelings flooded my brain, I doubt I was successful in getting my point across.

I knew in my heart the filmmakers meant well, but as far as this character description was concerned, it was as if they had gotten their talking points from Keith Olbermann. I had no way to fight this mindset. If the film is ever released, I am hopeful we'll see a fair representation of both sides.

These were but small illustrations of the consequences of the 2008 primaries and election. Many bought into the talking points fed them by their respective news sources and believed what they heard. We did not talk to each other. Not enough, anyway. Creating controversy has long been profitable to get ratings. It didn't profit me or anyone I knew out here on the ground.

I had a large media contact list and would write weekly to offer a different perspective. I was not part of the narrative and with few exceptions, received no response. My only way to communicate my frustrations was on the blogs. Several websites offered me a home to share my work. My transformation into a blog writer was an odd one. I got pulled into a world where my alter ego received a great deal of approbation in particular circles, but I was still too frightened to let go of my secret identity. I wanted to share that I was an anomaly – not fitting into a neat little box.

Considering my life just one year prior, co-producing and acting in a solo show, performing weekly, working on commercials, soaps, episodic TV, hosting parties for friends, I was social as hell. By the time September of 2008 rolled around, I barely left our home. I was still working as an actor but was far more occupied writing, researching, sending out letters to the editor and to legislators.

The Presidential election was the day after my 50th birthday. Not getting the Hillary present I was hoping for, I didn't want to socialize with anyone who wasn't a supporter of hers that week. I couldn't bear to hear the commentary.

Turning fifty did turn out to be a gift, however. And in some ways, I had the media to thank. The passion I felt for this cause helped me to draw a line in the sand as I never had before. I left polite by the side of the road. Other women friends who had turned fifty told me this was a by-product of this milestone under any circumstances.

Yet arriving at a place where I felt both enriched and blessed, more confident of my own voice, and even looks, only to see older women insulted in so many corners throughout the year was devastating.

It is said you will never know what your principles are until they become inconvenient to you. Learning to trust my own judgment, I saw that Party is not as important as integrity and transparency. I discovered yet again that a familiar or friendly label is not always backed up with matching principles or behavior.

Though I called the DNC out on the carpet for the first time in my life, this is not to say Republicans guilty of wrongdoing got a pass; far from it. But Republicans were never my party. I held Democrats to a higher standard because I stood with them for thirty years.

I was a diehard Democrat the same way I used to be a diehard New Yorker. When I hit thirty, I saw New York City turning into an oligarchy. The mom and pop stores were disappearing, chased away by high priced leases, much like apartment dwellers were chased to the other boroughs to escape Manhattan's outrageous rents. I still loved the electricity of the city, but it started to feel like an overpriced Disneyland and a place of privilege. In the current landscape, both political parties made me feel the same way. With the exception of some honorable public servants on both sides, many had fashioned themselves into some sort of intelligentsia and my input was no longer required or desired. My donations, however, would always be welcome.

I had a newfound willingness to listen to both sides without predetermining that one or the other is evil. In the past, when watching a panel show with Democrats and Republicans, no matter who the Republican speaker was, I was predisposed to think that he or she was full of it. Now I listen and go with who makes sense. And who has a record that backs up their rhetoric. When I allowed myself to hear the words without the pundit class or peers pressuring me into one type of thinking, the answers were often quite illuminating, as well as surprising. Common ground is possible, and in some unexpected places.

As Senator Clinton once said:

> "You know, our politics can get a little imbalanced sometimes. We move off to the left or off to the right, but eventually we find our way back to the center because Americans are problem solvers. We are not ideologues. Most people are just looking for sensible, commonsense solutions."[217]

I looked back at 2008 with great sadness, but not regret. I had to do this.

Being so involved in the campaign and addicted to the news, I felt like I'd gotten my childhood PTSD back. So many events spilled over one another in my mind that reminded of a funhouse gone awry.

In recent years, as my self-respect and sense of self-worth have increased, so, too, has my understanding that I am part of the global community. I have a legitimate voice in the debate and my participation does count for something, as does everyone else's. I am grateful to live in a country where I have the opportunity to voice my concerns and that I've become a more active citizen. I don't want consent to be a thing taken for granted.

Whether anyone agrees with me is far less important than whether they choose to get more involved as a result. Joining in the debate would be the greatest reward of all.

> "I am only one, but still I am one. I cannot do everything, but still I can do something; and because I cannot do everything, I will not refuse to do something that I can do."

> -- Edward Everett Hale[218]

17 INAUGURATION FRENZY AND THE REALITY GOING FORWARD

Watching the HBO pre-Inauguration concert entitled "We Are One," I was moved by the pomp and circumstance staged before the Lincoln Memorial, the dress guard and the choirs; to see Mary J. Blige so proud, singing "Lean On Me" and the one and only Stevie Wonder singing "Higher Ground," a song that has resonated with me for almost 40 years. I watched Bono and Sam Jackson and Denzel and Beyoncé and Latifah and Jack Black and Rosario Dawson and others making their statements and singing, so happy for the change to come.

While I did not want to deprive anyone of their joy in crossing this barrier, I cried as I realized I couldn't help but wish for them to have a more sincere hero upon whom to bestow the honor of this historic election. Yet I remained glued to our television throughout the day, watching the Inauguration, drinking in as much of Mr. and Mrs. Obama as I could, wishing and praying for them to do well, even if I felt conflicted at the outcome.

My favorite moment came watching the high school bands parading past the first couple. It was night time and surely freezing cold. I watched Mrs. Obama, impressed, shaking her head and mouthing the word, "Wow." The immensity of the moment was reflected in that one word and in her expression.

The next night, I met with five female colleagues, some Obama supporters, some Hillary and one McCain. I brought some sparkling cider and proposed a toast to President Obama, Vice President Biden, Secretary of State Hillary Clinton and Senator John McCain. Godspeed.

During the campaign, I took Barack Obama to task because I had problems with his tactics and veracity. Having great respect for the office of the Presidency, and a deep love of our country, I appreciated those who wished to give him carte blanche on the day of his inauguration, declaring a new dawn and a new day. But it has been said if you want a good indication of what someone is going to do, take a look at what they've done. I promised myself I would stay involved in the debate.

The election was in part a referendum on George Bush, the Iraq war and the rule of the neo-cons. The economic meltdown also got blamed on President Bush, while in truth there was plenty of blame to go around. Democrats must also bear some responsibility for fighting against regulation of Fannie Mae and Freddie Mac and likewise, a lack of regulation of risky banking practices.

> "The only way you can control [the out-of-control spending]," Obama said, "is if there is some sense of shame and accountability. The more we increase accountability the more we reduce the special interests in Washington."[219]
>
> – Barack Obama

Unfortunately, the influence of special interests in Washington continued unabated.

Due to the economic crisis in which we found ourselves, there was an urgent sense that we needed to pull together to get through a difficult time. Our situation smacked of what Naomi Klein discussed in her book *Shock Doctrine*, in which the powers that be, and we now know that includes Democrats as well as Republicans, used a crisis to mire Americans in fear, so that out of our fear, we would have no choice but to do what those in authority told us we had to do. They count on us getting tired and giving up, or becoming too overwhelmed by our circumstances to demand a different solution.

In the process, we forget to hold people's feet to the fire. I was not immune to this. Some scandal would be in the paper, perhaps an ethics investigation. Two weeks later, I had difficulty remembering who was on the chopping block. And soon, they were back at work as if nothing had happened. Few noticed. It was a familiar sensation.

Once elected, even President Obama admitted his promise of bipartisanship was not even being attempted. All legislative votes were strictly along strict party lines. Partisan bickering and a herd mentality in Washington were still choking us.

Independent thinkers are required, regardless of party. In our current system where there is no limit on campaign spending or fundraising, it is impossible for our public servants not to be slaves of the almighty dollar. When they are threatened with primary challenges if they do not kiss the feet of their respective party's establishment and follow their orders, how can they vote their consciences? Clearly, public service of this kind is not meant to be a lifetime career. Less focus on the gathering of power or securing re-election and more on doing the people's business is in order.

I didn't want to set the stage for yet another Administration suffering no consequences for their actions. President Obama believed in his ability to move mountains on the force of his personality. The Democratic elite and mainstream media enabled him at every turn to believe this was true. Our president has since discovered the difficulty of relying on that tool to get the job done.

During the campaign, the idol worship I witnessed toward Barack Obama both by the press and his supporters was troubling. No human being could match up to the messianic treatment he had received. It was irresponsible to pretend otherwise, inspirational speeches notwithstanding. However unintentionally, that self-same media set him up for a fall, and his supporters could not help but be in for a disappointment.

Over the years, the press had become less reliable as unbiased watchdogs of our government, trading objectivity for access. Certain top reporters had negotiated multi-million dollar book deals for the privilege of intimate entrée in order to cover the Obama White House for the 2012 elections. It was not surprising that 2008 became the year of the citizen journalist.

As mainstream news is now controlled by the entertainment divisions at their respective networks, it is has become less a public service than a piece of theatre. This theory was advanced by Chris Hedges, the Pulitzer Prize winning former mid-east bureau chief for *The New York Times*. Mr. Hedges penned an article entitled *Buying Brand Obama*,[220] criticizing our fascination with junk politics:

> "The consumption-oriented culture honors charm, fascination and likeability."

> ... It is about keeping us in a perpetual state of childishness. But the longer we live in illusion, the worse reality will be when it finally shatters our fantasies. Those who do not understand what is happening around them and who are overwhelmed by a brutal reality they did not expect or foresee search desperately for saviors. They beg demagogues to come to their rescue. This is the ultimate danger of the Obama Brand. It effectively masks the wanton internal destruction and theft being carried out by our corporate state. These corporations, once they have stolen trillions in taxpayer wealth, will leave tens of millions of Americans bereft, bewildered and yearning for even more potent and deadly illusions, ones that could swiftly snuff out what is left of our diminished open society."

Perhaps the best any candidate could do would be to move us a couple of inches in a more genuine direction. Watching the theatrics employed by news media in 2008 made me yearn for us to discard junk politics and demand character over personality and real leadership over branding.

Since being elected, at almost each press conference or public appearance, President Obama tried to tamp down people's expectations of him. Even he realized the dangers of the Frankenstein of hope created by such lofty campaign rhetoric.

At President Obama's first major press conference, a female reporter stood up to race-bait by asking if he felt he was being treated differently in office by virtue of his ethnicity. To President Obama's credit, he said he was being judged solely on his policies and actions. Whether I voted for him or not, I daily hoped his current actions would overcome my past reservations.

Eugene Robinson posted a column in the *Washington Post* entitled *What We're Not Talking About*[221]:

> "Not even three months have passed since President
> Obama's historic inauguration, and already it tends to
> slip the nation's collective mind that the first black
> president of the United States is, in fact, black. There
> may be hope for us after all."

President Obama has been treated with respect here and around the world, as Mr. Robinson noted. As he pointed out in his column, any criticism of Barack Obama had nothing to do with his race. It never did. That was just politics. Sixty-nine million voters proved that. Unfounded insinuations of racism were painful and costly to many. The ends did not justify the means.

It came as a surprise to a number of President Obama's media champions that in his first year in office, he had floated and/or adopted several policy proposals that he excoriated Senator McCain for suggesting during the campaign, finding himself not only to the right of Clinton and McCain but even President Bush on some of the actions he had already taken in office. Rhodes' Scholar Rachel Maddow of MSNBC must have been shocked to report that to the rest of us when she spoke of President Obama's call for "preventive detention."

Sadly, women were the first group to get thrown under the bus as Speaker Pelosi struggled with President Obama to pass sweeping health care reform in 2010.

> "You know what I don't want to hear right now
> about the Stupak-Pitts amendment banning abortion
> coverage from federally subsidized health insurance
> policies? That it's the price of reform, and pro-choice
> women should shut up and take one for the team.
> ..."

> -- Katha Pollitt, *The Nation*

NOW President Terry O'Neill also had choice comments about the way women once again got short shrift in the name of "passing historic legislation."

"Fact: The bill permits age-rating, the practice of imposing higher premiums on older people. This practice has a disproportionate impact on women, whose incomes and savings are lower due to a lifetime of systematic wage discrimination.

Fact: The bill also permits gender-rating, the practice of charging women higher premiums simply because they are women. ...Larger group plans (more than 100 employees) sold through the exchanges will be permitted to discriminate against women -- having an especially harmful impact in workplaces where women predominate.

We know why those gender- and age-rating provisions are in the bill: because insurers insisted on them, as they will generate billions of dollars in profits for the companies. Such discriminatory rating must be completely eliminated."

I had a hard time believing Senator Clinton would have stood for women being treated this way. Clinton was the true health care candidate, putting nearly twenty years of thought into getting this one right. She favored interstate competition between insurance companies to drive prices down, major tax breaks for small businesses, importing less expensive drugs and most important, that citizens could opt in to the same plan that Congress enjoys. A policy wonk, Hillary would not have outsourced the creation of this important legislation to Speaker Pelosi without a very clear prescription for its contents up front. Perhaps that's why I had the impression Mrs. Pelosi did not want Hillary for a boss.

Numerous sources have now declared Pelosi the most powerful Speaker in one hundred years.[222] Troubling when you consider Mrs. Pelosi making this comment about the health care bill: "We need to pass it so you can find out what's in it."[223]

* * *

It is easy to extol the candidacy and policies of someone who says they agree with you on every issue. Inhabiting the world of smoke and mirrors for many years as an actor, I knew that talk was worthless. Only actions mattered. President Obama's strongest supporters had taken to complaining of his broken campaign promises.

In 2011, two wars continued in Iraq and Afghanistan, a third military action was begun in Libya, and the Defense of Marriage Act (DOMA) remained the law of the land. Gitmo was still in operation, as was Blackwater, and the Patriot Act was renewed (yearly) with little fanfare. On the cusp of 2012, President Obama withdrew troops from Iraq. Contrary to his campaign promises, he had adhered to President Bush's original timetable.

Don't Ask Don't Tell (DADT) was at last repealed in 2011, but not until fully 80% of the country was in favor of the law being overturned. Congressman Patrick Murphy and Senator Joe Lieberman (erstwhile Democrat who was nearly thrown out of his Party for campaigning for John McCain in 2008), were the two most responsible for doing the heavy lifting to get the law repealed. They received an able assist from Republican Senator Susan Collins and Democratic Whip Steny Hoyer.[224] Up to that point, the Obama White House and Justice Department had repeatedly filed briefs in defense of both DADT and DOMA.

Glenn Greenwald of *Salon.com* complained that by taking over the Democratic brand, President Obama had ruined it, getting liberals, from a place of defensiveness, to support policies put forth by Obama that they themselves would have roundly condemned had they been proposed by his Republican predecessor.

In 2008, *Newsweek* editor Evan Thomas declared Barack Obama "is sort of God." In 2011, Thomas described President Obama's economic policies as "a profile in cowardice."[225] His stunning about face reflected the sentiments of many journalists who once exalted a candidate in direct proportion to their shocking condemnations of his primary opponent, Hillary Clinton.

* * *

Considering the derision those in my writers' circle received at the hands of pundits or opposing bloggers in 2008 for voicing our opinions, it became an uncomfortable pastime to note how, four years after the campaign many were coming to agree with our original concerns, though we would never be acknowledged for the same.

The issue was bigger than who got elected. It was about the way the election unfolded and what it said about the state of our democracy, our involvement, our knowledge or lack thereof, how we treated each other and the contributions of a biased press. How we got here mattered to me.

And we should not have gotten here by kicking women in the teeth.

18 GRADED AND DEGRADED: ON CLEAVAGE, CLOTHES AND COMICS

The date was February 1, 2009. The stock market had just lost half its value, two wars continued abroad, we had inaugurated a new president, and Congress was about to pass the $787 billion stimulus bill. CBS, along with other news networks, were wondering, "Will Jessica Simpson's Curves Hurt Her Career."[226] On CNN, "Jessica Simpson spoke out in her first interview since getting slammed for putting on a few pounds."[227]

A preposterous amount of attention was focused on this woman's waistline. In the midst of numerous crises, we were being offered bread and circuses.

Stories were and are daily filed by major newspapers and network media outlets about Hillary Clinton's pantsuits, Sarah Palin's wardrobe expenditures, and Michelle Obama's dress designers.

> "If I want to knock a story off the front page, I just change my hairstyle. "
>
> -- Hillary Rodham Clinton

> "We still live in a man's world. Otherwise, women wouldn't still be wearing make-up."
>
> -- Fran Drescher, FOX News interview

"The sexual references are pervasive: they come from left, right, and center, and range from gushing to highly offensive. *The Atlantic* asked, "Is Sarah Palin Porn?" as others quizzed the former governor about whether she had breast implants. Right Wing News compiled a list of the hottest conservative women in new media. *Playboy* even ran an outrageous piece titled "Ten Conservative Women I'd Like to Hate F--k," which read like a sick attempt to make rape cool. "We may despise everything these women represent," wrote the author, "but goddammit they're hot. Let the healing begin." Moron.

"Women in politics are used to being trivialized, and have tended to dress and behave soberly in response. The wisdom has long been that discussions about their sexuality are not just distracting and degrading, but also destructive."[228]

-- Julia Baird, *Newsweek*

In the early days of the presidential campaign, the Washington Post offered a story about "Hillary's dip into new neckline territory":

"There wasn't an unseemly amount of cleavage showing, but there it was. Undeniable."[229]

This tidbit was picked up by news outlets and pundits from here to Australia. Senator Clinton was discovered in her incriminating ensemble as she stood on the floor of the Senate discussing the burdensome cost of higher education. Her wardrobe had once again trumped her issue.

If the objectification of women was not endemic to our culture, it would find no quarter with the American people and those practicing it would have to find something else to talk about. We, too, are part of the problem.

We are daily reminded what the feminine ideal should be via airbrushed and otherwise "enhanced" images of beautiful women who grace magazine covers. It is also clear how easily any woman can be the target for humiliating treatment if for whatever reason, she does not match up to that ideal physically, socially or politically.

A woman's appearance can be used against her via demeaning images in novelty stores, airports, greeting cards, television ads, magazines. There is no escape: Hillary's head sticking out of a toilet. Hillary as dominatrix dolls. Hillary toilet paper. Chris Matthews teased about Hillary being a "she-devil," displaying a photo with horns coming out of her head on his show.

To complement David Letterman's references to Sarah Palin's "slutty flight attendant look,"[230] there were Sarah Palin orifice-accessible blow up dolls and 'naughty Sarah' action figures. Photographs were manipulated on the internet. The naked Sarah Palin and the naked VP Dick Cheney having sex, her legs up over his shoulders, was the nadir.

Ridicule. A woman's sexuality is abused as a weapon to demean and humiliate. It would appear the thinking is, "If I can screw it, I can own it."

One of the worst weapons is laughter. We are encouraged to listen to an endless litany of put downs with good humor and complain about none of it. Yet over time, it must have an effect on the way society sees women and the way women see themselves.

> "They fined CBS a million dollars for Janet Jackson's nipple. Just think what they could get for Hillary Clinton's cunt."
>
> --Bill Maher, HBO, "Real Time with Bill Maher"

Bill Maher also found it acceptable to criticize a woman's looks. He delivered sexist rants on his HBO show, calling women horrid names; flirting with the more "attractive" ones, distracting from the message and qualifications of his female guests.

And Mr. Maher was not the only comic who found Hillary to be a rewarding pastime:

> "In a fiery speech this weekend, Hillary Clinton wondered why President Bush can't find the tallest man in Afghanistan. Probably for the same reason she couldn't find the fattest intern under the desk."[231]
>
> --Jay Leno

"...Clinton has accused Obama and his people of trying to dump a bucket of water on her and make her melt."[232]

--Jimmy Kimmel

"Bill Clinton is the only ex-president who hasn't planned his own funeral. But, in his defense, in the past he has said he wants to be buried next to Hillary. I guess he figures he never slept next to her when they were alive, might as well try it now that they're dead." [233]

–Jay Leno

"[F]ormer President Bill Clinton says that most people don't know Hillary has the world's best laugh. Bill added, 'I get to hear it every time she pushes me down the stairs.'"[234]

--Conan O'Brien

"Kenyan women have vowed to withhold sex until their leaders stop bickering — they said they got the idea to withhold sex from a recent visit from Hillary Clinton." [235]

-- Jay Leno

"It's true, everybody is in the holiday spirit. Last night, Bill Clinton saw the 'Nutcracker.' Not the ballet. Hillary." [236]

--David Letterman

"According to a new survey, Hillary Clinton's popularity rating is down to its lowest point in over a year. When Bill Clinton heard this, he said, 'If there's one thing Hillary can do, it's bring polls down.'"[237]

--Conan O'Brien

"I'm surprised they did a portrait of Hillary. I thought maybe an ice sculpture would have been more appropriate."[238]

--Jay Leno

Frigid. Witch. Ball buster. Killer.

These men knew nothing of her sexuality. And if they used her husband's infidelity as a reason to deny her womanhood, research has been done stating that men who marry the most beautiful woman are often more likely to cheat on them.[239] Infidelity was not something that could be explained away by blaming the wife.

A few weeks before his sudden and most unfortunate death in 2008, Bernie Mac performed at a $2,300 a plate dinner benefiting Barack Obama:

> "[My] little nephew came to me and he said, 'Uncle, what's the difference between a hypothetical question and a realistic question?' "I said, 'I don't know,' but I said, 'I'll tell you what you do. Go upstairs and ask your mother if she'd make love to the mailman for $50,000.'"
>
> Mac's wife, in the joke, said she'd sleep "with anyone" for $50,000, and Mac's daughter said the same.
>
> Explained Mac: "Hypothetically speaking, we should have $100,000. But realistically speaking we live with two hos."

Mr. Mac received some heckling from the audience for his comments. Fifteen minutes later, Barack Obama went onstage to calm the crowd, admonishing Mr. Mac to "clean up his act next time." Yet in the next breath Senator Obama said, "By the way, I'm just messin' with you, man."[240, 241]

During the campaign, Dana Carvey premiered his new HBO special, most of it hilarious. He did the obligatory political riff, making fun of just about everyone: Reagan, Bush I & II, Gore. He took a tentative swipe at Senator Obama, calling him Urkel, but was otherwise almost reverential. The audience sat in stony silence through most of his commentary about Obama; protective, waiting. So after the "Urkel" snark, he raced off the subject.

The Clintons however, were not so lucky. Ten years after the fact, we were subjected once again to Bill Clinton's dalliance with Monica Lewinsky.

Dana Carvey then said, "Well, look at Hillary. Can you blame Bill for what he did?"

The audience laughed.

Since Hillary Clinton does not resemble Angelina Jolie, his theory was that she should expect this sort of treatment. Should all other women not likewise blessed to look like a raving beauty expect it, too? I wondered if women in the audience aged sixty or otherwise laughed along to protect themselves from being trashed as Hillary had been.

There are very successful comics, Sinbad comes to mind, who don't require misogyny to be funny.

It's not just the jokes themselves but their relentless, repetitive nature that is exhausting. Hearing someone described this way night after night -- how can this not eventually influence your opinion of them? Small wonder many women laugh it off. And if we didn't... "Lighten up, ladies!"

Men are encouraged to express themselves in these terms having seen thousands of grateful audience members laugh at comics who make jokes at women's expense. Female comedians laugh at men too, but the roles we perpetuate for them are different. We play Mommy: My hubby is Peter Pan. He cannot see in three dimensions. He is sloppy. He doesn't listen. He needs to watch the game.

My husband likes to have me narrate the refrigerator for him, which I can do from the other room. He stares into it and he still can't find the juice. *"Behind* the milk," I shout. It's an old Rita Rudner joke. Harmless.

Terrified of being left, cuckolded or criticized by women, male comics mount a preemptive offensive more difficult to fight against: You're not pretty enough. You talk too much. You don't suck my dick enough. You're a gold digger. You are old. You are fat. You are boring. Other women don't like you. You don't like each other.

2008 also proved once and for all women were not immune from trashing other women. It occurred to me they had been trained by watching men get such a good reception for doing the same.

> "[L]iberal radio personality Randi Rhodes called Clinton a "big [expletive] whore" and said the same about former vice presidential nominee Geraldine Ferraro. Rhodes was appearing at an event sponsored by a San Francisco radio station, before an audience of appreciative Obama supporters -- one of whom had promoted the evening on the presumptive Democratic nominee's official campaign website."[242]

> -- Marie Cocco, *Washington Post*

The divide and conquer scenario keeps us busy ripping each other's hair out instead of paying attention to those pulling the strings. A friend had said, "You know why you never have to put a lid on a barrel of crabs to keep them from escaping? Because as one crawls to the top, another crab reaches up and pulls it back down."

Some pundits were no better than comics during the primary:

> "When she comes on TV, I involuntarily cross my legs."[243]

> -- Tucker Carlson, MSNBC

> "She is a stranger to consistency, sincerity and (at a guess) oral sex...." "and (it was wittily observed on CNN this week) knows in the end about as much about the inner workings of executive government as the White House pastry cook. ...(Barack Obama) is, in short, the present world's likely saviour if he makes it through November and this yapping troll at his ankle may yet bring him down..."[244]

> -- Bob Ellis, "ABC Unleashed"

Kathy Griffin performed in Alaska and started in on Sarah Palin: "What? Did McCain meet her for like ten minutes before choosing her as VP? That must have been some blow job!"

I thought of Griffin's comment about Palin in contrast to a story she told about Bill Maher in one of her comedy specials years earlier.

She said that though they were friends, Maher did not take her seriously. 'What the hell do you know about politics, girlie' or sentiments to that effect.

Since she is someone who has entertained the troops in Iraq, she asked Maher, "When was the last time you were there, Bill?"

"Uhh, yeah, I've been meaning to go," he replied.

By perpetuating the idea that Palin only got to the top by getting on her knees, it appears Ms. Griffin was helping the very mindset that had allowed Maher to discredit Griffin as well.

Science Daily[245] reported:

> "Sexist humor is not simply benign amusement. It can affect men's perceptions of their immediate social surroundings and allow them to feel comfortable with behavioral expressions of sexism without the fear of disapproval of their peers," said Thomas E. Ford, a new faculty member in the psychology department at WCU. "Specifically, we propose that sexist humor acts as a 'releaser' of prejudice."

> "...The acceptance of sexist humor leads men to believe that sexist behavior falls within the bounds of social acceptability."

> The research indicates that people should be aware of the prevalence of disparaging humor in popular culture, and that the guise of benign amusement or "it's just a joke" gives it the potential to be a powerful and widespread force that can legitimize prejudice in our society, he said.

In one of their experiments, researchers shared sexist comedy skits with a group of men, showing women in demeaning roles. It was found that "men higher in sexism discriminated against women by allocating larger funding cuts to a women's organization than they did to other organizations."[246]

Brainwashing takes many forms.

Objectifying women, whether through humor or demeaning sexual imagery is celebrated more than it is protested. 22% of teenaged girls are now "sexting" – sending nude or semi nude photos of themselves via their cell phones. ABC News filed a horrific story of a girl who had hanged herself as a result of the hazing from her peers when an angry boyfriend decided to circulate these pictures far and wide.

Most devastating, misogyny is not confined to hateful words. Violence against women shows no signs of dissipating. One in three women report being physically or sexually abused by a husband or boyfriend at some point during their lives. More than 32 million Americans are affected by domestic violence each year. Domestic violence is the leading cause of injury to women,[247] to say nothing of other crimes against women committed by strangers. Other degrading behavior, discrimination and emotional abuse to which women are subjected cannot be quantified.

On April 30, 2009, Nicholas Kristof published an article in the *New York Times* entitled *Is Rape Serious?* detailing how many rape kits sit around gathering dust in labs for up to ten years without being processed, and the many cases that go uninvestigated and unprosecuted as a result.

> "As long as violence against women, sexual or otherwise, remains strictly and exclusively a women's issue, it will always be an issue. We men must own this and we must recognize it as vital to our own survival. And we must help our brothers to see it as such."
>
> -- Ben Affleck
> Vital Voices Global Partnership

The media would have done well to spend as much copy drawing attention to these unfortunate facts rather than focusing so much attention on a woman's cleavage or hip measurements. Likewise, it would be refreshing if the derogatory names used to describe women were no longer a protected class.

In his 2008 HBO special, "Kill the Messenger," Chris Rock shared what he thought of several celebrities, Michael Richards of "Seinfeld" fame among them, who had gotten in trouble for using the "N" word. He told the audience what circumstances would make it permissible for a white person to use that word.

I'll never tell this joke right, but he said if it's 4:00 am on Christmas Eve and you are standing in front of Toys-R-Us in a blizzard trying to buy the last Play Station 3 for your kid and a black guy mugs you, kicks the crap out of you and leaves you bloody on the ground, taking your Play Station 3 to boot, then in the five minute period between 4:27 am and 4:32 am, you may use the "N" word.

Maybe.

It's a word I wish would never be used. Interesting that it is so verboten in my mind, I cannot bring myself to write it on the page. Yet it is okay to call a woman a whore, a bitch, a cunt, fat, butt ugly, frigid, a nag and dried up twenty four - seven - three sixty five.

I remind myself it's just a joke.

19 HE'S A BIT OF ALL RIGHT

In the first few months of the New Year, I still felt bruised by what had transpired in 2008. I had to remind myself there were men who were nothing like Jack Cafferty or Chris Matthews. I started to wonder if other men I had worked with or befriended over the years had secretly felt it was okay to talk about a woman as Carlson, Olbermann, Maher, Rich and so many others had. The list was comprehensive.

Having long ago buried sexist behavior, the primaries brought it all back, along with every other piece of insulting and humiliating behavior that ever found me on the receiving end. I had to make another list as an antidote.

I reflected back on the night of the Indiana primaries, where Hillary had just managed to eke out a win. I was perched on a chair in our home office combing websites for the vote percentages while my husband, David, sat on the living room sofa, watching pundits blasting her since Obama had won a much bigger victory in North Carolina that night.

David stood up and shouted out to me, "Send Hillary another $100. I don't want her to think we've abandoned her!"

John, one of my best buddies, had made a wonderful video for Hillary that he put up on YouTube called "One Day More." He wore his Hillary hat everywhere, calling me every day so we could keep up on the latest news about our girl.

My 32-year-old talent manager pushed the idea of voting for Hillary to his friends. He was confident of her smarts on the economy and felt safe with her tough foreign policy. He had never before voted for a Democrat. I laughed when he said, "Men have been screwing it up long enough. Let's give a woman a chance." Right up until the second day of the Democratic Convention, he would call asking me if there was any hope Hillary could still get enough delegate votes to win the nomination.

Our dear gay friends surely voted for her in the Primary – she'd been marching on behalf of GLBT rights for years. Beyond that, they appreciated her smarts and grace under pressure.

I also considered myself fortunate to have men in my life who stood with and encouraged me without question. Thinking of those friends and family provided a welcome antidote to what could truly be called the boob tube.

I thought about my father for the first time in many years. While his abusive behavior made him the villain in our home, I still honored him. His horrid experiences in the war made him worse than he would have been otherwise. I wished he could have seen me thriving in a world he had forsaken. I'm sorry he was never able to ask forgiveness of my mother or sister. But wherever he was, off in the ether, I had hoped he was healed.

My dad used to say, "You will master everything you take into your hand." No matter how limited his imagination of what a woman could achieve in the world, he believed in me. It took a long time for me to hear his praise as a boost to my confidence rather than pressure not to fail. Six months before his death, he turned to my mother, pointed to me and said, "You know, she's worth three boys."

As I grew to have more faith in myself, his words resonated.

I can't prove it, but I would bet my last dollar that if he had watched Hillary in a debate, he would have looked at me, nodding, pointed his finger at her, raising his eyebrows in approval. Clearly, he liked a tough cookie. My father was crazy, nuts, and at times, cruel, but if you could prove to my dad you were smarter than him, that was something he did respect.

I was not ready to grieve for him until fifteen years after his death, coincidentally around the time *Schindler's List* came out. I knew without reading any reviews that Steven Spielberg would do a brilliant job with the film. Standing in line, it was the only time I was nervous before a movie. When I got to my seat, I balled my legs up under me and cuddled into my sweater in preparation for the three hours of crying I knew I'd be doing. I glared at anyone who had the nerve to bring popcorn into the theatre. Toward the beginning of the film, there is a close-up of molars with gold fillings piled high on a table. That said it all. I'm so sorry, Dad.

I set about writing a book of prose called *The Healing Rites* to work through feelings I had locked away about my family's troubled journey. It was never published.

After David and I had been dating for a few weeks, he sat in my apartment one evening as I read him about two hours of the book I had written. He musta wanted to get with me bad. Our first Christmas together he commissioned a friend to make a ceramic pin for me. It was in the shape of a girl with wings. She was reading from a book. On it were written the words *The Healing Rites*. He is one of a kind.

When David and I got married in 1997, his dad John was still working overseas as a civil engineer and did not attend our wedding. Perhaps since David's parents were divorced, David's father wanted to leave his mom in possession of the field. I wanted to find a way to include him so I corresponded with him to share our wedding preparations. He was happy to discover his beloved son was marrying a woman who could assemble a coherent paragraph.

When we later went to visit him at his new home in Florida, he presented me with a long stemmed rose. David tilted his head quizzically and said, "Dad, the rose is made of plastic!" John threw his head back and laughed, and made me laugh. He hadn't noticed.

On the drive home from the airport, I was sitting in the back seat with David riding shotgun, and we two lefty liberals from California were giving John the Republican what for on politics, since we were Clinton fans. I made some snarky remark, and while on the freeway, John half turned over his shoulder, doubling down on his pleasant Tennessee accent and growled, "C'mowon, Anita!"

The ice was broken. I started calling him Dad.

I loved the way he played angry, getting hot under the collar arguing politics with me. He held it all in rather jolly perspective. He'd seen too many 'pols' come and go to get himself worked up. He called me his bar of Octagon Soap. From what I gathered, Octagon Soap is not too far from lye, strong enough to take the flesh from your bones. He meant it as a compliment. At least, that's what he said. He liked getting the straight scoop from me. We could talk about anything.

Back in 2000, apart from doing my civic duty as a voter, I was not involved in politics, so his vote one way or the other was not a topic of discussion. But in 2004, after four years of President Bush, we did our level best to convince Dad and his new wife to cross party lines and vote for John Kerry.

Dad had still not forgiven Kerry for giving back his medals after Viet Nam. No matter how I kept pointing out that President Bush had lied about the intelligence that got us into Iraq, or how badly they were executing the operation, or government corruption, it was a bust.

We had gotten into a few heated arguments over it. Then Dad dropped the bomb on us that he and his new wife had voted absentee. Not only had they voted for President Bush. They voted early. In Florida. It was all I could do to make myself talk to him after that. After a year's time, the bruised feelings dissipated.

I didn't realize it at the time, but I think he was the first Republican with whom I had ever discussed politics.

I appreciated that his love was never conditional. Though I adored my own father, if we had fought like that, he would have "disowned" me. He did that once when I was a kid and dared to argue with him. "You are no longer my daughter. Get out of my vicinity." There would be no talking to him until I came around to his way of thinking, crawled on his lap and apologized.

My father-in-law never did that, though I think he used to hit me with the conservative talking points just to see if he could get me riled up. But I was the one intimating, as many liberals do, that he must be nuts for being a Republican. I had no right. In fairness, I have had Republicans sneer at me for being a Democrat. I didn't care for that either.

In the 2008 race, my father-in-law knew we were huge Hillary supporters and I was surprised to find out that he liked her smarts and had some respect for her. He preferred her to Bill.

Once the Primaries ended and my writing for *NoQuarter* started in earnest, I put Dad on my mailing list and sent him copies of my articles. He forwarded my work to friends and family. In some of our conversations, we were so much in agreement, I'll bet he chuckled to himself, pulled the phone away from his ear and stared at the receiver, wondering if he had dialed the right number.

I told him I put country before party and didn't feel Senator Obama was up to the task at this time. Dad was sympathetic to my frustration, and didn't make fun of my sudden shift.

When he died suddenly on February 11, 2009, I felt lost. Who else would call me his bar of Octagon Soap? Who else would double down on his Southern accent till he sounded like Foghorn Leghorn and give me crap about whooping his ass at Chinese Poker? Who would ask after every new acting job I had coming up and give me so much encouragement – and make me laugh every time he called some talking head on the news a "runnin' dumb ass?"

We hadn't gotten to visit with him nearly enough those last few years. He was a generous man who supported everything we did. He was proud of us. Since my own father died so many years ago, I was grateful I got to say the word dad again. I was also thrilled to be welcomed into such a kind family.

John had a full and fascinating life, and with David's strong and generous mother had raised four beautiful sons.

I am sure he died happy, entertained by the thought that someday my husband and I might turn into Republicans.

I thought to myself, "Don't get too happy, Dad. Independent is as close as we'll get."

20 SEXISM AND MICHELLE OBAMA

A forthright, successful professional reduced to a fashion plate
tilling a victory garden in designer jeans and Lanvin sneakers. What
was wrong with Mrs. Obama before her transformation? Answer:
nothing.

Michelle Obama is an outspoken, educated woman over-managed
with constant makeovers. Soon after the inauguration, she
advertised new "softer" eyebrows and huge false eyelashes. For the
record, gluing those whimpers to your eyelids is about as
comfortable as wearing feather dusters on your face. She was also
touted by the press as a fashion icon and the unofficial minister of
culture. If Mrs. Obama liked that role, fine. But it would be
unfortunate in this day and age if she felt hamstrung by her handlers.

> "I don't want to have a say. Really, there are a lot of
> times when I'm like, don't tell me what happened
> today at work. I just don't want to hear it, because I
> want the home space to really be free of that." [248]

> -- Michelle Obama

> "[W]hat is with American society that it cannot
> accept a working spouse first lady? ...[I]t reconfirms
> my belief during the last election attitudes toward
> race moved markedly forward, but gender-bias was
> allowed to remain politically correct." [249]

> -- Bonnie Erbe, U.S. News & World Report

Ambitious, powerful women are still depicted as bad mother, sex object, out of control or, in Mrs. Obama's case, 50s mom and fashion plate. Why do we still need to homogenize women, buffing away raw edges?

Smile. Keep smiling.

I have sometimes felt like I'm too much, too loud, too quick, too emotional, too funny, too something. Sssshhh. But smile. And wear big, false eyelashes.

After Mr. Obama's twenty year attendance at Rev. Wright's church was revealed, pundits Chris Matthews and Chris Hitchens floated the idea that Obama's presence there was Michelle's fault. So while candidate Obama remained exalted in their eyes, his wife was not so lucky. But how is it possible that a forty-seven year old millionaire, bestselling author, US Senator, father and front-runner for the Presidency of the United States did not have the presence of mind to leave a church that didn't suit him, regardless of what his wife was doing? It was far more convenient for Matthews and Hitchens to project the inconvenient qualities of the male onto the female.

I later wrote a blog post about Michelle Obama getting a taste of being "Hillary'd"[250] via an article in the *UK Telegraph*. In March, 2009, the British Prime Minister, Gordon Brown, and his wife visited the President. President Obama presented PM Brown with the gift of 25 DVDs in an unwatchable format. Author James Delingpole determined that this, along with other ceremonial slights, was somehow the First Lady's fault. He theorized that her Princeton thesis, written twenty-five years before, translated into contempt for British hegemony, thereby prompting the less than stellar treatment PM Brown received.

The article refers to Michelle Obama as Lady Macbeth, the same name they had coined earlier to describe Hillary Clinton both in the US and the UK. By branding Michelle Obama as the ambitious, evil wife, this article is intimating that Barack Obama is not capable of thinking for himself. Blame the wife. She is telling her "weak husband" what to do.

This was a milder version of the claptrap that plagued Hillary for years. It is a familiar pattern to say, "Oh, he seems nice, but that wife of his!!" I know all too well what it is like for a husband with an easygoing manner to be the guy doing all the glad handing, while refusing to be the disciplinarian. That role goes to the wife by default. She winds up looking like the harridan by comparison. Whether conscious or unconscious, this is image management on the part of the man and not necessarily an accurate picture of the relationship.

I've been at parties watching the sidewalk act of married couples where the wife gets referred to as some contemporary slang for the "old ball and chain." Another nail in the coffin: "She's got me whipped. I just say yes, dear."

The responses I received to my blog post were enlightening. Some expressed the view that "it's the wife's job to keep the husband from looking foolish." Not unlike me being in charge of remembering to buy all the presents, regardless of whose family it is.

On the Internet, Mrs. Obama was likewise subjected to some horrific vitriol about her appearance. Focusing on physical imperfection is an old and obsessive habit and the easiest way to take a woman down. A ghost knows whom to scare. I have never known a woman to look in the mirror and not find something in herself to criticize. I am still captive to those judgments as well.

During the Primaries, in the name of carrying the political water for her husband, Mrs. Obama made an unfortunate comment when asked if she would support Hillary's candidacy were she to be the nominee:

"I'd have to think about that. I'd have to think about that, her policies, her approach, her tone."

While I was unhappy with that, along with several other of Michelle Obama's statements, it was inappropriate in my mind that she be used as a buffer or scapegoat for the President's actions.

The day after the UK article appeared, Secretary Clinton and Mrs. Obama were together at the International Women of Courage Awards. I watched the thirty-seven minute press conference, and from the grace these two ladies exhibited toward each other, you'd never know anything at all happened between them or their spouses the previous year. They stood together, warmly, for an important cause and I was moved by it. Mrs. Obama has already asked Secretary Clinton for advice on rearing children in the White House.

That seems a far departure from her earlier comments worrying about Hillary's "tone."

I have read in many corners that Hillary seems to grow on people. The closer they look, the better she looks.[251] As Hillary is "one of the most misunderstood figures in politics"[252] she has pointed out that over the years, many have apologized to her, saying they misjudged her – probably buying into talking points first rather than getting to know the source.

Upon Hillary Clinton's appointment as Secretary of State, Chris Matthews said "her spirit seemed to be with Obama" and she has "sublimated her ego." He was characterizing Clinton as submissive. No wonder he found Mrs. Obama's wifely image so appealing.

Predictably, Chris Matthews and others portrayed Michelle Obama as the anti-Hillary and applauded her staying away from policy by choice, foregoing ambition to assume a more classically feminine background role tilling her garden, visiting with cabinet staff, federal employees and military families, a good will ambassador for her husband.

Matthews seemed to revel in Mrs. Obama's behavior because it reflected the role he felt comfortable seeing a woman assume, a role of quiet, steadfast support to her spouse. Since she was polling at 79% popularity at the time of his statement, it appeared many agreed with him. He enjoyed that Michelle Obama was "deferential" enough not to pick a policy issue of her own and go after it. In my view, she's a smart lady and we need all the help we can get.

Thus far, staffers have done a wonderful job protecting Mrs. Obama from being vilified the way Hillary was as First Lady. And what did they think was the best way to do it? Put an apron on her and let her play with garden implements.

There is something downright regressive about the image they wish to paint, relentlessly "softening" her for the American public. Even her rhetoric out in public is more soft spoken and yielding, even emotional.

Several weeks after Mr. Matthews made his pronouncements about the "deferential" Mrs. Obama, an article in the *Washington Post* stated the First Lady was discontent with her background role and was vigorously working to have a more vital voice in her husband's

Administration. A couple of articles appeared touting her heightened involvement in the health care debate. But soon after, we returned to Michelle Obama, fashion icon.

On *This Week with George Stephanopoulos*,[253] panelists Claire Shipman and Cynthia Tucker echoed the sentiment that we live in a post-feminist world. They applauded how comfortable Mrs. Obama was in her new identity, not feeling the need to prove anything, to be either Hillary Clinton or Laura Bush. This romantic notion of post-feminism is something to be enjoyed over drinks at some swanky beltway bistro, but has little to do with the real world.

> "There is no post-feminism—that's like saying post-democracy."[254]

> -- Gloria Steinem

A fellow writer pointed out that attaching a label like post-feminist is something researchers call "defining away the problem." By pretending that sexism is a thing of the past, we no longer need to address it.

I wrote to the network:

> For those who declare that feminism is dead and is no longer necessary as a movement, that we live in a post-feminist world, I can only say if post-feminism translates into trashing and defaming a qualified woman daily, a world in which an act of violence is committed against a woman every few seconds in this country, a world where the most obscene negative characterizations of women are excused without consequence, then yes, I completely agree, we live in a post-feminist world.

> If we were done with sexism, we would not look to blame a wife for a husband's transgressions, nor would she require molding to make her less threatening. I will know it is safe to enter a post-feminist world when violence and violent rhetoric against women ends, when women have equal pay for equal work and an equal opportunity to advance without mind-bending double standards that were so evident this past election cycle. We will no longer

need to homogenize, make vanilla or make-over any women who may be different, outspoken or off-center.

As of this writing, Mrs. Obama is continuing President Clinton's cause in the fight against obesity, particularly as it affects children. It is my hope that Mrs. Obama becomes the type of First Lady she wishes to be, without handling. She has an opportunity to be a role model for so many young women. As much progress as women have seen, the fact that misogyny was once again made cool in 2008 shows how far we still need to travel.

Mr. Delingpole would not be the first person to try to project the negative traits of the male onto the female. Perhaps the reason he and others chose to blame Michelle Obama and to a greater degree, Hillary Clinton before her, is more out of fear of a powerful woman than anything else. This irrational fear or envy in part explains why we do not have a woman president as we speak.

21 CARRY ON, MADAME SECRETARY

President Obama's decision to appoint Hillary Clinton Secretary of State came as a surprise to many, and to Hillary herself, to hear her tell it. Despite the treatment she enjoyed at the hands of her own party she stepped up to serve her country, which told me I was correct to admire her in the first place. She didn't have a bad word to say about the colleagues who had delivered her such painful insults. Everything I liked about Hillary – her indefatigable nature, class and dedication – were qualities that had shown themselves throughout this journey. The theme of the good soldier had emerged once again.

Yet she was required to prove her worth by bowing her head repeatedly. Arrogance is not troubling in a man, but confidence in a woman still makes us queasy. Men can be ambitious but women are "conniving." The fact that she took her lumps at the Convention, sucked it up to serve the nominee, being "subservient" to him, somehow pleased more people than it bothered.

In January 2010, Joe Scarborough offered his assessment of Hillary Clinton's bid for the presidency in the *Huffington Post*:

> "Character is rarely revealed in its sharpest contrast after a glorious victory. Instead, you find out what a person is made of after they sustain a soul crushing defeat. In her long, tortured march toward Denver, Hillary Clinton showed more character, more

resilience, and more true grit than any presidential candidate I can recall.

And in that losing cause, Secretary Clinton served as a great example of character not only for my young daughter, but for us all. It is that type of strength that we need in our leaders now more than ever."[255]

As *Washington Post* columnist Marie Cocco noted, "...This wasn't a breakthrough year for American women in politics. It was a brutal one."

What I witnessed in 2008 and beyond made it unlikely I would see a woman president in my lifetime. I agreed with Ms. Cocco's pained assessment that "the glass ceiling remains firmly in place"[256]

Women may now be free to pursue any field they wish, yet the ratio of males to females in positions of authority is still skewed. In a December 2009 study of 2,000 of the world's top performing companies, only 29 of those CEOs were women."[257] As of 2011, women in elected U.S. government positions numbered 16%, though women are 52% of the population.

Ms. Cocco quoted Barbara Lee, who owns a Boston based family foundation that conducts extensive research on gubernatorial races involving women: "There are no female Arnold Schwarzeneggers." "That is, no woman will ever burst into politics, capture the voters' imagination and be catapulted into high public office without a lick of experience." But Hillary Clinton wasn't a female Arnold. She was and is qualified to handle the office.

Barbara Lee also stated:

"Voters demand more experience of a woman candidate, and judge her competence separately from whether she is sufficiently "likable." "We heard that over and over again — that no woman is ever right. They like the concept of it but when it comes to a real, live, breathing candidate, they don't."

Hillary Clinton shared with reporter John Heilemann that she was mistaken in fixating on the commander-in-chief hurdle:

"I frankly made a wrong assumption about how to present myself to the country. This seemed to me to be looming over everything. I knew if I couldn't cross it, nothing else would matter. I believe that I've succeeded certainly in diminishing if not eliminating the commander-in-chief barrier for women candidates in the future."[258]

Whether she had made a wrong assumption on that score is open for debate, since one misty moment in New Hampshire led the attack dogs to declare that she was going to "cry her way back to the White House."[259] If she had instead presented herself as someone who had worked on behalf of children and families her entire life, as communications director Howard Wolfson and others on her team had advised, she might have been taken to task on that score, too, and condemned for having what Marc Rudov of FOX News called a "female agenda."[260]

In her book, *Cracking the Code – the Barbara Lee Foundation Political Intelligence for Women Running for Governor*, Ms. Lee clarified the butter:

> "For female candidates, personal qualities and performance often outweigh substantive issues with voters.
>
> A female candidate's mistakes at [unscripted] moments are more vivid and longer lasting than similar gaffes committed by male candidates.
>
> Title and executive authority matter... voters are even more confident in a statewide office holder who has exercised the power of her office, thereby demonstrating competence, authority and confidence."

If what Ms. Lee avers is true, then if Mr. Obama were a woman of any color running for president with his resume, he would not have been taken seriously. Did anyone ask what kind of a father Obama is? Or criticize his wardrobe choices? Or ask whether or not he was qualified to take this job at this most challenging time in our nation's history? No one would dare.

We were willing to elect a man on the basis of hope and vision. A woman would not get the benefit of the doubt.

Hillary Clinton could boast many accomplishments that never saw the light of day with the American people. In Richard Wolffe's book *Renegade: The Making of a President*, Obama was quoted as stating he knew from the middle of the primaries, when he was "pretty sure he was going to win," that he wanted Hillary for Secretary of State and thought she would be excellent in that position. Surely, her qualifications were as evident to him as they were to her supporters. Yet many voters were snowed by his assertions about her "tea parties" and her "claws" coming out.

By distracting ourselves with superfluous concerns, we distract ourselves from the woman's message. It is harder to see and hear what a woman stands for if appearance, character smears and vocal quality trump policy positions.

The Nation's Katha Pollitt wrote she was happy Hillary Clinton did not get elected because, among other reasons, she didn't want to listen to the endless sexist diatribes that would follow – blaming any flaws of her administration on the fact that she is a woman. I understood her sentiments. I had even worried that if we were to elect a woman president, violence against women would go up. Having viewed the violent pictorials aimed at Hillary Clinton and Sarah Palin on the internet, that was not an off the wall assumption.

Secretary Clinton would catch hell as the first woman in office yet I refused to hope she would lose just to spare myself the pain of watching. If she was willing to put up with it, what excuse did I have for hiding from what would inevitably follow? A woman cannot dispel old myths if I don't give her an opportunity to prove them wrong.

It appeared Ms. Pollitt also felt Hillary and Obama were interchangeable and would govern the same way. I was surprised she could assume they were cookie cutouts of one another when they had different experiences, disciplines and perspectives. If that was her way of reassuring herself for her decision, I could not agree.

While one might offer many reasons for not voting for someone, if the male ego cannot tolerate a woman having the last word in any circumstance, I have doubts he will ever vote for a woman. Further, if a woman is perceived as taking something away from the man that he might otherwise have, the male is not only competing with his own gender, but has to fend off the encroaching female. That threat has somehow to be addressed. And if a woman does not trust herself, she may not trust another woman to have the final word, either.

Women are now forever part of the Presidential debate. If we are ever to have competent female leadership then we need to stop trashing competent women, otherwise a qualified woman bruising her head on the "highest, hardest glass ceiling" is as close as she's ever going to get to the Presidency.

* * *

Celebrating Hillary's appointment as Secretary of State, I bristled at the media's revisionist history. Senior NBC Correspondent Andrea Mitchell, who gushed that this was the job Hillary was born to do, as if in apology, wasn't cutting it. Big media's new narrative, all's well that ends well, did little to blunt the injustice of their earlier coverage.

During her eight-year tenure, Hillary had built a reputation as a Senator for keeping her head down, being collegial and getting the job done. Yet in her nomination to this cabinet post, *Vanity Fair's* Christopher Hitchens appeared on MSNBC's "Hardball" and called her a "ludicrous embarrassment." That this lady held her head high and continued to do her job despite petty tyrants who were nipping at her heels said plenty.

I couldn't believe I had to listen to this horse hooey. Having watched her in action at press conferences, briefings and interviews, more often than not, she seemed to regard disrespectful remarks as little more than fly spittle. I made an effort to follow Hillary's example, with varying degrees of success. I still felt the urge to rush to her defense.

Then President-elect Obama's chief speech writer, twenty-seven year old Jon Favreau, showed himself to be a bit of a knuckle dragger, too. In December of 2008, flanked by another aide, Favreau groped the chest of a full sized cardboard cutout of Secretary Clinton while his pal stuck a beer to her mouth. Mr. Favreau posted this photograph on his Facebook page. The photo went viral.

Sharing the picture in *Vanity Fair*, former White House press secretary Dee Dee Myers offered the following:

> "What's bugging me is his intention. He isn't putting his hand on her "chest," as most of the articles and conversations about the picture have euphemistically

referred to it. Rather, his hand—cupped just so—is clearly intended to signal that he's groping her breast. And why? Surely, not to signal he finds her attractive. Au contraire. It's an act of deliberate humiliation. Of disempowerment. Of denigration.

And it disgusts me.

...Her spokesman, Phillipe Reinnes, tried to make light of the incident. "Senator Clinton is pleased to learn of Jon's obvious interest in the State Department, and is currently reviewing his application."

... At what point do people get punished in ways that suggest this kind of behavior, this kind of thinking, is unacceptable?"[261]

My concern was the eternal nature of the Internet. Never put anything on the web you don't want plastered on the front page of the *New York Times*. That picture might be viewed anywhere in the world. Was that the message a valued Presidential operative wished to send to foreign leaders about the lack of respect they had for President Obama's chosen Secretary of State? Was that a display of "Smart Power"?

* * *

Watching Hillary Clinton's confirmation hearings in January, 2009, one Senator asked her about Third World countries that modeled good use of their mineral rights. Without pausing, Hillary said, "Well, you know, Senator, in Botswana..."

"You tell 'em, Hill," I crowed.

I stood from the sofa, doing a two-armed baseball stadium type wave toward the TV. Our two tuxedo cats looked up at me. There she goes again.

I laughed as Hillary offered a detailed answer to the Senator's question. I enjoyed our Hermione Granger. I couldn't help it. She likewise answered Senator Boxer's query making clear her intention to put the rights of women worldwide at the forefront of her agenda. As Tina Brown put it, Hillary was an example of "what real female power looks like," a "dedicated policy wonk who worked on behalf of oppressed women in unpronounceable places long before it was fashionable."[262]

Reporting on the hearings, Dana Milbank of the *Washington Post* complained:

> "At Hillary Clinton's confirmation hearing yesterday, senators came up with a new interpretation of the Constitution's "advice and consent" clause. This one could be called the "admire and congratulate" clause."

It appeared Mr. Milbank could not bear the thought of Hillary receiving praise from her colleagues. But considering that the source was someone who later issued an apology to Secretary Clinton for saying she should be drinking "Mad Bitch Beer,"[263] his comment was understandable.

The snark just made all these guys, and the jealous gals who joined in with them, seem foolish. I wondered that they didn't know that. By Hillary's choice to kill 'em with kindness, put her shoes on and keep going, she made her detractors look tired and small. They could not defeat her. And for twenty years, many had tried.

As Maya Angelou said: "Rise, Hillary, Rise."

Even conservatives like former Secretary of State Henry Kissinger and Republican Senator John Kyl had praised her appointment. She was confirmed as Secretary of State by a Senate vote of 94 to 2.

> "At 11 this morning, Senator Hillary Clinton of New York will also take the floor to say goodbye. That'll be an emotional moment because everyone knows Hillary Clinton earned that Senate seat and very much loves that place. In fact, is loved a lot in the Senate. She has really become one of the members of that Senate club."[264]

> -- Chris Matthews, MSNBC
> from *Media Matters'* article, "Chris Matthews Eats Crow"

* * *

The day after his Inauguration, President Obama joined Vice President Biden, Secretary Clinton and envoys Mitchell and Holbrooke in presenting a united front. They appeared together before State Department diplomats ushering in a new day. Mr. Obama then said the nicest thing I have heard him say, "I gave you all a great gift. Her name is Hillary Clinton."

The tears came as I watched the video of Hillary Clinton being sworn in. I was relieved someone of her caliber would be representing us around the world and knew she would temper President Obama's naïve foreign policy notions with strength and common sense. Still, it was not the swearing in ceremony I wanted to see.

> "And finally, to my husband, who understands so well the awesome responsibilities resting on the shoulders of President Obama and Vice President Biden and all of us who serve with them. I am so grateful to him for a lifetime of... all kinds of experiences – (audience laughter) – which have given me a – (applause) – which have given me an extraordinary richness that I am absolutely beholden to and grateful for."
>
> -- Official Swearing-in Ceremony,
February 2, 2009

Commentator Peter Beinart touted her skill set but didn't want her to take the job, advising *Don't Do It, Hillary.*[265] Since cabinet positions are by appointment, he worried she would be made the scapegoat for any failures of the Administration and later fired, her political career over. Many of us out in the blogosphere were worried about that, too.

Some were furious she would be serving under an administration whose inside team had been disrespectful to her during the primary and felt she should walk away. I was one among a number of bloggers jumping in to defend her decision, sensing she would be far better than either Senator John Kerry or Governor Bill Richardson, two other hopefuls who desperately wanted the job.

In her Primary campaign, she reached out for every vote, whether she thought she would receive a cool reception or a standing ovation. As Secretary of State, she continued that tradition by employing her favorite forum, effectively holding town halls in cities around the world. She called them "town-terviews."

She had a much greater opportunity to affect change from within the administration than by skulking in a corner. Her rock star status and the warm receptions she received around the world have proved a bonus in efforts to alter perceptions of the U.S. formed during the Bush Administration.

Several books were published in the first year of Obama's Presidency touting him and belittling Hillary. This was odd considering she was so respectful of the chain of command. I couldn't help but sense that bruised egos needed once again to put the woman "in her place." If it wasn't about the issues, it was drivel.

The book *Game Change* by reporters John Heilemann and Mark Halperin stated that fellow New York Senator Chuck Schumer supported Clinton to her face, but behind her back told Obama "to take a 2x4 to Hillary." Secretary Clinton has since called Senator Schumer to say she believes no such thing ever happened. Gracious to the last, we will never know what she believes. As they say, in politics, if you want a friend get a dog.

If the statement is a lie, shame on the reporters for making it. If it is true, shame on Senator Schumer. And no, I will never forgive or forget what I witnessed.

In order to sell more copy and keep the Barack vs. Hillary drama alive, news outlets spread the word that Hillary was the most marginalized Secretary of State in modern history, a woman without portfolio, a ceremonial post.

In her first exclusive interview as Secretary of State, George Stephanopoulos mentioned special envoys Richard Holbrooke and George Mitchell who had been dispatched to the Middle East. Implying that Hillary had been pushed aside and had nothing to do, he said, "What is your role?"

I added my two cents. "She's their boss, George. She tells them what to do. That's her role!"

Secretary Clinton then smiled and offered her answer undeterred, "There's plenty of work to go around."

In truth, Secretary Clinton campaigned on the need to hire envoys for regions requiring special attention. She approached her new post the same way she approached the Senate, by keeping a low profile until she learned the turf. She mastered her brief. It became quite clear that, to use the words of CNN's Anderson Cooper: "She's large and in charge." Secretary Clinton has also been credited on many fronts as having, in short order, put diplomacy back under the charge of the State Department, rather than the military.[266]

On May 13, 2009, Secretary of State Hillary Clinton was presented an honorary degree from NYU as she gave their commencement speech. She spoke of the power of citizen diplomats and mentioned two college students who used the power of Facebook to organize 14 million people in Columbia against terrorism. She encouraged all citizens to become more involved to affect positive change. More and more, we seemed to be taking her advice. I prayed for the trend to continue.

She has received many prestigious awards and accolades that by and large go unreported in the American press. In 2009, Secretary Clinton received the Roosevelt Institute's Four Freedoms Medal, honoring "a lifetime of distinguished service and an unwavering commitment to freedom." Previous honorees include Presidents Truman, Kennedy, Carter and Clinton; Coretta Scott King; Elie Wiesel; Justices William Brennan and Thurgood Marshall, the Dalai Lama, Shimon Peres, Kofi Annan and Nelson Mandela.

Lack of media attention to her achievements bothered me a lot more than it bothered Hillary. Yet it is a troubling behavior. Young girls need to celebrate the achievements of women as they learn to celebrate their own accomplishments. You can't celebrate what you've never heard of.

During the 2008 campaign, the *Los Angeles Times*[267] had made this comment about Hillary's service as First Lady:

> "As for overseas travel, the papers show that Clinton did spend some time conferring with foreign leaders on strategic issues. But the records suggest she spent a lot more time fulfilling the traditional role of the first lady: meeting the leaders' wives and focusing on women's and children's issues."

As if in rebuttal, while addressing the Barnard graduating class on May 21, 2009, Secretary Clinton once again echoed her deeply held sentiments:

"Although not always acknowledged by governments, businesses, or society overall, women and girls bear a disproportionate burden of most of the problems we face today. In the midst of this global economic crisis, women who are already the majority of the world's poor are driven deeper into poverty. In places where food is scarce, women and girls are often the last to eat, and eat the least. In regions torn apart by war and conflict, women are more likely to be refugees or targets of sexual violence. . .

And women's progress is more than a matter of morality. It is a political, economic, social and security imperative for the United States and for every nation represented in this graduating class. If you want to know how stable, healthy, and democratic a country is, look at its women, look at its girls."

When a country's women thrive, their economy and society thrive also. To classify dealing with women's and children's issues as anything less than critical is the very definition of sexism. Some found this agenda unimportant. This was a sad indictment of the lack of value women have in society. It seemed fitting if unfortunate that a woman on the receiving end of so much bias was and is fighting for the rights of women elsewhere.

While she had often been referred to as mannish, Secretary Clinton has taken a feminine approach toward advancing women's rights around the world. There are still times a woman is not at liberty to be direct, so when dealing with societies where women are oppressed, Clinton looks for the way around, still aiming for the desired result. By appealing to foreign governments on the grounds that women's progress makes economic sense and will advance the interests of each respective society, rather than lecturing about morality, she is more likely to move this agenda forward.

A year into her tenure as Secretary of State, she was polled as the most popular person in President Obama's cabinet. In January 2010, the *Washington Post* indicated that he was our most polarizing president. I could only stare at the page in amazement. One year.

As her confidence built with her tenure, media coverage devoted more time to her "transformation." Yet it seemed they were the ones who had been transformed. Perhaps reporters had slowed down enough to take a deeper look, rather than contenting themselves with their prior judgments of her. They were finally witnessing the person Hillary was all along. Not the vile witch of their projections. There was an almost unspoken surprise in much of their writing.

The image of Hillary that had been cultivated in the media over eighteen years seemed to be rehabilitating. A glowing feature appeared in *Vogue* in December 2009, *Her Brilliant Career*, discussing Hillary's maternal nature, generosity to her staff, good humor and tireless work ethic.

Critique of the inner workings of Hillary Clinton's presidential campaign operation led some to make the accusation that she would not govern well. Yet in *Esquire*, she was credited with "running one of the most important departments in the federal government, and running it as if to reform it is to redeem it, and herself."[268]

Washington Post writer Lois Romano reported:

> "We have had other secretaries of state who have cared deeply for the institution," said Patrick F. Kennedy, undersecretary for management and a senior Foreign Service officer. "None who have done as much internal outreach."

> "She fully understands that when she came in there was a weak and degraded platform. You need it to be refreshed with new people and new blood, and that's what we are getting in now."

> "She has walked the halls and popped into offices unexpectedly, created an electronic "sounding board," and held seven internal town hall meetings... is taking steps to remedy overseas pay inequities and instituted a policy that allows partners of gay diplomats to receive benefits. She became a heroine to the Foreign Service when she went to bat to get funding for 3,000 new Foreign Service positions for State operations and the U.S. Agency for

International Development — the first boost of this magnitude in two decades."[269]

Clinton also had unprecedented hiring authority at the State department – about 200 political jobs "from the most senior level to the 20-something researchers" – usually it is the president who fills these positions.[270] Her budget briefing surprised many. Rather than being a pro-forma meeting, she turned it into "a line-by-line review that took three sessions to complete."[271]

Ms. Romano reported that Secretary Clinton had evidenced her leadership skills in other ways. Shamila Chaudary, 32, a "self-described backbencher" and "faceless expert on the Pakistan desk" was invited to brief Clinton on the importance of engaging non-governmental power centers in Pakistan. A heated debate between the two women followed, yet:

> [Chaudary] said that although she and Clinton "didn't necessarily agree . . . she said that it's very important for us to debate like this. . . . This is how she said she wants to do business."
>
> Within 48 hours of their meeting, Chaudary was promoted to a front-line job in the office of policy planning."[272]

One of her deputies confided to Tom Junod of *Esquire* that no matter how difficult a year it had been politically, "her loyalty to Obama has been incredible. She never says 'my agenda'; she says 'our agenda.' ... She is incredibly disciplined and she never complains. I couldn't fucking do it."[273]

As Mr. Junod notes, President Obama knew he needed a powerhouse to handle foreign policy to free him up to deal with his overwhelming domestic agenda:

> "One result of her loyalty is that she's made him look good. It's right there in the polls: Americans approve of Obama's foreign policy far more than they approve of his domestic agenda. Which means that she's also made him look bad."

And

"...the quality she brings to the job is not her celebrity but rather her unfathomable and almost unsettling doggedness."

From Junod's comments, her work ethic seemed downright intimidating to him. He also wrote of her "unforgivable competence." But isn't that what we want? Someone who knows what they're doing.

To whom was her competence unforgivable?

After trailing Secretary Clinton to write his feature story, Mr. Junod determined her revitalization and reformation of the previously "broken" state department probably proved she would make a great president "now," while in the same breath stating that she has "lost her chance forever" to get the job.

In 2016, at 68 years of age, she would be confronting sexism and ageism. Whether either ailment would be gone from the collective psyche by then was doubtful, so perhaps she would not have another chance at the Presidency. Yet I could not help but read Mr. Junod's assessment as his need to define her by the comfortable limits he had set for her.

Like many others, he gave himself the power to predict Hillary's future. Someone should have told him that Scorpios are good at reinventing themselves. Hillary had done this more times than most people can count. Like the Phoenix, she had risen from the ashes.

Junod also decided that if she were successful in "resetting the relationship" with Russia and securing a new arms treaty, it wouldn't be owing to her fame, but "because she knows how to deal with difficult men..."

I laughed reading this, remembering that as a Senator she'd built the reputation for working so well with older Republican males, who in past years had tried their best to function as her kryptonite. By all accounts, Mrs. Clinton's father was a tough character, too. Some survival skills never leave us.

She is now referred to as the "bad cop"[274] to Obama's good cop, and has of late been affectionately called "Hillary the hammer" and "the iron fist in the velvet glove" in more conservative circles. All have acknowledged her growing influence in shaping policy.

In the *New York Times*, Ross Douthat observed that in 1992 "much of conservative America viscerally recoiled from Hillary Clinton's career-woman persona. Now Clinton has become many conservatives' favorite liberal..."[275] Will wonders never cease?

The *Esquire* article concluded...

> "She is not soft. She simply hardens herself through her own rituals of endurance, and that makes her harder than her boss could ever be. The problem Barack Obama has faced abroad is the same one he has faced at home: For some reason, people have no qualms about telling him no."

* * *

Like her, hate her, the speculation and obsession about Secretary Clinton continues. As of June 2010, according to CBS' Sixty Minutes, her popularity stood at 77%, which was 26% higher than that of her boss. A Rasmussen poll then determined more Americans thought Hillary was more qualified to be president than Mr. Obama, or any other leading Republican contender for that matter.[276] Divisive and polarizing no more.

At around the same time, Secretary Clinton struck a populist tone and waded into the current economic situation:

> "The United States' huge national debt — now topping $13 trillion — is becoming a major threat to U.S. security and leadership in the world."

> "We cannot sustain this level of deficit financing and debt without losing our influence, without being constrained in the tough decisions we have to make," Clinton said, adding that it was time to "make the national security case about reducing the deficit and getting the debt under control."

Clinton emphasized controlling the budget deficit, saying it was "personally painful" for her to see the yawning U.S. spending gap after her husband, former President Bill Clinton, ended his second term in 2001 with budget surpluses.[277]

She also complained that "the rich are not paying their fair share" in taxes while making clear it was "only her opinion":

"...Brazil has the highest tax-to-GDP rate in the Western Hemisphere and guess what – they're growing like crazy," Clinton said. "And the rich are getting richer, but they're pulling people out of poverty."

"There is a certain formula there that used to work for us, until we abandoned it, to our regret in my opinion," she added.[278]

Predictably, some in the media and blogosphere read her remarks on the deficit, which had ballooned horribly since President Obama took office, as a rare shot across the bow. Yet all the postulating about what a backstabber she was or "what a problem" Bill Clinton and his global foundation would be proved baseless. None of these worries about "backstabbing" had come to pass.

All at once, pundits and insiders like John Fund, Leslie Gelb and Sally Quinn were clamoring for Hillary to help President Obama win re-election, as his poll numbers had dropped precipitously due to the continued troubled economy and the disaster of the BP oil spill damaging the gulf in 2010.

Once again, mommy's presence was required.

In her *Washington Post* editorial, Sally Quinn decided that Secretary Clinton and Vice President Biden should switch jobs, proclaiming that Hillary was "cheerful, thoughtful, serious and diligent." Like a puppy. Or a fifties housewife. Hillary was only there to serve the man. Quinn's outmoded comments made me think I was living inside an episode of "Mad Men."

These pundits were as much as admitting that her strength and leadership were critically needed, yet they couldn't bring themselves to admit she ought to have the top job. Hillary was the true visionary and the true progressive. Maybe she couldn't sell the brand as well, but I sensed she knew what to do once she got in there.

Long one of her detractors, Peggy Noonan of the *Wall Street Journal* offered her assessment of the sea change in Washington as the 2010 midterm elections approached:

"...[I]t's also true that among Democrats—and others—when the talk turns to the presidency it turns more and more to Hillary Clinton. "We may have made a mistake. She would have been better." Sooner or later the secretary of state is going to come under fairly consistent pressure to begin to consider 2012. A hunch: She won't really want to. Because she has enjoyed being loyal. She didn't only prove to others she could be loyal, a team player. She proved it to herself. And it has only added to her luster."[279]

If Hillary Clinton has had any sort of failing, it would be that she was and is too loyal. She has been lambasted many years for the same, for staying with her husband, for her loyal long-term staff – dubbed "Hillary-land." And even for her intense loyalty to the Democratic Party. She had nothing to prove on the loyalty front. These speculators hadn't a clue what made this lady tick. As Hillary herself said "At the end of the day, have you solved the problem or haven't you? Have you crossed it off the list or haven't you?"[280]

Mainstream media daily pondered her future, suggesting everything from a Supreme Court nomination, to running for Governor of New York to being named the new Secretary of Defense when Secretary Gates retired.

There was much spit balling about her distancing herself from the current administration to offer a primary challenge to President Obama, and still more about Secretary Clinton being asked to replace Vice President Biden on the Obama ticket in 2012, "thereby teeing her up for 2016."[281]

It remained to be seen if association with the policies of the Obama administration and current Democratic leadership would help or hinder her chances at another presidential run. Pundits touted Obama's brilliant "master stroke" of neutralizing the Clintons by appointing Hillary Secretary of State, thereby taking away her ability to campaign or raise money, since a cabinet member is prohibited from doing so. Yet, she was the one who had delivered the master stroke, by standing above the fray. Now it is Hillary, worker bee extraordinaire and diplomat who stands apart from the mess, the most popular person in President Obama's administration.

Even the *Wall St. Journal* was encouraging her to challenge Obama and run for President in 2012. From *The New York Times* to *The Huffington Post*, that cry grew louder across America. *The Chicago*

Tribune then delivered a hometown slap, proposing that President Obama "pull an LBJ" and step down in favor of Hillary.[282]

Secretary Clinton went on the record to say she was interested in doing none of this.

Needless to say, no one believed her.

22 THE COST OF INDEPENDENCE
AND OTHER RUMINATIONS

My mother taught me how to show up. I taught myself how to leave the subservient part of her legacy behind.

In May of 2008, my mom had a bad fall on the sidewalk in front of her apartment building. She was banged up and seriously shaken. It took her some time to recover. Her new frailty reminded me that my hero was mortal after all. The thought of losing her daily loomed large in my mind. I was grateful that after years of living so far apart, we could see each other regularly, but there hadn't been enough time. Please don't let her get sick now, especially not during such a depressing year.

I was both frustrated and terrified at being pulled back into an all too familiar situation of family illness. Especially since little miss fix it didn't have any power to fix it. Being involved in Hillary's campaign was a relief, somewhere to make myself useful since I felt helpless at home.

In the two years that followed, we underwent another odyssey with my mom's health. Confronting her mortality, I confronted my own. 2008 was quite a year to turn fifty. I remembered that's how old my mother was when she collapsed. I thought about the differences in our paths and how much easier my life was than hers.

By June 2010 she had once again recuperated. More fragile, perhaps, but still kicking. We got back to her apartment after her MRI and a bit of lunch at our favorite Mexican bistro. She got comfortable in her big chair as I fetched her blood pressure cuff. I sat on the floor in front on her, pushing her sleeve up to wrap the fabric contraption around her arm. She looked down at me with her party smile. That smile is a bit more tentative now, but still lovely. The angle of her face at that moment was the same as my favorite photograph of her, taken so many years before in a park on New York's Riverside Drive.

She wore a blue chiffon sheath that day, her long black hair upswept in a French twist. Alone in the picture, Mom smiled at my sister and me. Her loving expression was the way I always liked to think of her. I pushed the button to start the cuff expanding.

"Think happy thoughts," I said.

She laughed at me. I'm controlling as ever.

"How do you do it," she said. "You're some girl."

She probably thought I worked harder than I did. But I appreciated her words just the same. My mind wandered as I waited for the blood pressure machine to give us the readout. I thought back to the one time I had seen her happy.

After Mom was widowed and on her own in the eighties, it was a thriving time in the fur business. Her boss sent her, along with several others from the manufacturing staff, on weekend sales trips to high end department stores in the tri-state area to sell the coats. She worked a ton of extra hours, but loved the adventure of going on mini road trips. She had even made a female friend, Bea. I'd never known my Mom to have a friend. She talked about Bea all the time. And she talked about herself, for once, in a positive way.

Since my mother was such a stylish person, "the Countess" knew what coat would be flattering on any woman, no matter her build, just by looking at her. She became more social. Even better, she was selling more coats than anyone. Her melodic laughter filled the room as she marveled about how well she did, how much the customers favored her. "You know, they like talking to me!"

She stopped going to the bank for money orders and got a checkbook instead.

"Ani, I paid the bills just fine. *No problem!*"

She blossomed and for once, believed in herself. For a moment, she realized that what my father said about her wasn't true.

Seeing her grow in confidence had an effect on me. She was healthy and happy. She relaxed and I did, too. I felt free to chase my own goals. But confidence was something I developed mechanically and at a slow pace. Not long ago my mom told me she was glad I pursued my acting career since she was never able to follow her dream to be a singer.

Mom puts up with me hugging her now. As a child, I would sit next to her on the couch at the end of her long work day, wanting to embrace her. It wasn't long before she'd jump up, remembering something else that needed doing. But now she'll just sort of stand there with her arms around me and relax into my embrace. It's taken us a long time to get here.

It feels good to have her close, even though she has had to deal with my moods, defensiveness and gut grinding rage during the election. I'm sure she, like some of my friends, thought I'd gone off the deep end. If Chris Matthews were reviewing me, he'd have called me "strident." Well, he'd have called me worse if he knew what I'd had to say about him.

Most, if not all, of my friends were Hillary supporters. They'd voted for her in the primary and were unhappy she was not the nominee. A good portion of them decided to move on and vote for Senator Obama in the general election. That's the way things are done. During the primary, when I pointed out the differences between these two candidates, I could see a few of them shrinking away. They were going to vote for whoever had the (D) after his/her name, "even if he were a geranium," as one friend put it.

By the time October of 2008 rolled around, I was pretty sure what the result would be, whether I said so or not. After eight years of President Bush and the neo-cons, this was a no lose year for Democrats. As Senator McCain's campaign manager Rick Davis said the night before the election, "It's not a good year to be a Republican."

Barack Obama was my President, too, no matter my concerns about his readiness for the gig.

The issue of the egregious bias in the campaign was still in the forefront of my mind. Friends asked me what I'd been up to and I told them about my writing. While they wished to be supportive, I sensed one or two didn't want to hear it. They were talked out on the subject. Perhaps they regarded my work as an obsession that would bear no fruit, or, protective of me, they didn't want me to feel disappointment. I sensed they felt frustrated and didn't want to dwell on information they felt powerless to change.

I had a colleague tell me that the reason the events of 2008 so upset me was because of my dysfunctional upbringing. I found it hard to believe anyone would have enjoyed seeing a woman called some version of bitch on national television daily. So, no, I didn't buy her theory. Perhaps for her to admit what went on in 2008, she'd have to admit she had turned away while it was happening. We could no longer say it was only Hillary Clinton, or Sarah Palin, or Michelle Obama or Justice Sonia Sotomayor or Elizabeth Warren. The list was growing of women it was okay to demonize.

If I acknowledged newscasters' wrongdoing, how could I watch them again? If I acknowledged the abandoning behavior of Democratic Party elders while Hillary was being excoriated, how could I vote for them again? How could I believe they had principles when they allowed one of their own to be dragged through the mud because it served their purposes?

My newfound unwillingness to sip the Kool-Aid of either party made a few people uncomfortable. I could feel the tension in their bodies: "Gee, I hope she won't bring *that* up again!" They were struggling to get by like so many in our difficult economy and didn't want to hear anything but good news about those in charge. I understood. But still felt I had to speak up if I thought we were on the wrong path.

I called myself out on the carpet for all the times I had turned a blind eye to other abuses. Remembering Daddy was mean to Mommy did make me hyper aware and I reached my boiling point faster. My collected memories of injustice against women dictated my actions and my need to not turn away this time. Something in me was altered by what I saw. Many who are removed from politics may not have been aware it was happening, making it simpler to breathe easy now.

My own insecurity left me feeling like I was being laughed at for my need to put this on paper. As this is a diary of sorts, it would be dishonest not to share these feelings no matter how uncomfortable.

Acting was always enough of a calling for me. I was no longer sure where I fit in that world. Without pretense, discussing the need for real and open political dialogue with both sides, to stop bias from whence it comes feels like a mission worth the attempt. I had no idea who was listening. I felt the voice that was small. That was part of the reason I refrained from engaging sooner.

Who cares what I think? Just shut up and sit down. Shut up and sit down. Shut up and sit down.

I had nightmares I would be punished for my words. Someone would come to take me away. Dad's voice was still with me, though a bit softer.

I told myself 'Finish it. Finish what you start. Then you can kiss it up to God and be free. Don't be afraid even if you think David Axelrod is as big and scary as Dick Cheney and he's got a Gitmo list, too. Finish it. Tell the story. Like that irritating Nike Ad says: Just Do It.'

Close friends were present above and beyond the call of duty throughout my newfound activism and lent no end of support, even the ones who didn't agree with me.

My best pal, dealing with the stress of family illness these past several years, allowed herself a rare quiet moment by the beach in Santa Monica. On the tree lined street of Ocean Boulevard sitting in a gazebo overlooking the Pacific, she saw a lizard scurry out of the brush. He began to do pushups in the noonday sun.

"You must be joking," I said.

Then I Googled "lizards do pushups" and got 46,400 hits. They like to flex their pecs for attention, either to mark their territory or to attract a mate. I asked her why she thought to share this with me.

"Even the most delicate of creatures have muscle," she said.

When those dear to me offered encouraging words, I thanked them, even the shaky ones, for what they taught me about myself, my own doubts and limitations, my willfulness and my determination. Even my anger has been a gift because a funny thing happened on the way to the election. My principles became more important than being liked. Smoothing things over used to be number one on my agenda.

Looking back, the conclusions I came to are not as important as the fact that I came to a reasoned conclusion at all. The best weapon I have as a citizen is to think for myself and look past the easy sound bite, making decisions not based on what is convenient or popular, but by doing something that both Al Gore and the late George Carlin said corporate America doesn't want us to do – engage in critical thought.

I've surprised myself by realizing that while I am liberal on most issues, I am conservative on a few. I no longer dance to anyone's particular tune. I reflected on my old biases and attitudes and realized I parroted much out of unconscious habit via the influence of parents, peers or Party. It was threatening to challenge a belief system. I had seen people end longtime friendships rather than to rip open a sore.

I became free to investigate messages I had previously rejected. I may choose to reject them yet again but I will have made an informed decision. No party will be able to take my vote for granted.

My informed decision led me to Hillary, the practical choice. I appreciated how specific she would be with each state she visited. It spoke volumes that she took the time to learn and understand each audience, not just give a pat stump speech regardless of the realities on the ground.

My need to be practical in all things has been the antidote to my impractical career choice as an actor. The search for what is solid in my life was also a reaction to a childhood where the ground was forever shifting under my feet. It's no surprise that of my father's many proverbs, my favorite by far was "slow and steady wins the race."

Not knowing whether I was going to get kissed or slapped, peering underneath the surface was important to me. When observing a person or place that looked inviting, I'd ask, "What's that really like?"

Secretary Clinton also reminded me of the value of going the extra mile for something you think is worth fighting for.

As a rank and file actor, my buddies and I talked about leaving it all on the table when trying to get a job. No one likes rejection and would avoid anything to be told you didn't make it, you're not good enough. It is easier to make excuses. I didn't have the material long enough, my car broke down, I had a fight with my significant whoever, traffic sucked.

Like the lady said, she gave it everything she had. Many made note that Hillary taught boys and girls everywhere how to fight on till the buzzer sounded. Spending much of my life in fear of looking foolish or being wrong, it was a good lesson for me to learn.

Drinking my own special iced coffee concoction, setting several years' worth of outrage aside for a moment, I ruminated over a couple of things for which there are no obvious solutions on the horizon. One, we still treat women like crap when it suits us and many won't admit it. Two, both political parties currently do little more than pay lip service to their faithful. They spend less time doing the people's business and more time focused on their own.

I sipped slowly and wondered if those who did stop to notice and make noise, whatever their respective causes, were going to stay fired up. Would their grassroots efforts amount to anything? I appreciated anyone who had the ability to be heard over the relentless din pushing the latest diet pill that is guaranteed to make you into the object outside yourself that you desire.

* * *

Pondering the next step, I am floating. For once the tingling and the nerves stop. For one moment, nothing else to lose sleep over, no longer concerned with outcomes, no longer thrashing about in protest of the process in which I have reluctantly involved myself, unable to look away no matter how much I abhor the news.

I take a short break before writing the next article, making the next phone call, going to the next audition, doing Mom's next blood pressure check. I stop shaking my fist at the parts of life that are unfair or unjust, otherwise I'd never stop shaking my fist.

I stand tall, weightless and see them all doing their jobs from a great height. They don't see me. They can't touch me. Still so far away, I touch them.

I say thank you to sixty year old Caroline sitting in a call center in the Valley talking to Texas: "I strongly urge you to vote for Hillary. She represents change ... with substance." I smile at the blogger who always shared the most incisive words, and the sharpest New York-y sense of humor even though I knew he was from anywhere but. He made me laugh out loud more times than I care to count, my brother in the trenches.

I thank people I've never met who have written back words of encouragement.

I even smile at the misguided pundit who wrote fawning drivel, revealing his self-loathing, aching to be a member of a club that doesn't want him.

I stare at the copies of my own pile of words and my signature beneath all of them and I remember one of my college professors once asked, "What does it cost you to say that?"

"I'm going to stand up" costs more than "let someone else do it."

I ponder how much it costs to sign my name when my father, secretly terrified of being taken away again, told me to keep quiet. The greatest delight will come when I can look back to the exact moment I learned to sign my name without fear. How odd to be an American citizen for this long and to never take advantage of the freedoms afforded us here. Since our Democracy allegedly encourages speaking out, it was as good a time as any to test it.

My mother would have a cow if she knew what I was doing. "Anita. Keep quiet. What if they write you back?" Well, what if they do? I have something to say.

I see my husband share my opinions, though he came to them on his own. When we disagree, we hash it out. It isn't always pretty and we stick together anyhow, my partner in all things.

I know I will always be an idealist, looking for people's better nature and for everyone who disappoints me, I find three kind gestures to overtake them.

I had a wonderful experience back in May of 2008 protesting sexism in the media on a street corner in front of NBC. No kidding. It was a great day. I've got the pictures to prove it. I hadn't protested anything since I was barely out of junior high, protesting the war, or marching on the city to keep them from closing Hunter High School.

There must have been about eighty of us standing in Burbank that afternoon, holding our signs, chanting loud and proud. Men, women, black, white, Asian, Latina, gay, straight, Democrats, Indies, some Republicans and one Russian lady whose party affiliation I did not know, all chanting for Hillary, chanting to stop the sexist trash being spewed on that station daily.

There was a ten-year-old boy who brought his own mini bullhorn shouting "What has Hillary ever done to you? Put a woman in the White House!" Everyone marching there knew the reason they showed up. They could give you ten reasons. Sophie B. Hawkins made up a song for us to sing on her bullhorn. "DAMN. I wish you were my President." I think I overheard one lady say she was born the year before women got the right to vote. She had a cane, but she stood holding her sign, leaning against a tree for balance and support.

We raised our signs above our heads in the hot sun getting appreciative honks from passing cars. I wanted to ask everyone standing on the firing line: "How did you get here today? What made you leave your meeting early, get off of work, or leave your home to stand out here at 3000 W. Alameda at 3 o'clock on a Tuesday afternoon?" I learned many new names and promised myself I wouldn't forget them.

To find strangers in agreement, together in a common cause for a few hours, who straggled over from their lives and locations to make a beautiful noise fed me in a way few things could. The day was more rewarding because I had to drag myself kicking and screaming to get there.

I look back at my pile of letters, the scathing one I wrote to a Congressman who let his pledge be bought for campaign contributions. The kind missive sent in support of a fair journalist. The email sent to an African American mayor thanking him for his support of Hillary though he was receiving tons of hate mail. A letter written to a Democratic female Senator who had inadvertently said one of the most racist, condescending idiocies I'd heard in a long time. What happened to me? When the hell did I get so fired up?

I was a child in the late sixties when all the revolution was happening, and when most had joined the "establishment," where I had dwelled for a long time, I was standing up with my fist in the air. Perhaps I hadn't let my parents' legacy of fear become my own. I figured out what it means and what it costs to live in a free country. I am filled with admiration for anyone and everyone who stood up and asked for more than I have, daring to show their faces.

When asked about the lessons 2008 offered women around the world, Hillary Clinton said:

> "My campaign ...gave a lot of heart to many young women. It is still the most common comment that people make to me: 'your campaign gave me courage' or 'your campaign made a difference in my daughter's life' or 'I went back to school because of your campaign.' So, it is unfinished business, and young women know it is unfinished business."

Signing my name to this book means I have completed the journey a nine-year-old girl started one afternoon when she got brave in the kitchen. If the moment comes that I shrink in fear, I'll breathe and once more resolve to jump into the fray, never again content to watch from a safe distance.

23 THE MEDIA CONFESSIONAL AND THE CONSEQUENCES

The Press

"For months now, my e-mail box has been full of messages from women across the country, explaining what Hillary's run meant to them, why it was so important. The reasons vary depending on age and race and region, but the one element almost all my correspondents express in common is a furious resentment at the press for what they see as blatant misogyny in the coverage of Clinton."[283]

--John Heilemann
co-author, *Game Change*

Mr. Heilemann's statement was published in *New York Magazine* two weeks after the Primaries ended. He had chosen to comment on egregious media bias after the fact, and even then by using the qualifier "what *they see* as blatant misogyny."

"There's a reason for the resentment. The level of dismissive and condescending comments, not just about me—what do I care?—but about the people who support me and in particular the women who support me, has been shocking. Shocking to women and to fair-minded men. But what has really been more disappointing to me is how few voices that have a platform have spoken out against it. And that's really why you see this enormous grassroots outrage. There is no outlet. It is rare that you have anybody on these shows or in a position of responsibility at major publications who really says, 'Wait a minute! What are we talking about here? I have a wife! I have a daughter! I want the best for them.'"[284]

-- Senator Hillary Clinton, 6/15/2008

A website called WomenAmericans.com offered a clearinghouse of commentary on the primary battle between Senators Clinton and Obama. In 2008, from mid-May onward, there were over sixty articles written for major publications devoted to discussing the sexism visited upon the campaign. From January through May 15th, there were three.

While other writers or bloggers may have discussed the subject during this period, they got little traction. The disparity in the ratio was clear. The bulk of the attention paid to the subject came too late to change the behavior or the outcome.

"The media coverage was deplorable. In fact, it was so biased in some quarters that more than a few living legends of broadcast news privately shared with me the embarrassment they felt toward their own profession."

-- Joe Scarborough, MSNBC, 1/10/10

In keeping with the trend to report on the obvious after the fact, John King, CNN's chief political correspondent, gave an interview that aired on October 30, 2008, and offered his critique of his network's 2008 election coverage. In King's words:

"I think there's some very legitimate criticism that we did not treat all of the candidates in the Democratic race, but particularly the top two or three equally, because of the Clinton obsession in the national media. It is a very fair point. We need to learn that lesson."[285]

King further stated said CNN's obsession with Hillary caused them to ignore any "thorough investigation" of Obama. He did not say how they were obsessed with her. His only excuse was that they had first assumed Hillary was "inevitable" and Obama's candidacy just snuck up on them.

Since Senator Obama had won the all-important Iowa caucus on January 3rd that should have been a wakeup call, offering plenty of time for vetting in the weeks and months that followed. Their course remained unchanged.

Mr. King accused the media of not adapting to the digital age, since "the electorate now has the ability to decouple themselves from the mainstream media":

> "They can learn everything they want to learn about these candidates without us."[286]

CNN was not the only culprit guilty of biased coverage, nor were they the only ones paying the price in terms of their bottom line. MSNBC's ratings were likewise on the decline. In the fall of 2008, the *New York Times* revenue plunged 50%, ad revenue collapsed by double digits,[287] and the *New York Times'* debt had just been rated "below investment grade" — or what is known in the investment business as "junk" — by the Standard & Poor's bond-rating agency. The *Washington Post* posted a 77% loss in revenue in 2008.[288]

The encroachment of the internet was not the only reason. Many walked away from mainstream news forums complaining they were not getting both sides of the story.

King continued the critique of his colleagues:

> "[T]here are a lot of people who sit … in New York or Washington and they don't come to South Carolina or North Carolina or Ohio or any other swing state out here and actually talk to human beings or watch what it's like to stand outside of a factory that just shut down with people."

> "And so their attitudes are influenced by the fact that they live in Washington or New York and they don't travel enough. And the criticism is that makes them elitist. I would just say sometimes there are some

people who are very influential in our business who are somewhat out of touch." [289]

Mark Halperin, editor at large of *Time Magazine,* and Mr. Heilemann's writing partner, was interviewed[290] by MSNBC's Joe Scarborough on October 28, 2008:

> HALPERIN: History and the story is just – it's great for us. It's been great for us. He's a great story. But I think, I think mistakes have been made and people- and people will regret it....
>
> ...Even if he goes – If Obama wins and goes on to become a hugely successful president, I think, still, people will look back and say it just wasn't done the right way.

Michael Malone presented a comprehensive article at ABC News on the *Media's Presidential Bias and Decline*[291] on October 24, 2008:

> "The traditional media are playing a very, very dangerous game -- with their readers, with the Constitution and with their own fates.
>
> "The media have covered this presidential campaign with a bias and that ultimately could lead to its downfall. The sheer bias in the print and television coverage of this election campaign is not just bewildering, but appalling.
>
> "I've spent 30 years in every part of journalism, from beat reporter to magazine editor. And my oldest son, following in the family business, so to speak, earned his first national byline before he earned his driver's license.
>
> So, when I say I'm deeply ashamed right now to be called a "journalist," you can imagine just how deep that cuts into my soul."

On November 6, 2008, CNN's Wolf Blitzer aired an interview[292] with Howard Kurtz, Host of CNN's "Reliable Sources":

> WOLF BLITZER, CNN ANCHOR: But, as you know, Howie, there are journalists out there who no longer go by the so-called old school rules. They

want to show their opinions out there openly, not only on television, but in the print media, as well.

KURTZ: ...If Obama is not successful because of either incompetence or extreme ideology, then I would hold the media mostly responsible for that because they were the ones who gave him a near free ride to both the Democratic nomination and to the White House without asking a lot of tough questions.

The Daily Beast, an Internet publication edited by Tina Brown, formerly of both *Vanity Fair* and the *New Yorker*, conducted a poll of 1,000 voters after the election. Results were published in their article, *The Barrier That Didn't Fall*,[293] on November 18, 2008:

• By an overwhelming 61% to 19% margin, women believe there is a gender bias in the media.

• 4 in 10 men freely admit sexist attitudes towards a female president. 39% of men say that a male is "naturally more suited" to carrying out the duties of the office.

• Only 20% of women are willing to use the word "feminist" about themselves. Only 17% of all voters said they would welcome their daughters using that label.

• 48% of women thought Hillary Clinton received fair media treatment and only 29% believed Sarah Palin was treated fairly. In contrast, nearly 8 in 10 voters thought the press gave fair treatment to Barack Obama and Joe Biden.

• More than two-thirds of women said they were being treated unfairly in the workplace (68%).

The Daily Beast noted "the heightened perceptions of how women were treated this cycle just may drive more votes by women for women next time around."

On October 11, 2010, Mark Halperin penned an article in *Time Magazine* where he stated:

"With the exception of core Obama Administration loyalists, most politically engaged elites have reached the same conclusions: the White House is in over its head, isolated, insular, arrogant and clueless about how to get along with or persuade members of Congress, the media, the business community or working-class voters. This view is held by Fox News pundits, executives and anchors at the major old-media outlets, reporters who cover the White House, Democratic and Republican congressional leaders and governors, many Democratic business people and lawyers who raised big money for Obama in 2008, and even some members of the Administration just beyond the inner circle."[294]

On June 29, 2011, Mr. Halperin was suspended from *MSNBC* for calling President Obama "a dick" on the air. Halperin was unhappy with the President's conduct during a press conference in which he was being pressed on skyrocketing spending and our continuing involvement in three wars. Apparently, he had become less of a fan.

In December, 2011, panelist John Heilemann appeared on MSNBC*'s Morning Joe* to blame Hillary's loss, in part, on her failure to focus on the historic nature of her candidacy, conveniently forgetting that when she dared do so, she was ridiculed by big media for playing the "gender card." Tina Brown offered a different theory:

> "...the press wanted a new narrative...[a]nd in the end, Obama's story of the first black president ... trumped the exceptionalism of her being the first woman president. It was bad luck for her that happened. But it was also a much more fun idea to have this new narrative to write about. Everyone was bored with the Clintons. They didn't want to have another Clinton story." [295]

Did the media's "fun idea" include bashing Hillary Clinton to entertain itself?

ABC's Chief White House Correspondent Jake Tapper later made the tepid observation that: "You had the media, perhaps, tilting on the scales a little bit."[296]

In December, 2011, Paul Bedard of *U.S. News & World Report* reported on two scholarly studies from University of Utah researchers, published in the prestigious Political Research Quarterly. Both concluded that Hillary "was doomed by media sexists." That, more than ideology, "drove the media's anti-Clinton theme." They exposed a "lopsided reliance on male reporters" who "first belittled her effort against Barack Obama, then jumped the gun to push her out of the race earlier than any other recent strong primary challenger."[297]

Bedard reported that while many examples of sexism were shrugged off at the time, the press included "nasty name calling" in their "bag of tricks" along with the more subtle tactic of referring to Clinton only by her first name; this had nothing to do with her marketing her campaign as "Hillary." 127 leading news people referred to her by her first name four times more than they did with Barack Obama. When men use their first name in their campaign, reporters still refer to them by their last names; a sign of respect and gravitas. Using the first name of a former First Lady and two-term sitting Senator was familiar and common, indicating she was not to be taken seriously.

The second study found that the media often quoted unnamed sources who went "overboard" in suggesting Clinton exit the campaign early, citing sexism as a motivator, while no male primary contender had faced such treatment. Ted Kennedy and Gary Hart fought on until the Convention when they contested as potential nominees, yet these gentlemen both indicated Hillary should get out early "for the good of the party."

Almost four years after the fact, CNN featured an article confessing that the creative delegate math used by Obama, the DNC and the bulk of big media to push Clinton from contention was a fiction.[298]

According to ABC News, almost one million voters have since fled the Democratic Party in key battleground states.[299] A number of voters left the Party over this very issue.

There is a price to be paid for a lack of vetting. Not one journalist or pundit will pay it.

* * *

The Party

On November 23, 2008, DNC Chairman Howard Dean was filmed at a Presidential Election Analysis Forum sponsored by Smithsonian Associates. The event was covered by C-Span2.

He noted the irony of being one of five men invited to speak on the panel of this event when the topic under discussion was "diversity." There were no women on stage to offer their views or experiences in the political arena.

Howard Dean, silent throughout the primaries, confessed to the audience that "sexism was the untold story of this election season."

It was curious that Mr. Dean had found new lung power on the issue of bias. Not unlike telling us we shouldn't burn innocent women at the stake for being witches after they are already dead.

At the same time, the Democratic leadership insisted we let bygones be bygones and stop "rehashing the political arguments of this last year." However, their version of the "get over it" mantra did nothing to prevent this type of debacle from happening again, in either Party. It is romantic to hope that candidates regardless of age, gender or race will run on issues and nothing else, yet that is far from reality. Since capitalizing on sex-based hate is a campaign technique still being utilized today, there is no advantage to looking forward without an examination of what happened in 2008 and why.

The why may take many forms but is likely the result of conditioning and even brainwashing. We are so accustomed as a society to derisive descriptions of women, they make less of a dent and are seen first as fact before being questioned. Examining the behavior of big media in the 2008 election cycle, an emotional, grasping, conniving or irrational characterization of a woman was the norm. A smart, logical, compassionate and accomplished executive was the exception.

These antiquated views are a self-serving model based on preservation of the status quo and sloppy reporting rather than an examination of each woman's individual merit.

While the media is the main culprit here, Democratic Party elders must accept responsibility for standing idly by while it happened and in some cases, using the very same tactics to discredit a female candidate. Both the left and right have made chauvinism a part of their arsenal, but for "the party of women's progress" to be so comfortable employing sexism to discredit women belies their basic credo.

The American people also bear some responsibility as too many, consciously or unconsciously, allowed themselves to be influenced by innate preconceptions that made such attacks an acceptable part of our political discourse. Such behavior would otherwise have been found offensive and roundly rejected.

The Women

Quoting 2010 studies commissioned by the Women's Media Center, the WCF Foundation and Political Parity (a non-partisan coalition of women's advocacy groups), *USA Today*'s Susan Page found that calling a female candidate "ice queen" "mean girl" or "prostitute" were very effective in damaging a woman's election hopes. Democratic pollster and strategist Celinda Lake said she was "stunned at the magnitude of the effect of even mild sexism."[300]

One would think that referring to one's opponent as a prostitute would damage the accuser more than the accused. Not so. It was found to be even more damaging if these women did not fight back. Responding directly to misogynist attacks worked much better than ignoring them and silently "toughing it out." The study found that sexist language affected women in both parties:

> "This year, an opponent of Sen. Lisa Murkowski, R-Alaska, sent a tweet that called her a member of "the oldest profession." A talk show host referred to Sen. Mary Landrieu, D-La., as a "high-class prostitute.""[301]

Swanee Hunt of the Political Parity Project noted that Massachusetts Attorney General Martha Coakley was referred to as an "ice queen" and a "babe" during her 2010 Senate campaign "yet [her Republican opponent] Scott Brown's nude photo in Cosmopolitan was barely mentioned.[302] A woman with a centerfold spread, no matter how long ago it was taken, would almost certainly have been knocked out of the running immediately.

It was found that women who were taunted on the basis of sexuality or sexist slurs were damaged by twice as large a percentage as they were by policy based attacks. The mere suggestion that a woman is cold, a diva, mean or a "whore" is enough to turn people from her, facts notwithstanding. And is there a male version of any of these taunts?

In her California gubernatorial race, Republican Meg Whitman was derided by career politicians as someone with no experience though she was a highly successful executive, turning eBay from a tiny start up into an $8 billion company.

The *Los Angeles Times* reported that Whitman's democratic opponent Jerry Brown or one of his aides called Whitman a whore in a campaign strategy discussion, caught on tape by a police union official when Mr. Brown's phone call to him was inadvertently not terminated. They later identified the voice as Mr. Brown's wife. So because a woman called another woman a whore, was this seen as acceptable? During their taped discussion, Mr. Brown did not offer any objection to the slur. And there is no excuse for context.

In a debate the following evening, journalist and moderator Tom Brokaw questioned Mr. Brown, asking if Brown thought calling a woman a whore was on a par with calling someone the "n" word. Mr. Brown stated that calling a woman a whore was a lesser offense. No matter one's opinion of degree of the crime, neither is excusable. The idea that slandering and degrading a woman is considered the lesser evil evinces a mindset that women are somehow lesser beings, or alternately, that they should not take insults to their persons or character as seriously. To conclude such verbiage is not as damaging leads me to wonder if some think a woman has no character to damage.

Florida Democrat and then Congressman Alan Grayson also publicly referred to Linda Robinson, an adviser to Fed chairman Ben Bernanke, as a "K-Street whore." Men are not referred to in such a manner – whores or not.

Six weeks before the mid-term elections of 2010, New York's junior Senator Kirsten Gillibrand had the privilege of being referred to as the Senate's "hottest member" at a Democratic Party fundraiser by none other than Senate Majority Leader Harry Reid.[303] While he later saw fit to mention her other attributes, such as her "extremely deep" knowledge of securities law, one wonders why being "hot" should be the lead off when discussing her qualifications for re-election.

Current research indicates that while media bias might not stop a woman from getting elected, the slanted coverage makes it less likely that a woman will run in the first place. Many women do not want to put themselves through the meat grinder of sex-based attacks or an overemphasis on their appearance.

As of this writing, the U.S. ranked only 82nd in the percentage of the women serving in national legislatures worldwide, behind Uganda for example. Women hold more than half the bachelor's and master's degrees, yet the percentage of women holding statewide executive offices has declined from 28.5% in 2000 to 22.9% in 2009.[304, 305]

Erica Falk, author of *Women for President: Media Bias in Eight Campaigns* noted that women are still treated as "novelties instead of serious contenders" and while she acknowledged that Hillary Clinton made far more progress in this arena than any before her, she detailed how Clinton's coverage was similar to that of Victoria Woodhull, a successful stockbroker and women's rights activist who ran for president almost 50 years before women had the right to vote.

In 1872, the *New York Times* discussed Woodhull's "dainty high-heeled boots" in their editorial "A Lamp Without Oil."[306] Her "carefully parted hair" and "blue silk stockings" were noted far more than her impressive successes in business – a precursor to the endless ruminations over Hillary Clinton's pantsuits 136 years later.

Ms. Falk's research on eight prior women presidential candidates from 1872 through 2004 indicated women got less coverage in the media than their male opponents. "The press included physical descriptions of men in just 14 percent of articles about them. For women, it was a whopping 40 percent...." adding to the impression that women are "objects" where men are "actors."

Media coverage of female candidates was also less substantive, less about the issues. More fluff, less stuff, as if women were not to be given equal weight. Falk found that men had 68 percent more paragraphs written about issues than did the women and "[b]etween 1872 and 2004, a substantial change in the media's pattern did not occur." This uneven coverage was evidenced at the start of the Clinton and Obama campaigns in 2007, when the six most popular

U.S. newspapers ran over 50% more stories that mentioned Obama in the headline than Clinton.[307]

Ms. Falk shared various researchers' strategic prescriptions for future women candidates to compensate for bias. It is shocking that such "strategies" would still be required. Qualified women candidates had already put their suggestions into practice, yet the attacks continued.

Strategists' advice was to "emphasize issues," but no female candidate runs on her hairdo. They advised projecting an image that emphasized "rationality" (doesn't that imply that they are innately irrational?) and to "minimize emotional expressions." Might they then not be referred to as automatons? Hillary Clinton would have some feedback to offer on that score. They told women to "fight back against sexism" – but they'd better not seem emotional or "irrational" while they're doing it.

Finally, researchers advised that "women should frame their candidacies as normal, natural and common in order to overcome the mainstream press's propensity to portray them as unusual." Again, we are suggesting that females be homogenized. A woman is still told to "behave." Trapped in an uncomfortable container, she maintains a cookie cutter appearance lest she seem too threatening. Hillary Clinton well remembers an early debate where she arched her brow and spoke forcefully to her male opponents. Pundits depicted her as an angry virago.

For the all the strides made by both Clinton and Palin, women made no gains in representation nationally in 2008 and are not currently running in numbers commensurate with their credentials for office. Women may have been motivated or inspired by the battles and fortitude of Hillary Clinton and Sarah Palin, but even if more women run for and win office, they continue to battle the same weapons, peculiarly aimed at females. I can only conclude that society at large has learned nothing. Yet the various pollsters, strategists and researchers quoted in these articles remained hopeful.

In the 2010 midterm elections, conservative women found success running on a platform of fiscal responsibility and transparency. Triggered by a backlash to what was viewed as the Obama administration's unsuccessful economic policy and egregious spending, female conservatives made strides forward. Journalist

Jessica Rettig shared that the traditional model of successful female candidates tending to be Democrats who emphasized "women's issues" was falling by the wayside. Rettig quoted pollster Kellyanne Conway. Complaining that women had long been insulted by the male dominated political establishment as only focusing on abortion and unable to handle economic issues, Conway shot back: "We *can* do the math and girl talk 2010 is all about fiscal issues."

The 2010 midterms were being billed as "the year of the woman." Chris Matthews, Hillary Clinton's primary "man handler," declared that these ladies had Hillary to thank. Perhaps he was right. There were many more women standing up, unafraid to speak out.

Four gubernatorial and senate primaries held in June 2010 were won by women and by convincing margins. Meg Whitman, Carly Fiorina both in California, Sharron Angle in Nevada and Nicky Haley in South Carolina. The theory being espoused across the political spectrum for their victories was that women were perceived as outsiders to corruption and more trustworthy than their male counterparts. However, all these women are Conservatives. Martha Coakley, a Democrat, lost her Senate election bid in 2010. A number of Democratic women incumbents in Congress were considered vulnerable in 2010,[308] but that was less a product of sexism than being damned by their votes for some of the current administration's policies.

Women have typically had better success in political campaigns during times of economic uncertainty. Does this trend indicate that only after "the guys have screwed it up" are we willing to take a chance on a woman? Another theory is that women are thought of as better able to control the purse strings since they typically manage the household budgets. If that is so, bring on the women!

In New Mexico, two women vied for Governor and history was made in 2010 as a Republican, Susana Martinez, became the first woman to hold the state's highest office. Mary Fallin of Oklahoma and Nikki Haley of South Carolina were likewise elected Governor. Gender took a backseat in their campaigns. Results mattered. Gender didn't.

Sarah Palin was influential in helping a number of conservative women to get elected, yet she did so as a private citizen. In the year prior, Governor Palin was hit with at least eighteen different ethics complaints in Alaska. Apparently, the frenzy to discredit her had not abated. No matter how specious the claim, Alaskan law at the time dictated that she was responsible for answering and defending against all of them, incurring huge legal fees in the process. Citing her unwillingness to burden Alaskans with slowing down the work of government, she made what many thought a questionable choice and resigned. She would forever be labeled a quitter for doing so.

In June of 2011, perhaps out of a fear that she would run for President in 2012, various news networks obtained approximately 24,000 pages of Sarah Palin's email correspondence, trawling for dirt while she was Governor. Drew Griffin, in a special investigative report for CNN, shared his findings in an interview with T.J. Holmes.[309]

Griffin stated that the thousands of pages revealed Palin to be a hard-working executive involved in the business of state. There was no evidence that her husband Todd Palin was the "shadow governor" as some had insinuated. Although Holmes probed for negative information, Griffin's almost sheepish demeanor indicated he had nothing damning to report. Griffin stated that Governor Palin had no email correspondence on "TrooperGate" – another scandal designed to take her down in 2008; further, that Palin typically took responsibility for any media criticism leveled at her staff.

There was an audible groan of disappointment on the airwaves that week as a smoking gun was not discovered.

Using Google and several other search engines hunting for a print article attesting to these findings in writing, I found none, though this news consumed big media for a number of news cycles. If it were not for a website that saved a video of the actual CNN interview detailing Griffin's reportage, one would be challenged to find evidence of it.[310]

The smear was the story. The exoneration was not newsworthy.

Entering the 2012 election season, disparaging women remains a popular sport, as evidenced by the treatment of female presidential nominee and conservative firebrand, Congresswoman Michelle Bachmann. In a guest appearance on NBC's *Late Night with Jimmy Fallon,* his band introduced her by playing part of the 1985 song "Lying Ass Bitch." Susan Milligan commented in *U.S. News &*

World Report, "Bachmann's an easy enough target on other, policy-related matters. Belittling her for her gender is not just offensive, it's lazy."[311]

Newsweek earlier featured a cover story of Bachmann, marring her attractive appearance by selecting a picture of her looking positively wild eyed. Aha! Another crazy woman! *Newsweek's* cover article on her was entitled "The Queen of Rage."[312] Her male counterparts may have received fierce critique on the issues, even their personal behavior, but did not endure the same visual vilification by the media.

Progressive women, too, were still on the receiving end of professional slights and personal insults. Per Suzanna Andrews of *Vanity Fair*, "[m]illions of Americans hoped President Obama would nominate [Harvard law professor] Elizabeth Warren to head the consumer financial watchdog agency she had created. Instead, she was pushed aside."[313] Warren then chose to run against Republican Scott Brown for his Massachusetts Senate seat in 2012. Since he had done a *Cosmopolitan* centerfold years before, Warren commented that she would not have taken her clothes off to pay for college. Responding to the comment in a Boston radio interview, Senator Brown said, "Thank God."[314]

* * *

At the start of my journey, and this book, I had asked the chicken or the egg question: was sexism the motive or merely the method of discrediting a qualified woman? Apropos of this, I encountered a man who confessed that while in college, he and his buddies knew the fastest way to defeat a smart girl who had gotten the better of them. Ridiculing her as being hysterical, frumpy, "on the rag" and either frigid or a slut were effective ways to isolate and discredit her.

Having witnessed a number of pundits who trashed Hillary behind her back only to find themselves somewhat flustered in her presence, it became clear that they knew her depth but resorted to crass maneuvers nonetheless. Therefore, to my mind, method won out over motive. Media culprits had years of empirical evidence that such attacks would achieve the desired result. A picture emerges of men who made a conscious choice rather than being engulfed by their own unconscious gender bias. Worse still were women in positions of influence, conditioned to participate with gusto in gender assassination that they themselves had likely been subjected to at one time or another.

The *Wall St. Journal's* Peggy Noonan had a good take on why women receive such vitriol, as exemplified by the still fresh hatred both in the U.S. and abroad for former British PM Margaret Thatcher:

> "Because she was a woman. Because women in politics are always by definition seen as presumptuous: They presume to lead men. When they are as bright as the men they're disliked by the men, and when they're brighter and more serious they're hated." [315]

Hillary Clinton was the first woman to have ever made a huge dent in a Presidential contest. She tested the limits and tested all of us to unpack every stereotype rattling around in our brains about the concept – and reality – of female leadership. Perhaps it was too much to hope that the first time out, the country would be brave enough to turn history, and so many years of male dominance, on its ear.

For me, forewarned is forearmed. Convincing perpetrators to stop misogynist rhetoric can only be accomplished by starving the beast. If a candidate, media outlet or Party tries it – I withhold support, financial or otherwise. The purse sends a powerful message. I also withhold my vote, otherwise the guilty might well ignore the lesson, brazenly paying lip service to the very issue about which they do nothing.

The faster I make a loud noise, boycott, protest, stop buying the magazine, block the TV station, the faster the message will be received. Zero tolerance. Perhaps then we can approach a place where neither race, gender, sexual preference nor age can be used as a weapon against a candidate, or as a tool to advantage him or her.

In future, if a qualified woman should contemplate a run for the Presidency, my fond hope is that she will be undeterred by the Hillary/Palin hazing from hell that occurred in 2008.

Reflecting on the Primaries once more, I remembered how candidate Obama's speeches were touted as more inspiring than anyone who came before him. It was clear the press had a short memory for a woman whose words had been ranked as truly historic:

"For too long, the history of women has been a history of silence. Even today, there are those who are trying to silence our words.

"It is a violation of human rights when babies are denied food, or drowned, or suffocated, or their spines broken, simply because they are born girls. It is a violation of human rights when women and girls are sold into the slavery of prostitution. It is a violation of human rights when women are doused with gasoline, set on fire and burned to death because their marriage dowries are deemed too small. It is a violation of human rights when individual women are raped in their own communities and when thousands of women are subjected to rape as a tactic or prize of war. It is a violation of human rights when a leading cause of death worldwide among women ages 14 to 44 is the violence they are subjected to in their own homes. It is a violation of human rights when women are denied the right to plan their own families, and that includes being forced to have abortions or being sterilized against their will.

"Women's rights are human rights. Among those rights are the right to speak freely—and the right to be heard."

-- Hillary Rodham Clinton,
1995 UN World Conference on Women in Beijing,
in defiance of the U.S. State Dept and Chinese Government

"[N]ot long ago, a woman handed me a photograph of her father as a young soldier. He was receiving the Medal of Honor from President Truman at the White House. During World War II, he had risked his life on a daring mission to drive back the enemy and protect his fellow soldiers.

"In the corner of that photo, in shaking handwriting, this American hero had simply written, "To Hillary Clinton, keep fighting for us." And that is what...that is what I'm going to do, because America is worth fighting for. You are worth fighting for.

"It was in this city that our founders declared America's independence and our permanent mission to form a more perfect union. Now, neither Senator Obama nor I, nor many of you, were fully included in that vision, but we've been blessed by men and women in each generation who saw America not as it is, but as it could and should be, the abolitionists and the suffragists, the progressives and the union members, the civil rights leaders... all those who marched, protested, and risked their lives, because they looked into their children's eyes and saw the promise of a better future.

"Because of them, I grew up taking for granted that women could vote. Because of them, my daughter grew up taking for granted that children of all colors could attend school together. And because of them, and because of you, this next generation will grow up taking for granted that a woman or an African-American can be the president of the United States of America."

-- Senator Hillary Rodham Clinton
victory speech,
Pennsylvania Primary, 4/22/2008

* * *

Hillary Clinton put on her pantsuit every day and in her typical plain spoken manner, declared her intention: "Bloom where you're planted."

She was and is unapologetic about her goals, her work ethic or her drive. She has never allowed anyone to shame her or talk her out of being who she is. I find the tone of Hillary Rodham Clinton to be quite inspiring, actually.

I am proud to have supported Hillary in 2008. She'll always have my vote.

In truth, I don't know that she will ever run for President again. If not, that would be our loss. Perhaps she was meant to be the pioneer who put 18,000,000 cracks in the ceiling so some other qualified woman would eventually break through.

As I write this, I throw down the gauntlet and challenge her to prove me wrong.

Run, Hillary. Run.

ABOUT THE AUTHOR

As an actor and native New Yorker living in Los Angeles, Anita Finlay has worked primarily in television for over twenty years, on such network series as "Castle," "Perception," "Brothers and Sisters," "24," "Hannah Montana," "Boston Legal," "Gilmore Girls," "Vanished," and "Judging Amy." She spent seven years on "The Young and the Restless" as Dr. Nora Thompson and starred in a number of feature films and made-for-television movies including "Alternate Endings," "The Last Place on Earth," "Two Voices," "Prison of Secrets, "and "Visions of Murder."

Anita has done scores of commercial campaigns and worked in the theatre as a solo artist, writing and performing *The Devil Takes a Wife* to acclaim in Los Angeles theaters. She has also performed in regional theatres throughout the United States and had long running spokesperson contracts for a number of Fortune 500 companies.

Moved to action by the biased coverage of the historic 2008 primaries, she became a staff writer for *NoQuarter*, a website recognized for its excellent political coverage. Her work has been featured on *Real Clear Politics*, *MemeOrandum*, *BlogHer*, *Media Bistro/FishbowlDC* and several other widely read political blogs. She is a senior contributor at *The New Agenda*, a bi-partisan organization dedicated to improving the lives of women and girls. This is her first book.

She lives with her husband David and their two furry children, Nicky and Caruso.

Website: http://www.anitafinlay.com
Facebook: http://www.facebook.com/AnitaFinlayAuthor
Twitter: http://twitter.com/#!/AnitaFinlay

ENDNOTES

[1] Gough, Paul J., The Hollywood Reporter, Clinton vs. Obama: A Must See, January 31, 2008

[2] Healy, Patrick, New York Times, Laughing Matters in Clinton Campaign, September 28, 2007

[3] Sweet, Lynn, Chicago Sun Times, Sweet: Clinton, Obama Hollywood debate. Kodak Theater Jan. 31, 2008. Transcript, Feb. 1, 2008

[4] Calderone, Michael, Politico, Chris Matthews sorry for 'sexist' comments, January 17, 2008

[5] Associated Press, CBS-TV News, Obama, Clinton Debate At Kodak Theatre, January 31, 2008

[6] Bennetts, Leslie, Vanity Fair, Leslie Bennetts on Michelle Obama, December, 2007

[7] McEwan, Melissa, Shakesville.com, Shut Up, Maureen Dowd, January 2, 2008

[8] Quote originally attributed to Allen Saunders, 1957. Made popular by John Lennon.

[9] Williams, Tennessee, Eccentricities of a Nightingale, 1964.

[10] Meacham, Jon, "Letting Hillary Be Hillary. Newsweek. 1/21/2008

[11] Mitchell, Cleta, Wall St. Journal, Are You Qualified?, September 17, 2008

[12] Ibid.

[13] Carlson, Margaret, with August, Melissa and Blackman, Ann, TIME Magazine, Hillary Clinton: A Different Kind of First Lady, Nov. 16, 1992

[14] Ibid.

[15] Ibid.

[16] Ibid.

[17] Rajghatta, Chidanand (January—February 2004), "First Lady President?", Verve magazine

[18] Carlson, Margaret, with August, Melissa and Blackman, Ann, TIME Magazine, Hillary Clinton: A Different Kind of First Lady, Nov. 16, 1992

[19] Ibid.

[20] Ibid.

[21] National First Ladies Library, Hillary Rodham Clinton

[22] National First Ladies Library

[23] Estrich, Susan, Newsmax, Good Parenting Shines Through in Chelsea Clinton's Wedding, July 30, 2010

[24] Transcript, ABC News, Obama and Clinton Debate, April 16, 2008

[25] HBO, "Real Time With Bill Maher," October 29, 2008

[26] http://www.stripes.com/article.asp?section=104&article=26085; Donald Rumsfeld later changed the practice after receiving public criticism.

[27] Serrano, Alfonso, CBS News, Hillary Clinton: "Give Me A Chance", Jan. 22, 2007

[28] Sullivan, Amy, Washington Monthly, Hillary in 2008? Not So Fast, July/Aug. 2005

[29] Ibid.

[30] MSNBC, "Chris Matthews Show," January 28, 2007

[31] Vennochi, Joan, Boston Globe, That Clinton Cackle, September 30, 2007

[32] Ibid.

[33] CBS' 60 Minutes, Hillary Clinton's Run For The White House, Feb. 10, 2008

[34] Jamieson, Prof. Kathleen Hall, PBS, Bill Moyers Interview, December 7, 2007

[35] Healy, Patrick, The New York Times, Caucus Blogs, The Clinton Sunday Show Blitz, September 23, 2007

[36] Media Matters, Reporting on Clifford May, Tucker Carlson, MSNBC, October 16, 2007

[37] Herszenhorn, David M., New York Times, Senate Approves Resolution Denouncing MoveOn.org Ad, September 21, 2007

[38] Eagan, Margery, Boston Herald, Sexist Coverage of Hillary Brings Women to Her Corner, February 10, 2010

[39] Scarborough, Joe, Huffington Post, The True Character of Hillary Clinton, January 12, 2010

[40] PBS, Tavis Smiley Interviews Hillary Clinton, Feb. 1, 2008

[41] "Clinton fought back, but she needs a radio-controlled shock collar so that aides can zap her when she starts to get screechy." --Joel Achenbach, Washington Post, 1/08

[42] "...Hillary Clinton is Glenn Close in Fatal Attraction. She's going to keep coming back, and they're not going to stop her." -- NPR's Ken Rudin, on CNN's Sunday Morning 4/28/08

[43] Conason, Joe, Salon.com, How Bashing Hillary Backfired, January 10, 2008

[44] Ibid.

[45] Transcript, New York Times, The Democratic Debate in New Hampshire, January 5, 2008

[46] In 1972, Shirley Chisholm won a non-binding president primary in New Jersey.

[47] http://michaelgraham.969fmtalk.mobi/2008/01/09/michael-graham-michael-plays-comments-made-by-msnbcs-chris-matthews-and-takes-reaction-calls-from-listeners.aspx

[48] http://www.noquarterusa.net/blog/2009/03/30/some-apologies-from-the-obamamedia-are-in-order-for-falsely-accusing-new-hampshire-primary-voters-of-racism/

[49] Blumenthal, Mark, Pollster.com, What Happened in NH, AAPOR's answer, March 30, 2009.

[50] Media Matters, Russert falsely claimed to show "exactly what President Clinton said," aired truncated quotes from both Clintons, January 13, 2008

[51] Ibid.

[52] Ibid.

[53] Ibid.

[54] Ibid.

[55] Ibid.

[56] Wheaton, Sarah, New York Times, 'Iron My Shirt', January 7, 2008

[57] Ibid.

[58] Media Matters; "Matthews asked about Clinton endorsers' "willingness" "to become castratos in the eunuch chorus," December 17, 2007; Huffington Post, Chris Matthews Asked About Clinton Endorsers' Willingness "To Become Castratos In The Eunuch Chorus," March 28, 2008

[59] Media Matters, Buchanan: Clinton's raised voice is one "every husband in America ... has heard at one time or another", February 26, 2008

[60] Dowd, Maureen, The New York Times, The Nepotism Tango, September 30, 2007

[61] Daum, Meghan, Los Angeles Times, She's Gotta Have It, January 12, 2008

[62] CNN Transcripts, Howard Kurtz interviews Joan Walsh, May 4, 2008

[63] Media Matters, MSNBC's Buchanan compounded sexist comments, misquoted Samuel Johnson , February 27, 2008

[64] Novak, Tim, Chicago Sun Times, "8 Things You Need To Know About Obama and Tony Rezko," January 24, 2008

[65] Appelbaum, Binyamin, Boston Globe, Grim proving ground for Obama's housing policy, June 27, 2008

[66] Novak, Tim, Chicago Sun Times, 8 things you need to know about Obama and Rezko, January 24, 2008

[67] Malcolm, Andrew, Los Angeles Times, Obama's small donor base image is a myth, new study reveals, November 28, 2008; *see also* CFI, November 24, 2008

[68] Montanaro, Domenico, MSNBC First Read, Obama unsure Hillary can get his voters, February 1, 2008

[69] Seelye, Katharine Q., The Caucus, New York Times, Obama Criticized Over Singer, October 22, 2007

[70] Stein, Sam, Huffington Post, Obama Compares Himself To Reagan, JFK...But Not Bill Clinton, January 16, 2008

[71] Edwards, John, Real Clear Politics, John Edwards Concession Speech, January 30, 2008

[72] Zeleny, Jeff, The Caucus, The New York Times, Missouri Senator Endorses Obama, January 13, 2008

[73] Cohen, Richard, Washington Post, Hillary's Diminishing Returns, February 26, 2008

[74] Tapper, Jake, ABC's Political Punch, Obama-Backing Senator Calls for Clinton to Drop Out, March 28, 2008

[75] Ibid.

[76] Associated Press, London, Obama adviser resigns; called Clinton 'monster', March 7, 2008

[77] Media Matters, So that's why NBC and MSNBC wanted Clinton's schedules?, March 20, 2008

[78] Ibid.

[79] Wilson, Joe, Smears and Tears: How Obama's National Security Week Turned into the Mendacity of Hype, Huffington Post, March 26, 2008

[80] Mr. Wilson also gave credit for his Huffington Post piece to the research of blogger "eriposte."

[81] Wallace-Wells, Ben, The New York Times, A star strategist offers Democrats a new vision, March 30, 2007

[82] Wallace-Wells, Ben, The New York Times, Obama's Narrator, April 1, 2007

[83] Wallace-Wells, Ben, The New York Times, A star strategist offers Democrats a new vision, March 30, 2007

[84] Bernstein, 2007, p. 105, A Woman In Charge

[85] Stein, Sam, Huffington Post, Obama Outspending Clinton 2.3 to 1 In Pennsylvania. April 21, 2008

[86] Collins, Gail, New York Times, Hillary's Smackdown, April 24, 2008

[87] Smith, Ben, POLITICO.com, Kennedy: No Veep slot for Clinton, May 09, 2008

[88] http://www.pbs.org/moyers/journal/12072007/transcript1.html, PBS, 12/7/2007

[89] lentinela, Huffington Post, 11:38 PM on December 27, 2007

[90] Kurtz, Howard, CNN Reliable Sources, Transcript, Hillary Clinton Complains About Media's Treatment of Women, May 25, 2008

[91] Abcarian, Robin, Los Angeles Times, Drift Away From Clinton Frustrates Many Women, March 3, 2008

[92] Leavitt, Steven D., The New York Times, So Much for One Person, One Vote, August 6, 2008.

[93] Vedantam, Shankar, Washington Post, The Oprah Effect, September 1, 2008

[94] Interview on This Week with George Stephanopoulos.

[95] Ross, Brian, Tapper, Jake, Wolfson: Edwards' Cover-up Cost Clinton the Nomination, August 11, 2008

[96] Ibid.

[97] The Sunday Times, Interview: Tony Allen-Mills talks to George Clooney, Dec. 11, 2005

[98] Media Matters, November 11, 2007

[99] http://www.cbsnews.com/blogs/2008/02/15/politics/fromtheroad/entry3838093.shtml

[100] ABC News' Sunlen Miller

[101] Erbe, Bonnie, US News & Word Report, Obama's Sweetie Problem, April 4, 2008

[102] Halperin, Mark, The Page, TIME, Obama Woos Clinton Supporter I'll Give You A Kiss, April 1, 2008

[103] Paglia, Camille, UK Telegraph, Why Women Shouldn't Vote For Hillary Clinton, April 20, 2008

[104] Paglia, Camille, Salon.com, Hillary Without Tears, January 10, 2008

[105] Ibid.

[106] Abcarian, Robin, Los Angeles Times, Drift Away From Clinton Frustrates Many Women, March 3, 2008

[107] Clinton, Hillary and Richards, Cecile, New York Times, op-ed, Blocking Care for Women, September 18, 2008; Fox, Maggie, Reuters, Family planning groups object to abortion plan, Jul 16, 2008

[108] The New York Times, July 2008

[109] Parker, Kathleen, National Review Online, Palin Problem, September 28, 2008

[110] Wakeman, Jessica, Huffington Post, On Sexist Media Coverage of Hillary Clinton, April 27, 2008

[111] Media Matters, GOP strategist on Hannity & Colmes: "[S]omeone is going to have to go out there and take [Clinton] behind the barn", February 26, 2008

[112] http://www.clevelandleader.com/node/4666

[113] Stein, Sam, Huffington Post, Matthews Calls Clinton Press Shop "Lousy," "Kneecappers," February 15, 2008

[114] Kaus, Stephen, Huffington Post, Sister Frigidaire Tries to Ice MSNBC, Feb. 12, 2008

[115] Media Matters, MSNBC's Shuster, Carlson discuss purported "cackle," laugh over "Hillary laughing pen", April 22, 2008 8:27

[116] Transcript, MSNBC, Countdown With Keith Olbermann, April 25, 2008

[117] Ibid.

[118] Hart, Gary, Huffington Post, Breaking the Final Rule, March 7, 2008

[119] Reference.com, United States Presidential Election, 1984

[120] Raum, Tom, USA TODAY On Politics, Obama criticizes Bush, McCain on economy, February 28, 2008

[121] Tapper, Jake, ABC News, Political Punch, Democratic Party Official: Clinton Pursuing 'The Tonya Harding Option', March 25, 2008

[122] Milbank, Dana, Washington Post, Ask Tough Questions? Yes, They Can!, March 4, 2008

[123] Politico, Wright's Controversial Comments, March 17, 2008

[124] Hannity, Sean, FOX News, Obama's Pastor: Rev. Jeremiah Wright, March 7, 2007

[125] Seelye, Katharine Q., New York Times Caucus Blogs, Clinton Acknowledges: 'I Misspoke,' March 25, 2008

[126] Jay Newton-Small, TIME, Obama's Foreign-Policy Problem, Dec. 18, 2007

[127] Robberson, Tod, Dallas Morning News, Hillary's Sniper Incident in Context, April 01, 2008

[128] Huffington Post, "If she gave him one of her cojones, they'd both have two," May 4, 2008

[129] Kornblut, Anne E., Cohen, Jon, Washington Post, Poll Shows Erosion Of Trust In Clinton, April 16, 2008

[130] Kornblut, Anne E., Washington Post, Clinton Told True Tale of Woe, Says Kin, April 7, 2007

[131] Fowler, Mayhill, Huffington Post, Obama: No Surprise That Hard-Pressed Pennsylvanians Turn Bitter, April 11, 2008

[132] Bai, Matt, New York Times, Working for the Working Class Vote, October 15, 2008

[133] Weisman, Jonathan, Washington Post, Obama's Uncle and the Liberation of Auschwitz, May 28, 2008

[134] CNN, Political Ticker, Obama incorrectly claims membership of Senate committee, July 23, 2008

[135] Transcript, ABC Obama and Clinton Debate, April 16, 2008

[136] Ibid.

[137] Snow, Kate, ABC News, Hillary Clinton Mentions RFK Assassination in Relation to '08 Race, May 23, 2008

[138] Seelye, Katharine Q., The New York Times, Clinton Defends R.F.K. Remarks, May 25, 2008

[139] Ibid.

[140] Eagan, Margery, Boston Herald, Sexist Coverage of Hillary Brings Women to Her Corner, February 10, 2010

[141] Media Matters, Taking lead from Drudge, conservative echo chamber hypes Clinton photo, December 18, 2007

[142] In '08 Race, the Other Clinton Steps Up Publicly, New York Times, Dec 17, 2007; http://www.nytimes.com/2007/12/17/us/politics/17bill.html

[143] Moyers, Bill, PBS, Journal, Interview with Kathleen Hall Jamieson, December 7, 2007

[144] Stephen, Andrew, NewStatesman, Hating Hillary, May 22, 2008

[145] Ibid.

[146] Rhee, Foon, Boston.com, Political Intelligence, Not So Fast, Clinton Supporters Say, May 20, 2008

[147] Heilemann, John, New York Magazine, What Hillary Won By Losing, June 15, 2008

[148] MSNBC First Read, Obama Limping Toward The Finish Line, June 3, 2008

[149] Guttman, Robert, Huffington Post, Obama: Limping Across the Finish Line, June 3, 2008

[150] NoQuarter, Paulie Abeles interviews Newsweek editor Evan Thomas

[151] The New Yorker, One Angry Man, Peter J. Boyer, June 20, 2009; http://www.newyorker.com/reporting/2008/06/23/080623fa_fact_boyer?currentPage=6

[152] Cocco, Marie, Washington Post, Misogyny I Won't Miss, May 15, 2008

[153] Sen. Ted Deutch, Palm Beach Post, Democrats' ballyhooed rules offer fix, April 6, 2008

[154] Mayer, Lindsay Renick, Center for Responsive Politics, Closing the Books on '07: Part IV, February 05, 2008

[155] CNN, Democrats withdraw from Michigan 'beauty contest', October 9, 2007

[156] Associated Press, Michigan Senate Refuses To Restore 4 Democrats To Ballot, Leaving Hillary Clinton , November 27, 2007

[157] CNN, Source: Obama not embracing Michigan revote, March 19, 2008

[158] http://www.lynettelong.com/CAUCUSFRAUD/

[159] Gaston, Gigi, Documentary: We Will Not Be Silenced, 2008

[160] Roberts, Cokie and Steve, Jewish World Review, Why the Dems Could Lose, May 6, 2008

[161] Smalley, Suzanne, Newsweek, A Caucus Fight - Clinton forces charge Obama camp with irregularities, March 4, 2008.

[162] Lopez, Kathryn Jean, National Review Online, Clinton Texas Caucus Complaining Continues, March 04, 2008

[163] www.wewillnotbe silenced2008.com

[164] YouTube links, We Will Not Be Silenced, Parts I through IV: http://www.youtube.com/watch?v=EGZFgMNM-UU;

http://www.youtube.com/watch?v=BXNqFQmGxDU;
http://www.youtube.com/watch?v=o4XFvq5XMk8;
http://www.youtube.com/watch?v=cnclKiHwatw

[165]Media Matters, More Media Attacks on Clinton: Makes "some want to drink a gallon of rat poison," March, 22, 2007

[166] Heilemann, John, New York Magazine, What Hillary Won By Losing, June 15, 2008

[167] Whitlock, Scott, Newsbusters, Editor of Time on Fawning Obama Coverage: Media Will Regret This, October 28, 2008

[168] Lerner, Gilda, Women and History, 1986, 1993

[169] Murray, Mark, MSNBC, Obama Outspent Hillary 5:1 on WI-TV, February 22, 2008

[170] Mooney, Alexander, CNN, Poll: Some Clinton supporters still not embracing Obama, July 5, 2008

[171] Walsh, Kenneth T., U.S. News, Despite Obama's Efforts, Clinton Supporters Won't Fade Away, August 7, 2008

[172] Ibid.

[173] Ibid.

[174] Lovley, Erika, POLITICO.com, Report: 237 millionaires in Congress, Nov 6, 2009

[175] Evgenia Peretz, Vanity Fair, Going after Gore,

[176] Cafferty, Jack, CNN, Cafferty File, April 30, 2008

[177] Kurtz, Howard, CNN Reliable Sources, Transcript, Hillary Clinton Complains About Media's Treatment of Women, May 25, 2008

[178] Shipman, Tim, UK Telegraph, Barack Obama under fire for ignoring advice on how to beat John McCain, September 13, 2008

[179] Fox News, June 24, 2008, Greta Van Susteren Interviews Nancy Pelosi

[180] Editorial, New York Times, Public Funding on the Ropes, June 20, 2008

[181] Newport, Frank, If McCain vs. Obama, 28% of Clinton Backers Go for McCain, March 26, 2008

[182] Tapper, Jake and Snow, Kate, ABC News, Sparks Fly at Black Caucus Meeting, June 20, 2008

[183] Lane Lea, Huffington Post, Eat Crow? Hell Yes, to Win this Election, September 17, 2008

[184] Berg-Andersson, Richard E., Research and Commentary, TheGreenPapers.com, 2008 Presidential Primaries, Caucuses, and Conventions, September, 2008

[185] Ibid.

[186] Nicholas, Peter, Los Angeles Times, Some Clinton delegates say the unity show was forced, September 04, 2008

[187] Ibid.

[188] Ibid.

[189] Ibid.

[190] Seelye, Katharine Q., New York Times, Live From Denver: Watching Hillary Clinton, August 26, 2008

[191] Becker, Bernie, Democrats Revisit Presidential Race Rules, Dec. 30, 2009

[192] Cannon, Carl M., Washington Monthly, Why Not Hillary? She can win the White House, July/August 2005

[193] Dowd, Maureen, New York Times, A Flawed Feminist Test, February 13, 2008

[194] CBS, "Hillary Is A Tortured Person," June 5, 2008

[195] Dowd, Maureen, New York Times, Begrudging His Bedazzling, February 27, 2008

[196] Dowd, Maureen, New York Times, Deign or Reign, January 2, 2008

[197] Dowd, Maureen, New York Times, Duel of Historical Guilts, March 5, 2008

[198] Media Matters, Matthews and others on NBC networks have repeatedly linked Clinton to fictional Nurse Ratched, December 7, 2007

[199] Hitchens, Christopher, Slate Magazine, January 7, 2008

[200] Collins, Gail, New York Times, Hillary's Free Pass, January 10, 2008

[201] Maureen Dowd, New York Times, The Hillary Waltz, April 2, 2008

[202] Dowd, Maureen, Dallas News, Shoulder Pad Feminism Lifts Hillary, March 6, 2008

[203] Dowd, Maureen, New York Times, Yes, She Can, August 13, 2008

[204] Dowd, Maureen, New York Times, Visceral Has Its Value, November 22, 2009

[205] Dowd, Maureen, New York Times, Isn't It Ironic, June 11, 2010

[206] Johnson, Kaylene, author, Sarah, How a Hockey Mom Turned Alaska's Political Establishment Upside Down

[207] Breslau, Karen, Now This Is Woman's Work, Newsweek, Oct. 15, 2007, http://www.newsweek.com/id/42534,

[208] Quinn, Steve, Alaska Governor Shows Fearlessness, AP, USA Today, Dec. 26, 2007, http://www.usatoday.com/news/nation/2007-12-26-1665591074_x.htm

[209] Yardley, William, Novice Stands Her Ground On Veterans Turf in Alaska, NY Times, October 29, 2006,

[210] Safire, William, New York Times, Language: You break it, you own it, you fix it, October 18, 2004

[211] Davey, Monica, New York Times Caucus Blogs, G.O.P. Women Call Palin Criticism 'Sexist', September 3, 2008

[212] Linkins, Jason, Huffington Post, Sarah Palin Battles The Internet (And The Rest Of Your Scritti Politti), June 29, 2009

[213] Miller, Tracy, Daily News, Sandra Bernhard issues 'gang rape' warning to Sarah Palin, September 19, 2008

[214] Original internet reference/website no longer exists; cite cannot be found.

[215] Stephanopoulos, George, ABC News, Sarah Palin to Hillary: Let's Have Coffee, November 15, 2009

[216] Ibid.

[217] Klein Joe, Time Magazine, What Hillary Believes, November 7, 2007

[218] Quote often misattributed to Helen Keller.

[219] Interview, Obama, Barack, Reno Gazette Journal Editorial Board, January 15, 2008

[220] Hedges, C., Buying Brand Obama, Truthdig, May 3, 2009; http://www.truthdig.com/report/item/20090503_buying_brand_obama/

[221] http://www.washingtonpost.com/wp-dyn/content/article/2009/04/02/AR2009040203286.html

[222] ABC News, Diane Sawyer Interview, March 2010

[223] Speaker.gov, March 9, 2010

[224]224 Seifert, Lauren, CBS News, Political Hotsheet, Rep. Patrick Murphy: Momentum in the Senate for DADT Repeal, December 15, 2010

[225] Sheppard, Noel, Newsbusters, Newsweek's Evan Thomas: Obama's Budget a 'Profile in Cowardice', February 19, 2011

[226] Yahoo News, Has Jessica Simpson's Weight Gain Helped Her Struggling Career?, January 30, 2009

[227] CNN, Transcripts, February 11, 2009

[228] Baird, Julia, Newsweek, Too Hot To Handle, July 3, 2010

[229] Givhan, Robin, Washington Post, Hillary Clinton's Tentative Dip Into New Neckline Territory, July 20, 2007

[230] Sheppard, Newsbusters, Letterman Attacks Sarah Palin's 'Slutty Flight Attendant Look', June 9, 2009

[231] Kurtzman, Daniel, About.com, Late-Night Jokes About Sen. Hillary Clinton

[232] Ibid.

[233] Ibid.

[234] Ibid.

[235] Ibid.

[236] Ibid.

[237] Ibid.

[238] Ibid.

[239] Fuller, Bonnie, Hollywood Life, Why Beauties Get Cheated On Big Time!, May 24, 2010

[240] Miller, Sunlen, ABC News, Comedian Jokes About 'Hos' at Obama Fundraiser; Obama Condemns, July 12, 2008

[241] Heher, Ashley M., Huffington Post, Bernie Mac Makes Off-Color Joke At Obama Event, July 12, 2008

[242] Cocco, Marie, Washington Post, Misogyny I Won't Miss, May 15, 2008.

[243] Harris, Lynn, Salon.com, Sexist coverage? What sexist coverage?, May 27, 2008

[244] Ellis, Bob, ABC.net, Hating Hillary Clinton, April 29, 2008

[245] Western Carolina University, Science Daily, Sexist Humor No Laughing Matter, Psychologist Says, November 7, 2007

[246] Special thanks to blogger American Girl in Italy for her research in re Science Daily.

[247] Joyful Heart Foundation, Homepage

[248] Erbe, Bonnie, US News, What's Wrong With American that Forces Michelle Obama to Tone Down, May 21, 2009

[249] Ibid.

[250] Adapted, Ani, NQ, March 6, 2009

[251] Sen. Chuck Schumer, on Hillary's departure from the Senate.

[252] Meacham, Jon, "Letting Hillary Be Hillary. Newsweek. 1/21/2008

[253] This Week With George Stephanopoulos, June 7, 2009

[254] Nussbaum, Emily, New York Magazine, In Conversation: Gloria Steinem and Suheir Hammad, September 28, 2008

[255] Scarborough, Joe, Huffington Post, The True Character of Hillary Clinton, January 12, 2010

[256] Cocco, Marie, The Glass Ceiling Holds Strong, Real Clear Politics, November 20, 2008

[257] Ibarra, Herminia and Hansen, Morten T., Harvard Business Review, Women CEOs: Why So Few?, December 21, 2009

[258] Heilemann, John, New York Magazine, What Hillary Won By Losing, June 15, 2008

[259] Dowd, Maureen, New York Times, Can Hillary Cry Her Way Back To The White House?, January 9, 2008

[260] Rudov, Marc, FOX News, The Factor

[261] Myers, DeeDee, Vanity Fair, Favreau's Sexist Photo Is No Laughing Matter, December 8, 2008

[262] Brown, Tina, The Daily Beast, Burqua, ?? 2009

[263] Huffington Post, "Dana Milbank Suggests Hillary Should Drink "Mad Bitch Beer","August 31, 2009

[264] Media Matters, Chris Matthews eats crow, January 15, 2009

[265] Beinart, Peter, Don't Do It, Hillary, The Daily Beast, Nov. 15, 2008

[266] http://www.cbsnews.com/stories/2009/06/23/politics/politico/main5106650.shtml

[267] http://www.latimes.com/news/politics/la-na-clinton21mar21,1,7812759.story

[268] Junod, Tom, Esquire, Hillary. Happy., May 12, 2010

[269] Romano, Lois, Washington Post, Hillary Clinton Widens her circle at the State Department, March 11, 2010

[270] Ibid.

[271] Ibid.

[272] Ibid.

[273] Junod, Tom, Esquire, Hillary. Happy., May 12, 2010

[274] Hirsh, Michael, Newsweek, Obama's Bad Cop, April 23, 2010

[275] Douthat, Ross, New York Times, No Mystique About Feminism, June 13, 2010

[276] Rasmussen Polls, June 22, 2010

[277] Quinn, Andrew, Christian Science Monitor, Clinton spotlights U.S. debt as diplomatic threat, May 27, 2010

[278] Mooney, Alexander, CNN Political Ticker, Clinton: Rich aren't paying fair share, May 28, 2010

[279] Noonan, Peggy, Wall Street Journal, A Snakebit President, June 18, 2010

[280] Hirsh, Michael, Newsweek, Obama's Bad Cop, April 23, 2010

[281] Alter, Jonathan, Vanity Fair, Woman of the World, June, 2011

[282] Chapman, Steve, Chicago Tribune, Why Obama Should Withdraw, September 18, 2011

[283] Heilemann, John, New York Magazine, What Hillary Won By Losing, June 15, 2008

[284] Ibid.

[285] ETV South Carolina, CNN's John King Says Sometimes the Media "Whines Too Much", air date Oct. 30,2008

[286] Ibid.

[287] Schonfeld, Erick , TechCrunch, The Wounded U.S. Newspaper Industry Lost $7.5 Billion in Advertising Revenues Last Year, Mar 29, 2009

[288] Ahrens, Frank, Washington Post, Post Co. Quarterly Earnings Fall 77%, Feb 26, 2009

[289] ETV South Carolina, CNN's John King Says Sometimes the Media "Whines Too Much", air date Oct. 30,2008

[290] Whitlock, Scott, Newsbusters, Editor of Time on Fawning Obama Coverage: Media Will Regret This, October 28, 2008

[291] Malone, Michael S., ABC News, Medias Presidential Bias and Decline, October 24, 2008

[292] Blitzer, Wolf, CNN, Transcripts, Situation Room, Howard Kurtz Interview, Nov. 6, 2008

[293] Daily Beast, The Barrier That Didn't Fall, November 18, 2008

[294] Halperin, Mark, TIME, Why Obama Is Losing the Political War, October 11, 2010

[295] Poor, Jeff, The Daily Caller, Morning Joe: 'The press was in the tank for Obama' [VIDEO], December 21, 2011

[296] ABC, "This Week with George Stephanopoulos," Jan 8, 2012

[297] Bedard, Paul, US News & World Report, Media Sexism Doomed Hillary's 2008 Bid, December 23, 2011

[298] Sracic, Paul, CNN, For Democrats, second thoughts about Obama?, October 4, 2011

[299] Bingham, Amy, ABC News, Voters Flee Democratic Party in Key Swing States, Dec 7, 2011

[300] Page, Susan, USA Today, Sexist jabs scar female hopefuls, September 23, 2010

[301] Ibid.

[302] Kusnetz, Nicholas, Miller-McCune, Stagnating Gains for Women in Politics, October 8, 2010

[303] Haber, Maggie, Politico, Reid calls Gillibrand the 'hottest' member at fundraiser, September 20, 2010

[304] John Fritze, USA TODAY, Women pounding on governor mansions' glass ceilings, 6/24/2010 , Mary Ann Chastain, AP??

[305] Lawless, Jennifer, AFL-CIO Media center, Why More Women Don't Hold Office, 2012

[306] Falk, Erica, Women for President: Media Bias in Eight Campaigns, 2007

[307] Falk, Erica, Cutting Women Out: The Media Bias Against Female Candidates, Mar 15, 2008

[308] Cogan, Marin, Politico, Democrats Fear Wipeout for Women, 10/12/2010

[309] The Right Scoop, attaching CNN video interview between T.J. Holmes and Drew Griffin, June 10, 2011

[310] Ibid.

[311] Milligan, Susan, US News & World Report, Michele Bachmann's Nuttiness Is No Reason for Sexism, November 28, 2011

[312] Flock, Elizabeth, Washington Post, Newsweek Michelle Bachman Cover Article "Sexist" and in Bad Form?, August 8, 2011

[313] Andrews, Suzanna, Vanity Fair, The Woman Who Knew Too Much, November, 2011

[314] Geiger, Kim, Los Angeles Times, Scott Brown: 'Thank God' Elizabeth Warren didn't pose nude, October 06, 2011

[315] Noonan, Peggy, Wall St. Journal Opinion, Oh, Wow!, December 24, 2011

Made in the USA
Middletown, DE
08 August 2015